CW00666486

A FRENZY OF
INDIFFERENCE

A FRENZY OF INDIFFERENCE

Tales of a TV Journeyman

Harry Turner

The Book Guild Ltd
Sussex, England

The Book Guild Ltd
25 High Street,
Lewes, Sussex

First published 2000
© Harry Turner, 2000

Set in Times
Typesetting by Keyboard Services, Luton

Printed in Great Britain by
Bookcraft Ltd (Bath) Avon

A catalogue record for this book is
available from the British Library

ISBN 1 85776 530 3

CONTENTS

PREFACE

I could have stayed in the army of course. With a fair wind and a decent haircut, I might have become a Major-General. Or not, as the case may be.

Instead, I earned a living in commercial television for over three decades, and for a large part of that time it was about the most fun you could have with your clothes on.

That I blundered into commercial television as a callow 26-year-old when serious pundits were predicting that it would be no more than a flash in the pan, was in itself an act of naivety and blind faith. Not to say a desperate desire to meet my mortgage commitments.

'Hardly a serious career choice,' my late father said, who'd spent 27 years as a London policeman.

'How silly of you to choose such an unimportant and trivial pursuit,' said my old headmaster, Guy Boas of Sloane School in Chelsea.

Well, was it?

There are those who not only think it is unimportant, but positively baleful. Listen to columnist Peter Simple in the *Sunday Telegraph* on 11 August, 1991:

It is arguable that television is the greatest single evil in the world today. This most superfluous of inventions first became noticeable in England about forty years ago. At first it seemed a fascinating toy, a comparatively harmless novelty. What a transformation! Since then it has developed, with the horrible, irresistible swiftness of a nightmare, into a monstrous, all-pervading plague.

Obedient to the laws which govern our society, it has

become an ever-proliferating industry employing hundreds of thousands of people in the task, by now routine, of purveying ever more and more of its illusory images. Making thousands of talentless, often vacuous people rich, famous and powerful merely by being connected with it; perverting and corrupting everything it touches. It represents the lowest common denominator of our world, it is the unmistakable voice of the sub-human.

A pretty apocalyptic view to be sure, but sadly with a soupçon of truth concealed amidst the rhetoric.

That viewing the telly is still the third most important single daily activity in most households is beyond dispute. Research of multifarious stripes confirms that next to working for eight hours and sleeping for eight hours, slumping in front of the magic box for three to three and a half hours is an easy third.

It was once said, and probably still is, that television would kill the reading habit. However, leaving aside the fact that the great British public have never been excessively bookish, the growth of paperback sales has been boosted by television which continues to whet people's appetite for new experience and fresh knowledge. Re-run *Brideshead Revisited* and sales of Evelyn Waugh will twitch into life again. No bookshop in the high street is without its shelf of television-derived titles and television is the spur for people to explore new hobbies and leisure activities.

Television news is now the main source of information for a large slice of the population, but this hasn't prevented new newspapers and magazines proliferating. Nevertheless, I believe that the images of world events on both BBC and ITV news have created an appetite for information that the written word can never match. To many, television is the reality. Their own lives are by comparison drab and without incident. This may be sad, even regrettable, but it is the way of the world for many of our fellow citizens.

People, it is true, do just 'appear' on television, often with negligible talent, but the act of appearing confers on them celebrity beyond the dreams of avarice. This is merely an inevitable product of the medium itself: as fire cannot but produce smoke, so television cannot help but manufacture celebrities. Such fame, often transient, carries with it a serious responsibility. In my old region, the South-West of England, our on-air personalities had the same stature as a Wogan or a Rantzen had nationally. They were recognised in the street, in the supermarket, in the pub. Wherever they went, fame hung over them like a perfumed cloud. Ludicrous though it seems, they were expected to be somehow 'different'; they were the people invited into hundreds of thousands of homes every night. To a minority of the very old and very isolated, they were the only source of human contact in otherwise lonely lives. All on-air personalities receive mail – most of it flattering, some of it eccentric, a minority of it frankly disturbing. It goes, as the Americans would say, with the territory.

Television has also given gloss to activities that, left untouched by its magic eye, would perhaps wither on the vine. Darts as a spectator sport? Amazing. Fat men with tattooed forearms bigger than a sprinter's thighs chucking feathered spikes at a cork board. This is entertainment? Well, television has made it so. No other medium can reach the parts that other media scarcely glance at. Television is part of the fabric of our lives. An integral part, woven inextricably into our culture and our consciousness.

I remember Sir Brian Young, the erudite Director-General of the IBA giving a speech at Hatfield House to an audience of hard-boiled television professionals some years ago. 'There is *good* bad television,' he said, 'and there is *bad* good television.' What did he mean? I do believe he encapsulated the true philosophy of this extraordinary medium in that puzzling phrase. *Good bad* television is that which appeals to the simpler, less educated taste. A game show perhaps, or a weekly soap opera. Bad because it is without intellectual pretension, but also *good* because it is created with love and care by television professionals who can reach people without patronising them. That's *good* bad television.

And *bad* good television? An obscure opera chucked into the schedule, cynically, by a programme controller who is trying to fulfil his quota of 'culture'. Or a pretentious discussion programme where men and women talk in stilted, pseudo-intellectual jargon on subjects so obscure as to defy description.

Then of course there is *good* good television. It is that which is made with love and passion and considerable skill and appeals to huge audiences across the whole social spectrum. From duke to dustman, as the phrase goes. *Only Fools and Horses* was such a show, as was *Upstairs, Downstairs* from LWT.

There is another development in current television programming that should give cause for concern. It is, for want of a better description, the steady relentless 'proletarianising' of virtually all drama, children's programmes and light entertainment on both BBC and the commercial channels. Put bluntly, the celebration of yob culture is now prevalent in speech, behaviour and appearance. Children's presenters seem, for the main part, to have been selected for their poor speech and self-consciously down-market dress code. Children must now believe that the glottal stop and the dropped aitch, not to mention the semi-literate construction of sentences, is an ideal to be aspired to.

EastEnders is undeniably a popular soap and it is perhaps inevitable that most of the characters it features are coarse, oafish, sad or bad tempered. Is life in London's East End really such a catalogue of unpleasantness? *Birds of a Feather* mimics this trend and of course the one character whose speech is what could be described as a shade 'upmarket' is the subject of ridicule and pity. She's middle class so she's *bound* to be a nympho. See what I mean, squire?

Does Danny Baker, unshaven, unkempt and dressed by Oxfam really represent the best of chat show hosts? He was a card all right and a bit of a cheeky chappie, but at least he was occasionally funny, unlike the wretched Terry Christian on Channel Four's *The Word*. His famous nasal mumblings made him an icon of the young. Thankfully, he has now vanished from our screens, but God's teeth, we still have Chris Evans.

And does British Telecom really believe that Bob Hoskins in his ripest yobbo accent will persuade us it is 'good to talk'? And does it matter? Is it of no concern to us that the English language, so rich and colourful, should be so poorly treated by those who appear on our screens night after night?

This slide downwards to the vernacular of the street corner seems to have spread its virus even to those presenters whose natural speech patterns are close to standard English. On a recent *Gladiators*, I saw and heard Ulrika Jonsson, the ex-TVAM weathergirl, descending into verbal 'blokishness' and deliberately shedding the occasional aitch – just, I suppose, to underline her street cred and demonstrate that she too can be as verbally constipated as her contemporaries.

I accept the risk of being assaulted in the Groucho Club by a posse of unshaven TV producers wearing baseball caps back to front who will accuse me of 'élitism', 'snobbery', 'fascism' and probably 'ageism' as well. So be it, but I still think it would make a nice change if we lifted our noses from the trough and reached for higher things – just occasionally.

In the 1990s, the proliferation of channels through cable and satellite, the extension of broadcasting hours to 'round the clock' programming and the looming approach of digital broadcasting mean that soon the ordinary viewer at home will be faced with a cornucopia of choice undreamt of by those early pioneers at the old BBC and the original ITV network. However, 'more', as we have already seen, doesn't necessarily mean 'better'. Indeed, to my admittedly jaundiced eye, what is on offer, increasingly, is a jumble of tat and shlock, a gross and Gadarene rush to serve what is traditionally described as the 'lowest common denominator' in taste and appetite.

This inexorable slide into mediocrity and sensationalism is the result of the deeply flawed broadcasting legislation of the

1980s, plus the relentless corrosion of the BBC's public service ethic.

ITV was always about money. But *not* exclusively. Monopoly franchises were given in a Faustian contract that required the commercial companies to provide 'quality' and to pursue excellence in broadcasting in return for the right to sell advertising in their respective geographical regions – without competition. A curious British compromise. But it worked. When such a delicate balance is disturbed, as it was by the Conservative government's obsession with shaking the TV industry out of its alleged complacency, chaos ensues.

The seeds of this obsession have now borne poisonous fruit. Creative executives have been sidelined or even superseded by gimlet-eyed accountants whose focus is exclusively on the bottom line. A 'return' for the shareholders takes precedence over service to the viewer.

Part of the reason is the fragmentation of audiences across the range of channels – people 'graze' with their remote controls or 'time shift' their favourite programmes on video recorders. It is getting increasingly hard to lasso *big* audiences for the duration of a programme unless it is, frankly, down-market.

A glance at the TV schedules any day of the week reveals that what we have in the large part is tabloid television. The importation of shows like Jerry Springer's 'victim' TV is a prime example. Most programmes that tax the intellect or are aimed at an educated, perceptive audience are bunged out late at night as if the schedulers assume that anybody with more than two O levels is an insomniac. Daytime television is now so gross or so bland as to defy further description.

And what of dear old Aunty herself? The 'nation's' British Broadcasting Corporation. A once respected institution admired throughout the world has begun a gradual process of self-inflicted corruption. Drenched in political correctness, blatantly left-wing in all its public affairs programming and stifled by its own bureaucracy, this huge, lumbering monolith is trying to compete with its sharp, nimble commercial brothers in ITV, cable and satellite. Vast sums of money are squandered on management consultants and – equally damaging – on a network of 'local' radio and TV stations which try to compete with the profit-driven commercial radio and TV companies.

If the BBC concentrated its efforts and its resources on BBC 1, BBC 2, Radios 1, 2, 3 and 4 and *nothing else*, it would be able to afford the finest programming on earth without sliding down-market like some middle-aged hippy in order to establish its own street cred.

Unless power and authority is returned to the creative programme makers, unless top-quality writers are encouraged and supported, and unless the fatuous management jargon and psycho-babble of the consultants is reduced, the slithering collapse into bathos will continue.

At the time of writing, the prognosis is gloomy, but perhaps I'm wrong. Perhaps my vision is that of one of yesterday's men, one who is out of touch with the brave new world of computers, Blairism, Cool Britannia, the Internet, Vanessa Feltz and men with shaven heads and earrings who present children's programmes. Only time will tell.

This book is not just a memoir about the television business, it is the story of the adventures one practitioner enjoyed over a span of more than 30 years in the trade. Some of the events chronicled were peripheral to the actual process of making television programmes or the running of a television enterprise, but they were, I suggest, unlikely to have occurred had that time been spent in accountancy, cement manufacturing or the production of canned dog meat. This not to cast a slur on these trades, which I am sure in their own way offer their incumbents a lifetime crowded with incident.

Television, however, is unique. It is a business that brings together a kaleidoscope of talent, ranging from actors, musicians, writers and producers to salesmen, engineers and financiers. From such a melting pot, steam always rises and if I may be permitted a double metaphor, sparks occasionally fly upwards. I have been privileged to work in television during the 1960s, 1970s, 1980s and 1990s and was both spectator and participant in the convulsions that were an inevitable part of its growing-up process.

The little box in the corner of most living rooms is now an accepted part of the furniture. It is still the ultimate window on the world, the dazzling mirror which, although sometimes distorting, we hold up in order to see ourselves and our changing environment.

This is a tale that ranges from the earlier, golden years right up to the angst-riddled present. It touches on the arcane process of awarding television franchises in the early 1980s, a process likened to the anointing of a medieval pope, and it reflects on the harsh and sometimes Byzantine machinations of the 1991 'Blind Auction'.

It traces the flawed legislation that climaxed with the handing out of ten-year licences to a lucky few, and with the dramatic intervention of Margaret Thatcher, whose letter to the Chairman of TVAM admitted that she was 'painfully aware' that she was responsible for the legislation that led to the current debacle.

No writer of fiction would have dared construct such a plot, even though the events of recent months might well have been gleaned from the pages of a Victorian penny dreadful. My adventures as a TV journeyman were occasionally bizarre, often precarious, but invariably exciting. They have not been presented in precise chronological order, but I felt this mildly erratic structure might assist narrative flow and more importantly enhance the enjoyment of the reader.

I am grateful to the numerous people who have helped jog my memory about past events and restrain my natural instinct for mild hyperbole. There are too many of them to make a comprehensive list and omissions might give offence as indeed might inclusions. Therefore the opinions expressed are my own, and I stand by them, even though a few friends and fewer enemies may feel bruised by them.

Harry Turner, Autumn 1999

CHAPTER 1

*Early days – in which the board of Westward
Television attempt to remove their founder,
Peter Cadbury, and high jinx ensue revealing
the IBA in all its petulant, bureaucratic glory.*

As I flipped through the glossy photographs on my desk, I felt
a tingle of anticipation. Here was glamour, here was power,
and above all here was fun.

I was 25 and working as an advertising salesman for *TV
International* magazine in London's Clifford Street, a confident young man keen to 'belong' and become part of that
spurious, swinging London that had been so cruelly over-
hyped by *Time* magazine. The photographs in front of me
were of a new breed of entrepreneur, the ITV tycoons, who
had secured franchises in the late 1950s to run Britain's new
commercial television system. They were partying, drinks in
hand, surrounded by an abundance of mini-skirted girls at
some festival in the South of France. An older colleague
glanced over my shoulder and snorted disapprovingly. 'And
they call that work,' he said tartly, and walked away.

For the best part of my 30 years in television, people have
continued to glance over my shoulder and say much the same
thing. To get so much enjoyment from one's work, and be
handsomely paid too, seems to bring out a puritan streak that
lurks in the British character and cause acid disapproval.

London in the early 1960s was a city pulsating with a sense
of its own importance, particularly if you were young or at
least under 30. The explosion of popular music and the growth
of fashion seemed to suggest a life of permanent carnival was

1

available just for the asking. The blight of unemployment was still no more than the rumble of a distant drum and to many of us a whole new raft of opportunities were opening up in the mushrooming services industry.

Careers did not have to be boring. It wasn't necessary to manufacture things or work in gloomy factories on gloomier trading estates to become successful. You could have fun too. I had left the British Army in the middle of the 1950s with no real sense of purpose. My clutch of A levels pointed me in no particular direction and my career plans were haphazard in the extreme. However, I could talk, persuasively. This, I suppose, was my only talent and it was perhaps inevitable therefore that I became a salesman, but more importantly a television salesman.

After a short spell hawking baked beans in the Commercial Road for Crosse & Blackwell, I chanced into Fleet Street with a job on the old *Daily Herald* selling advertising space. This in turn led to a similar job on Roy Thomson's *Sunday Graphic* and then, wonder of wonders, the advertising managership of a new magazine devoted to the glittering, seductive, irresistible world of television. It was then, as the first issue, on its heavy art paper, rolled off the presses, that I knew I was hooked, not on publishing, but on television itself. My fate to become a TV journeyman was sealed and from that moment, and I have never wanted to work in any other business.

TV International was a brave attempt by three young people (Derek Hoddinott, an ex-editor of *TV Today* magazine, Margaret Cowan, a freelance journalist and myself, an itinerant huckster) to capitalise on this new, immensely exciting industry. Our magazine, 'For TV executives throughout the world', was a shade naïve and probably a touch ahead of its time. The established journal was a dull little publication called *Television Mail*, but it was *there* and it was the only trade magazine to cater for the new breed of producers, writers and directors.

Our backer – and Indian millionaire improbably named Justin Cohen – understandably wanted a return on his investment and when it was not forthcoming after two years, the

2

magazine folded, pitchforking the three of us back onto the job market.

There was an exquisite innocence about commercial television in those days. Every night in darkened sitting rooms, black and white images flickered over minuscule screens and the faces of Michael Miles and Hughie Green were known throughout the land. Even more fascinating, to me at least, were the commercials themselves. Actresses with Roedean voices and pleated skirts romped coyly on top of huge replicas of fruit gum packets, and disc jockey Alan Freeman winked and grimaced his way through countless soap powder vignettes.

I knew little of this esoteric world of images and fantasy but was eager to learn. The salesmen employed for the ITV companies were different from those I had worked with in Fleet Street on the *Daily Herald*. They wore shiny, mohair suits and smoked little cheroots with an air of insouciance. Their hair was longish, their shoes Italian. They sported identity bracelets on their wrists and spoke in accents which were dangerously transatlantic. One of them, the legendary Pat Henry, ATV's Sales Director, of whom more later, was reputed to be earning £30,000 a year – a vast sum in those days – and his car was the latest Rolls.

I scanned the job pages of a now moribund journal called *World's Press News* in search of openings in this new Valhalla. After some weeks of fruitless endeavour applying in desperation for jobs I didn't really want on trade magazines like *Cage Birds* and *The Local Authority Journal*, I spotted a small advertisement for a salesman with a brand new contractor called Westward Television. Its London office, where the sales team were located, was off Bond Street in an old building adjoining the Keith Prowse record store. The ad was quite specific. The person being sought needed 'grit, determination and a vibrant personality' and should apply in writing to Peter Cadbury, the Chairman, a man whose reputation as a swashbuckler was well-known. Westward's studios were in Plymouth as its franchise was for the South-West of England, but the job advertised was London based.

The interview with Cadbury was a curtain-raiser for the sort of industry I was destined to work in. Tanned and supremely confident, he occupied a vast office with lots of black leather furniture and a huge Great Dane that lolled at his feet throughout. Before being ushered into his presence, a uniformed commissionaire in reception had introduced me to the company mascot – a parrot called Jackson who swore softly in an upper-class drawl that I later identified as being a perfect imitation of Cadbury himself.

Ten minutes into the interview, Cadbury lit his pipe and strolled over to the window, leaving the Great Dane eyeing me with what I thought was an unnecessary degree of lasciviousness.

'If you've sold advertising space on the bloody *Daily Herald*, you can sell anything,' he said. 'You're hired. When can you start?'

And so in December 1962 I joined Westward as a junior sales executive at £1,600 a year, more than twice what I'd ever earned before.

Let us now fast-forward 18 years to the leaden heat of a West Country summer. It is 14 July 1980 and I enter a small conference room at the Rougement Hotel, Exeter. The sky outside is hung with brassy clouds and a warm sticky wind nags at the loose casements of the old building. A long table has been laid with meticulous care. Carafes of water, crystal tumblers, notepads and sharpened pencils are laid out with geometric precision. I notice a small vase containing, perhaps prophetically, one dead rose. An elderly hotel servant in black carries it solemnly from the room on a tiny tray.

I light a Monte Cristo cigar and take one of the three vacant chairs around the table. The board of directors of Westward Television is gathered in full strength – well, almost full strength – as they wait in discreet silence for the arrival of the man who founded their company in 1960 and whose name has been inextricably linked with it for good or bad ever since.

On my immediate left sits Lord Harris of Greenwich, magisterial in his solemnity. He has a button missing from his cuff

4

and a light dusting of dandruff on his collar. He acknowledges me politely, but avoids any attempt at conversation.

I glance around the table and nod towards my other colleagues. First is Ronnie Perry, the Managing Director, ex-floor manager, theatrical agent and stage manager at Glyndebourne. Ronnie looks pale and drawn and his hands rest on a pile of documents. George Lidstone, Vice-Chairman, is a fine West Country man with many years of service to the company. Then Sir Robert Cooke, ex-Member of Parliament and owner of the medieval stately home, Athelhampton, in Dorset, the house featured in the Laurence Olivier movie *Sleuth*. Robin, as he is known, manages a grin as our eyes meet. Michael Heathcoat Amory, inheritor of a famous political name, looks boyish, but solemn. The Right Honourable Simon Lennox-Boyd, son of an ex-colonial secretary, is rich, assured, even relaxed. He nods at me like a priest about to take confession from a particularly raffish member of his flock. Dr Harry Kay, Vice-Chancellor of Exeter University, appears stunned that he should be part of the cut and thrust of a television boardroom power struggle. Rodney Brimacombe, now a Director of Harrods since his family business became a part of that exclusive empire, looks very young, redeemed slightly by his greying hair.

Terry Fleet is Programme Controller, ex-journalist and ex-editor of Westward's daily diary programme. Terry, as always, shows no signs of outward stress, but I know he has been under immense pressure for months. Ken Holmes, Managing Director of Renwicks, is a recent addition to the board: a shrewd accountant with a rounded, faintly oriental persona. I feel sure he thinks most television executives are slightly loony – a reasonable assumption as far as any accountant is concerned. They crave order, discipline, predictability. There hasn't been a lot of that knocking around in the last few months. Penny Phillips, another relative newcomer to the board, is a holder of the Croix de Guerre for her dauntless exploits in France during World War II. I experience a twinge of apprehension that such a distinguished lady should be embroiled in the executive butchery we all know is about to take place.

The minutes tick by. A hotel maid, even more ancient than the flower remover, enters the room backwards carrying a tray of teacups which rattle like old bones as she negotiates the door. She is politely waved away. Blood must flow before thoughts of tea and biscuits many be entertained.

I know Peter Cadbury is in the building. He was with me five minutes earlier when I arrived alongside his faithful deputy, the Earl of Lisburne. His sense of drama makes it vital that he enters last of all, like the Prince of Darkness in some sixteenth-century morality play.

The doors open again and there he is. Immaculate, lightly tanned, those incredible ice-blue eyes blazing like diamonds. He carries a bulky leather briefcase in one hand and his pipe in the other. A pace behind follows Lord Lisburne, limping slightly, his general demeanour not unlike the astronomer Patrick Moore, exuding a reassuring, honest-to-goodness, faintly crumpled decency. With them is Anne Whatley, Cadbury's personal assistant with whom, earlier, I had journeyed in a helicopter from London to be at today's Roman circus.

Cadbury sits at the head of the table with Lisburne on his right hand, as always. There is a brief murmur of perfunctory greetings. Cadbury smiles at me and I am reminded of the countless occasions when that smile, mischievous, challenging and wicked, has broken the ice at many a solemn moment. He snaps open his briefcase and removes a few papers and as he does so the smile fades, leaving his face set in another familiar mask. The mask of a relentless, supremely self-confident autocrat who is about to deal with a temporarily irksome item on an already boring agenda.

Lord Harris adjusts his spectacles, a gesture that only he and Roy Jenkins can invest with the deep significance of the Pope blessing a multitude of 30,000 souls in St Peter's Square.

Cadbury glances at Harris and the blue eyes are hard as bullets. Less than a year ago the two men seemed almost inseparable. An extraordinary chemistry had sprung up between them: the swashbuckling Cadbury with his vast estates, aeroplanes, fast cars, effortless style; and Harris, the ex-junior minister, ex-journalist, with his measured speech and fondness for witty political gossip. Of course we all know why Harris had been brought in. It was Cadbury's simple, uncomplicated belief that the inclusion of such a political nabob would impress the IBA and secure a renewal of the franchise on 29 December.

And Harris tackled his new role with zest. It is easy now, sitting in the cathedral-like calm of the Rougemont Hotel, to forget just how zestful he had been. His master-minding of the written franchise application was a model of hard relentless attention to detail. Nothing, it seemed, would split asunder this brilliant duet of free-wheeling millionaire and well-connected ex-socialist Mr Fixit. Until today.

The meeting commences, without histrionics, and George Lidstone begins by saying how sorry we all must be that such a meeting should be necessary in the first place. The directors have been convened by telegram to a 'special' gathering of the board for which the agenda is bleak: 'To consider the position of the Executive Chairman and the future of the company.' Every one of us in that room knows that this bland euphemism is a mask for the meeting's true purpose – to dump Peter Cadbury. It is franchise year of course, and nerves are somewhat frayed – not least among the newer directors who have had merely a foretaste of the Cadbury style.

A few days earlier Cadbury had ignited a spark that would eventually contribute to a Wagnerian conflagration. He issued a statement, on Westward headed paper, in which he claimed he was being driven to quit his Queen Anne West Country mansion 'because of police harassment'. When pressed as to why he was not taking any official action to back his complaint, he said pugnaciously, 'It didn't do Blair Peach* any good, why should it do me any good?'

The Devon police, in the meantime, accused him of wasting their time over his concern that there might be corruption in high places on the Plymouth City Council ('wasting police

*Blair Peach, a man who suffered the ultimate humiliation in police custody.

7

time' is a rare action invoked under an ancient law). The plot did not merely thicken, it positively congealed when Cadbury claimed '100 per cent backing' from the board for his technicolour outburst.

The effect of all this on an already sensitive board of directors was predictable. They had not seen the famous press statement and neither were they consulted about it. It was despatched with flourish on a Thursday preceding a board meeting, even though Cadbury maintained stoutly that it was merely an error, a 'secretarial' mistake and that he intended to show a draft to his colleagues anyway. This doesn't cut any mustard with Lord Harris, ex-Minister of State of Broadcasting in the Labour government, who professed 'horror' at the press release.

After his opening remarks, George Lidstone defers to Lord Harris who then launches into a funereal vignette about the 'grave embarrassment' caused to the board and Cadbury's 'unforgivable behaviour'. It escapes nobody's notice that in addition to being a non-executive Director of Westward, Harris is also Chairman of the Parole Board and a friend of Devon's Chief Constable, John Alderson.

All of us have been witness to Peter Cadbury's recent joust with the Devon authorities. It is no secret that his relations with both the Plymouth Council and the police have been strained. There was the strange affair of the 'Canada geese' during which the police received an anonymous tip-off that Cadbury had turned a blind eye to his estate staff shooting at a flock of protected Canada geese on the estate lake. Cadbury was away at the time, but nevertheless received a visit from the boys in blue on his return. Subsequently, they called again, 'late at night', according to Cadbury, 'to inspect my gun licence'.

Trivial stuff, perhaps, but didn't somebody once start a war over a man called Jenkins and his ear?

Harris completes his address, which bears all the hallmarks of relentless rehearsal and then sits back in his chair, fingers steepled like a Renaissance wood carving of John the Baptist.

Cadbury, to my surprise, doesn't leap up immediately at the

8

throat of his adversary. 'I'm sorry,' he says, 'if I embarrassed the board. It was not intentional. The letter shouldn't have been issued without prior consultation; it was a genuine mistake.' He backs up this uncharacteristically dove-like statement by producing a sworn affidavit from his secretary, Sue Baldwin, admitting the error.

There is a brief silence, punctuated only by the shuffling of papers and the rasp of a match as Cadbury lights his pipe. I experience a feeling of relief. With luck and goodwill all round, maybe we can emerge from today's meeting in one piece.

My elation is short-lived, however, when it becomes apparent that Harris and his supporters don't believe or accept the Cadbury version of events. Blood is what they seek and blood is what they intend to spill. Harris professes outrage at the way Cadbury has attacked John Alderson, 'a fine public servant' and dragged the company's name into what must surely be a 'purely personal and misguided dispute'. This is total cobblers of course, but Harris specialised in such nonsense.

The temperature of the meeting nudges up a few degrees as Harris rounds off his second address and draws support from other members of the board. Michael Heathcoat Amory, his face set in hard lines, echoes Lord Harris in his 'deep disapproval' of the Cadbury statement, and Simon Lennox-Boyd tempers his remarks with the prefix that it 'pains' him to have to agree with what has already been said. Then, with the slow inevitability of a runaway hearse, a motion is proposed that Peter Cadbury be removed from the office of Chairman.

One by one the directors vote in favour. Some silently, others with obvious pain, their memories of past triumphs, enjoyable years of success and good comradeship with Peter Cadbury still undimmed. Only Lord Lisburne and I vote against the motion and to Lord Harris's obvious irritation I utter a few words in support of Peter Cadbury. The motion is carried and Cadbury's face is granite now.

Lord Lisburne, then, as always, the perfect gentleman, takes the chair to succeed the dethroned king, but he does it with a

9

heavy heart. He asks for the next item on the agenda to be placed before the board and it is a motion calling for his own head on a plate. Clearly, the board intends to finish the business of the day with Borgia-like thoroughness.

I vote against the motion, but it is supported by all the other directors. Lisburne stands down with grace and dignity. His only crime, it seems, is his loyalty to Cadbury and his unwillingness to ditch a friend in times of hardship.

George Lidstone takes the chair and with chilling swiftness the board elects Lord Harris of Greenwich as their new chairman. I abstain. For a moment I wait to see if I will be next on the chopping block. I am, however, spared.

In spite of my support for Peter Cadbury, the board seems unwilling to shed its Sales Director. In truth, they have no quarrel with me or I with them, save on this one fundamental issue – should Cadbury be ditched? The deed is done, however, and with a sense of occasion that couldn't be more British, we break for tea, although stronger stuff is available in the adjoining bar.

Much of what follows has the hollow unreality of anticlimax. Cadbury and Lisburne sweep out to waiting cars. They are still full directors of the company, but are stripped, nonetheless, of their exalted rank. I follow, driving Peter Cadbury's sleek, black BMW.

My last impressions of the meeting are of little knots of directors standing around trying to look utterly normal. Other hotel guests, however, have sensed that a tiny smudge of commercial history may have been made this day and they stare balefully from high-back armchairs in the residents' lounge as the fallen Caesar exits.

Cadbury, Lisburne and I regroup at another nearby hotel and are greeted not only by a clutch of reporters, but a fair number of Westward staff from Plymouth who have turned out to show loyalty and support for Peter Cadbury. This loyalty is his spur. Within a few days he is announcing 'massive support' from shareholders and staff for his reinstatement and he begins his spectacular counter-attack.

'Under the circumstances,' he says in the *Daily Express* on

10

18 July, four days after his sacking, 'I have no alternative but to requisition an Extraordinary Meeting of the shareholders'.

His plan is clear. He will seek a shareholder mandate to turn the tables on Harris and restore himself as Chairman. His support among many shareholders is well-known and the *Sunday Times* reports on 20 July that 'Quite soon, Peter Cadbury is likely to be restored as chairman, sacrificing Lord Harris'.

Cadbury is now firing on all cylinders. He calls a press conference on Saturday 26 July in a small Chelsea café, Foxtrot Oscar, and there, perched on a plastic crate, he tells the specially invited journalists from the Sunday 'heavies' that the 'fight is over' and Harris is 'finished'. It is rousing stuff, set against a backdrop of torrential summer rain, chilled white wine and a lot of marvellous euphoria.

I am pleased and surprised to see a number of my most junior sales staff showing up to support Cadbury, together with the sales management team.

After the press conference, we emerge from Foxtrot Oscar into bright sunshine and several of us take lunch in a Kensington trattoria where, over lasagne and Frascati, we ponder Cadbury's words: 'It's in the bag, boys – all over bar the shouting!' It is true that he now commands 'well in excess' of 50 per cent of the company's crucial 200,000 voting shares, but as subsequent events prove, there is still a lot of shouting to be done on both sides.

The rest, as they say, is not only history, but history that has been flogged to within an inch of its life. What this narrative will concern itself with, therefore, is the effect that these bizarre events, and what led up to them, had on the morale and performance of staff, particularly in my own domain, sales.

That Cadbury was a popular leader in Plymouth is undeniable. His visits by helicopter, aeroplane, yacht or blood-red Ferrari had over the years been charged with a great sense of occasion. Cadbury is a man who has perfected the art of 'arrival'. He is physically impressive, always suntanned, and his clothes look as if 50 tailors in Savile Row have toiled all night to bring the cloth to sartorial perfection. The drill in

11

Plymouth, after his spectacular arrival, would be a meeting in the Managing Director's office, usually punctuated by phone calls to or from people whose names clog Debrett's like hyphenated frog-spawn.

Any business other than that conducted at formal board meetings would be performed 'on the hoof'. I have had some of Cadbury's very best decisions made in my favour while walking, flying, driving or even swimming. From the Managing Director's office he would make a beeline for the staff canteen. Here, in the bar, Cadbury's magic for identifying with the employees of Westward would be at its zenith.

He would drink lager and play the fruit machines, inevitably winning, to the huge enjoyment of the onlookers and he would talk freely, often too freely, to anyone willing to listen. His indiscretions were legion, but sprang from his belief that Westward was one big family and if father couldn't say outrageous things in front of his own flesh and blood, then what the hell.

While popular, Cadbury never for a moment ceased to be the Boss. He has an intimidating style when he senses anybody becoming too familiar and his famous blue eyes can freeze boiling oil at 60 paces.

In London, the form was different. Although never attracted by the crass nonsense of actually coming to the office every day, he did maintain a sort of royal court, consisting of secretaries, PAs and chilled white Chablis just in case he fancied a visit. My own sales team recognised him for what he was: a nineteenth-century buccaneer with a magnificent upper-class drawl that made Norman St John Stevas sound like Alf Garnett by comparison. He never interfered with the marketing operation other than to support what I wanted to do with gusto.

Occasionally, I would irk him and his displeasure was sharp, but brief. I do believe the chemistry between us enabled the sales operation to blossom and bear fruit in a very special way. Sales people are sensitive. They have to be. They can tune in to bad vibrations with speed and accuracy. Generally they knew that the 'Old Man' was on 'our' side. He understood the vital importance of sales and enjoyed nothing better than a few drinks with the members of the department – especially when they were pretty girls.

His self-confidence (some would describe it as arrogance), provided the seeds of his own destruction. In the 19 years I worked with him I don't ever recall him admitting he was wrong about anything. I suppose from childhood he was used to getting his own way and it's hard to break the habits of a lifetime.

He failed to read the warning signals early in 1980 when the board, with some justification, began to worry about his public outbursts, his 'rows' with the police and his increasingly eccentric behaviour. I shared the board's concern, but didn't believe we were approaching the subsequent apocalypse. Cadbury's ill-fated move to Plymouth, to Lyneham House, a pretty mansion with a lake and a farm, was made in the teeth of strong advice against such a move. In fairness, and to set the records straight, Ronnie Perry, the Managing Director, urged him not to set up in the West Country, but he ignored this counsel. I told him I thought it was a crazy move and that the IBA were not so naïve as to be impressed by such a blatant piece of public relations. He just laughed and moved anyway.

But he hated it. He missed his friends and he loathed the wind-lashed Devon winter. Then the nonsense began – the obsession about police persecution, the belligerent press releases, the gradual rupture of his relationship with the board – and all in franchise year. It was as if Westward had developed a death wish and was offering its throat to Lady Plowden's sacrificial knife.

When Lord Harris, Ronnie Perry and others decided enough was enough and Cadbury had to go, I was violently opposed to the public execution they proposed. I thought then, and still believe now, that if we'd avoided that fateful Exeter board meeting, with its gallows logic and inevitable bloody aftermath, we might have saved the day. How? By opting for a private, informal meeting with Peter Cadbury and slugging out the differences early in the year. It sure as hell wouldn't

13

have been an easy route and I cannot place my hand on my heart and say it would have been certain to succeed. But firing him and Lord Lisburne was like igniting a powder keg. The fight was exhausting and ultimately self-defeating and staff were stunned and hurt by such an unseemly spectacle. In short, I didn't believe that it was fair to drop the skipper just because we'd struck a patch of bad weather.

My sales team didn't like what was happening one little bit. Every day they would face agencies and clients who wanted to hear the latest blow-by-blow account of the Westward troubles. Inevitably, morale suffered. The entire sales team signed a petition urging the reinstatement of Peter Cadbury as Chairman and it was presented to Lord Harris. He was not impressed.

I found my day-to-day contact with the man faintly surreal. Up until the 'great row', when he was the apple of Peter Cadbury's eye, we'd had a perfectly amiable rapport. He enjoyed Havana cigars, good wine and pithy conversation laced with malice. I found those things agreeable too. Once the 'troubles' started and he'd succeeded Cadbury, our relationship, not surprisingly, underwent a metamorphosis. He conducted our brief meetings as if I were some sort of fairground huckster peddling snake serum. I don't think he really understood the commercial reality of airtime sales upon which the company totally depended.

He gathered around him advisers, accountants, mysterious PR men. The atmosphere in his office was like Whitehall. He would only act after 'advice' – shades of his old ministerial career no doubt. The standard staff joke was that if you asked Lord Harris the time he would require written notice of the question and six civil servants would draft a reply so obtuse as to defy comprehension. An exaggeration, of course, but placing political animals with little commercial experience into the hot seat to succeed men like Cadbury was bound to cause ripples and it certainly did that.

It was late summer 1980. The Day of Judgement was rapidly approaching. The IBA was girding its collective loins for the Great Franchise Bonanza. Television companies

14

throughout the length and breadth of the kingdom were contemplating, nay executing, rate increases. We at Westward held back. We felt that we had troubles enough.

Almost every day the national press carried an item about the affair. No breakfast was complete without seeing the company name twinkling up from the Nigel Dempster column in which Lord Harris was invariably described as 'scruffy' and Cadbury as 'ousted' – such is the potency of language in Fleet Street.

Rumours abounded, some of them extreme. Harris ate at the Mirabelle every day. Untrue. Cadbury was planning an 'SAS'-type raid on the shareholders to enlist their support. Grossly exaggerated. Harris had his laundry sent to Plymouth by hearse; Cadbury had taken up ju-jitsu; the queen and Harold Wilson were going to intervene; a plague of boils had visited the West Country; Harris would be pursued by Cadbury 'beyond the grave'; Cadbury was getting tired and emotional – well, so were we all. And so it went on, day after day after day.

The sales team tried to ignore the publicity that burst like mortar fire all around them, but it was hard going. Uncertainty hung like a pall over their heads. Would Cadbury really pull it off and make a comeback? And if he did, would the IBA welcome him with open arms and a warm franchise? Did Lord Harris have special influence with the Authority? Would Roy Jenkins succeed Sir Brian Young in the not too distant future?

Most evenings when I got home, shareholders of various sizes and persuasion would telephone me and ask for action replays of the day's events.

Later, during that fateful summer, I am in the boardroom of a large manufacturer, a traditional and heavy user of television. We have consumed a lunch of Beef Wellington accompanied by an extraordinarily rare claret. My planned ratecard has scarcely been discussed, but my instincts warn me that a troublesome matter is about to be raised.

A senior director of the company announces that he wishes to speak frankly, an infallible sign that some sort of unpleasantness is afoot. Surely, I ponder, he will not concern himself with the fine detail of cost per thousands? He clears his throat and fixes me with a cool stare. I brace myself.

'I'd like to know,' he begins, 'just how stable your company is.'

The matter that has exercised his mind is, of course, the Cadbury/Harris drama and he is wondering if the product launch planned for our area should now proceed. I reassure him that boardroom wrangles notwithstanding, we remain a viable, fully operational television contractor. The staff, I emphasise, will continue to perform their professional tasks even if the entire board collapses, writhing, into the River Tamar.

The atmosphere unfreezes and cigars are produced from a gleaming humidor. Extraordinary though it now seems, those senior marketing men around that table were actually worried that their carefully laid plans might be aborted by the contortions at Westward. Dark rumours had been circulating that the IBA would 'close us down' – or at best, intervene and run the station themselves. Visions of ethnic knitting symposiums and two-hour epilogues flash before my eyes.

On the train journey back to London I reconsider the day's events and experience a chill of apprehension. It is clear that our credibility as a company is being damaged by the current dispute. Is it, however, actually losing us money? I recall the previous day's sales meeting in London when instead of the usually cheerful and confident group of sales executives gathered in my office, I saw a row of solemn, unhappy faces. If sales people are unhappy, I reason, their performance must eventually suffer. Thus, the wretched dispute will cost us money. I alight from the train in a state of deepest gloom.

Later, at home, I reconsider the reasons why my board colleagues chose to remove Peter Cadbury as their Chairman. 'He was unable to separate his own private life from that of the company,' George Lidstone, Vice-Chairman, has already explained. But what George failed to understand was that Westward *was* his life. And he, Peter Cadbury, *was* Westward.

Cadbury had also chosen, in contract year, to pick this extraordinary quarrel with the Chief Constable of Devon and the

16

Chief Executive of Plymouth Council. When Cadbury picks a fight with somebody there is no pussy-footing around, it's a hell of a rollercoaster ride with a touch of metaphorical gouging thrown in for good measure. He is also confident that there is no way we will lose the licence. 'It is not,' he announces royally, 'a matter I am even prepared to contemplate.'

Now, while it is true that Peter Cadbury did allow his own personality to fuse itself to that of the company he founded, this is no recent phenomenon. He's been doing it since 1960 and nobody, least of all his board colleagues, should be surprised that he's still doing it in 1980. The row with Plymouth Council, however, is a dangerous development and one which is increasingly embarrassing for the board. What all this has to do with whether Westward is a fit company to run a television franchise in the South West is never satisfactorily explained.

Cadbury sees no connection: 'My private life may be colourful,' he says to me over dinner at Lyneham House in Devon, 'and I know I'm not an easy man, but I want Westward to retain its licence as much as anybody.'

I believe him, in spite of the fact that his close aides know he has grown bored with it in recent months and is hungry for new challenges. Herein lies the key. All his life he has grown restless with familiar territory. He is rich; his goal isn't just money; it's excitement, novelty, a new game. Like many successful and powerful men, he is an unconscious seeker after stress. And stress, in bucketsful, is what he gets.

I resolve to try to do what I can to heal the breach which now yawns between him and his colleagues. I find myself acting as a sort of unofficial conduit between the board and Peter Cadbury, during which time he grabs the headlines in the national press and appears dressed in a 'JR' type stetson on BBC television; the *Money Programme* also devotes an entire programme to the dispute. Cadbury's charisma remains undimmed.

Loyal staff from the Plymouth Studio gather clandestinely at Lyneham House; they range from managers to studio electricians. The Cadbury plan to call an Extraordinary General

17

Meeting and fire virtually all the 'rebel' directors seems a real favourite to succeed. He will hear no talk of conciliation.

Sir Robert Cooke, who voted with those who wanted him removed as Chairman, meets me for tea at the Savoy and in a spirit of genuine concern discusses various ways in which we might salvage the situation even at this late hour. The possibility of Cadbury taking up a new non-executive role as President is kicked around and suddenly it seems worth giving it a try.

Cadbury continues to dominate the media with a battery of statements, press releases, off-the-cuff remarks, pavement interviews and stage-managed feature articles that are designed to encourage his supporters and break Lord Harris's nerve. In late July, the *Observer* reports that 'bronzed and stripped to the waist in his Chelsea penthouse [he] told a press conference that he now controls 108,430 shares – just over 54 per cent of Westward's voting capital'. Cadbury also points out, still stripped to the waist, that he has telegrams and letters of support that will be turned into 'irrevocable proxies' and thus armed with these powers of attorney he will 'boot out Harris and his gang' in September, or earlier if they run scared and quit.

Private Eye gives the dispute extraordinary prominence, running two long articles in consecutive issues headed 'A Tale of Two Shitties'. The first deals with Cadbury and is less than eulogistic. Its closing paragraph on Friday 15 August reads:

As the deadline gets nearer, Mr Peter Cadbury will need all his public relations expertise to get himself out of this one. Indeed to lose this battle to Mr Peter Cadbury in his present state would require in his adversary a combination of political mediocrity and personal vanity unknown in any living Englishman with the exception of Lord Harris of Greenwich.

In the following issue, Harris received the *Eye* treatment with knobs on, but tells me in his office – I am summoned to

18

brief him on sales – that he will ignore 'these scurrilous attacks.'

Price Waterhouse, the world-famous accountants, have already been called in by Harris to 'investigate Westward's internal procedures and financial control'. The timing of this move suggests that the board's lofty motives may be tinged with the desire to expose Cadbury's faults and weaknesses and his rather swashbuckling approach to running the company. In any event, the London office is besieged by accountants of all shapes and sizes who sift through every scrap of paper they can find, driving the chief accountant, Bert Maillardet, almost to nervous breakdown.

Incredibly, business continues as usual, but Harris becomes so remote from the day-to-day operation as to be virtually invisible. He issues ponderous bulletins which I have no doubt he considers to be both diplomatic and forceful. He draws up a statement for the 11 rebel directors to sign which says:

We regret the decision by Mr Cadbury to seek to convene an Extraordinary General Meeting of Westward share-holders. This can only damage the company's reputation. The board at its last meeting came to the conclusion with both reluctance and regret that it was no longer possible to conduct the business of a public company in the manner found acceptable by Mr Cadbury. In addition, we believed that unless a change was made in the chairman-ship of the company, Westward Television would lose it licence. That remains our view.

Cadbury has called for his shareholders' meeting to take place on 10 September at the Carlton Tower Hotel in Knightsbridge, but Lord Harris, his office six-deep with lawyers, accountants, foot jugglers and soothsayers, dismisses the meeting as being invalid. He will call a 'proper' meeting on 17 October when the 'full facts' of the affair will be placed before the shareholders. There follows a rapid series of events which can only be described as Byzantine in their baffling complexity.

19

Lord Harris, for reasons which may remain a mystery until the end of time, calls a board meeting at the old hotel adjoining Paddington station and there we sit, listening to the rumble of westbound trains as we deliberate on the weighty matters in hand. When I question the advisability of the present collision course, Harris rebukes me and announces that he is an 'honourable man'.

It is a sad day to see fine men like George Lidstone and others in dispute with the man who founded their company. I experience a feeling of personal failure and uselessness that I can't shrug off. I know I am at odds with my colleagues and as for Lord Harris, the outsider, what can be said of him? He is certainly active. The prospect of Cadbury's September meeting has clearly rattled him and, with the board's consent, he applies to the High Court in order to try to get the meeting banned.

Cadbury retaliates by issuing a writ against Lord Harris and the Westward board. The significance of the Harris meeting on 17 October, is clear to him. It is a week after his own appearance in a Barnstaple court on the charges of wasting police time. He is also aware that Harris is trying to find a 'legal' way to transfer the Cadbury voting shares elsewhere. An obscure clause in the company's Articles of Association suggests that such a move may just be possible.

Cadbury has machine-gunned off a series of letters to the shareholders, one of which reads:

> I am left in no doubt that the dominant intention of your board in delaying the requisitioned meeting [10 September] until 17th October was to enable it to disenfranchise the shares held by Lord Lisburne, myself and members of my family... In the circumstances, I am advised that your directors have (i) failed to comply with their statutory obligations under the Act leaving Lord Lisburne and myself free to convene the requisitioned meeting and (ii) exercised their powers under Article 30 (4) in breach of their fiduciary duty and wrongfully for the purpose of depriving the existing majority of mem-

bers of your company entitled to attend and vote at general meetings of their right to constitute the board.

The Harris response is swift:

The meeting convened by the board for 17 October following Mr Cadbury's and Lord Lisburne's requisition was properly convened. The date was approved by leading counsel. Mr Cadbury and Lord Lisburne are not therefore entitled to call the meeting which they have tried to convene for 10 September. If this meeting takes place resolutions passed at it will have no effect.

On 5 September, a week prior to the 'Cadbury' meeting, the wrangle actually reaches the Chancery Division and to Peter Cadbury's great delight, Mr Justice Dillon rules that his meeting may indeed take place. He warns sternly, however, that unless some sort of truce is agreed between the two parties, there is a risk that the Official Receiver could be put in to run the company.

I am sitting in court listening to all this and pinching myself lest I think it is just another Gothic nightmare. A number of my sales executives reveal themselves in the public gallery to observe these truly weird events. There is, after Mr Justice Dillon's ruling, talk of some kind of 'ceasefire' between the warring parties. Cadbury magnanimously announces that he is 'willing to agree to anything reasonable or sensible that will save Westward'.

Nevertheless, the Carlton Tower meeting proceeds on 10 September in a veritable blaze of publicity. Camera crews, journalists, shareholders and bemused Arab visitors all jostle with each other in the lobby of the hotel until Cadbury, scenting victory, arrives with his wife Janie.

It is an extraordinary meeting in the literal as well as the legal sense. With flash bulbs popping, Cadbury proposes the removal of Harris, Perry, Lidstone, Cooke, Heathcoat Amory and Lennox-Boyd from the board and all motions are carried. However, the voting at present is only a technical manoeuvre

21

made for legal reasons pending the further special meeting of Westward shareholders in Plymouth on 17 October, when the same resolutions for dismissal will be put.

Harris concedes he might still lose in October, but adds, typically, that if Cadbury returns it will mean 'certain death for the company'. Harris also says, in a now notorious remark: 'With Cadbury as Chairman, we don't stand a snowball's chance in hell of winning a renewal of our franchise'. (Much later, after losing the licence anyway, he is to receive a ferocious telegram from Cadbury which says: 'What does it feel like to be a snowball in hell?')

Summer turns to autumn and Cadbury continues to pile up ammunition. I see him regularly in his penthouse in Chelsea which has been converted into a battle headquarters with copying machines, electric typewriters and filing cabinets. It is here that his 'irrevocable proxies' are counted and a veritable flood of letters in the abrasive Cadbury style is dispatched to shareholders, supporters and dazed spectators. His mood is changing; he laughs a good deal less and talks darkly of vengeance and retribution. I suggest that magnanimity in victory might be preferable and receive a thunderous glare in response. His wife Janie looks tired and no wonder. Her home is like an elegant transit camp with well-wishers, lawyers and journalists coming and going all day long.

Frequently, I call at the house at about 8.30 a.m. and Cadbury is in his dressing-gown typing letters with two fingers while Janie organises a ceaseless flow of coffee. One morning he swings round to greet me with a look of absolute glee on his face.

'I've got Bill Cheevers to pledge his shares in my support,' he says. 'How's that for a coup?'

It is an extraordinary piece of generalship, for Bill Cheevers is the Managing Director Cadbury fired over a decade ago after another boardroom row. What was the other row about? Oh, just that Cheevers and his supporters thought Cadbury was unsuitable to continue as chairman of a public company, etc, etc. A feeling of *déja vu* sweeps over me as I digest this news.

However, it is an undeniable coup and it is not long before

22

the press pick up on the story. With Cheevers's support, plus the other proxies, the result of the forthcoming shareholders' meeting seems now a foregone conclusion.

Cadbury begins to plan his cabinet reshuffle after what he now believes will be his triumphant return to the chairmanship. Heads will roll, that is for certain, and others will be raised up to positions of greatness, not least of all his secretary and PA, Anne Whately, who is rather impetuously promised a seat on the board by Cadbury. An efficient lady, without doubt, but her appointment to the board will be unpopular with the staff, who feel others are more deserving.

Meanwhile, an IBA spokesman says that they are 'keeping a very beady eye' on what's happening. But by now, even Cadbury's closest supporters realise that merely 'knocking out Harris and his gang' on 17 October, after what has been a long and undignified wrangle, is only a minor hurdle. The water jump will be the IBA.

Cadbury refuses to consider caution or compromise. It is as if he believes the IBA will give us a renewal, come what may. No amount of argument, it seems, will prevent a head-on collision with Harris in October and a virtually new board structure being presented to the IBA at the famous 'interview' where ITV companies are grilled about past performances and future plans.

On 23 September, in Plymouth, the IBA holds its public meeting and the hall is packed to capacity. Cadbury is conspicuous by his absence and the Westward team is led by Lord Harris, later criticised by a local paper for not having cleaned his shoes. It is here that I see, for the first time, some of the TSW colleagues that I am destined to work with. The other faction, led by Simon Day, do not overwhelm the audience with their sparkle. We leave the meeting feeling a shade low, although the general consensus is that Westward has 'done OK'.

On 25 September, the *Guardian* reports that I am attempting to 'throw a frail bridge over the chasm' and that we must stem the blood-letting before the shareholders gather on 17 October. I talk to Peter Cadbury and he does seem ready to seek a formula for ending the wrangle. Catch 22, however, is that the board won't have him back as Chairman, at any price, and the nebulous role of President would need defining by lawyers, priests and probably a brace of cardinals as well.

Some of Cadbury's friends are privately advising him to drop the whole thing. He goes away for a short holiday to the South of France, but even the sumptuous luxury of the Hotel Cap Estel is not enough to soften his resolve.

Harris has become an obsession with him. The noble lord is referred to as 'that bugger Harris' and this is one of the more polite appellations. Harris plays it long and refuses to be drawn; indeed, his stance is one of Buddha-like reticence. It's obvious he feels that given enough rope, Cadbury may hang himself.

Meanwhile, back at Sloane Square House, the sales department faces up to the autumn with a sigh or three of desperation. I know what is going through their minds. Just what sort of lunatic asylum are we actually working in? I brief them regularly on the state of play and wish I could give them more encouraging news.

On 25 September, the IBA finally intervenes in what the *Daily Mail* describes as an 'unprecedented move'. They announce that they will decide on 9 October – eight days prior to the fateful 17th – which of the rival factions will run the company. The Authority is intervening under a clause of the ITV franchise which allows a company to forfeit its contract if there are substantial changes in its management and ownership.

Bryan Rook, secretary to the IBA, has written to both Cadbury and Harris asking for certain assurances, adding:

> The Authority feels it necessary to consider whether there has been, or is likely to be, a change affecting the nature and characteristics of Westward Television or in the persons having control or interests in it, such as to justify the Authority evoking the provisions of Clause One of the programme contract.

24

From this moment, events accelerate quickly, flashing and glimmering like a speeded-up film.

On 6 October, Cadbury appears before magistrates in Barnstaple to hear charges that he has wasted police time. This bitter dispute has hung over his head since early in the year and is one of the many ingredients that make up the present wildly theatrical impasse. In court, Cadbury admits that his 'vendetta' against the Chief Executive of Plymouth Council was 'misguided' and that his belief that there was corruption among local government officials untrue. He is fined £200 and ordered to pay costs. The *London Evening News* of that day runs a blazing headline on the front page: 'The Shame of Peter Cadbury' above a photograph of him and his third wife, Janie. The picture itself is captioned 'Sent forged letter to the Lord Mayor'.

It is a bad day for all of us. The success of Cadbury's planned coup on 17 October now seems less of a sure thing. Mysterious supporters for his cause spring up from unexpected quarters. I find myself having a drink in the bar at the House of Lords with Cadbury and one of Westward's earliest shareholders, Lord Willis, the creator of *Dixon of Dock Green*. Ted Willis is a pro-Cadbury man, although their connections seem tenuous.

As we sip our drinks, Lord Harris is discussed in slightly less than rapturous tones. I glance up, and to my discomfiture see Westward board member Robert Cooke at a nearby table drinking with a clutch of unknown peers. What drama. I feel I am part of some grotesque medieval farce. Will Robin (Sir Robert) ignore us or saunter across and offer to buy us a gin and lime? Cadbury either fails to see him or chooses to turn a blind eye.

I drive home slowly and at Sunbury on Thames I am flagged down by a policeman who tells me only one of my stop lights is working. It has been a day packed with incident and I am glad it is drawing to a close. When I arrive at my house in Surrey, no less than three shareholders have phoned leaving messages asking whether they should sell and if Cadbury will swing it on the 17th. I decide not to phone them back tonight and after rereading those awful headlines in the *Evening News* I hit the sack.

I believe now, and believed then, that even if the shareholders' meeting had taken place on the 17th, we would have needed a lot of luck to win a renewal of our licence. Two rival contenders for the South West franchise were in the field, one of them (TSW) with a skilfully prepared manifesto and powerful support within the region. As they presented their credentials with increasing confidence, Westward appeared to be bent on nothing more edifying than a highly publicised suicide.

On 9 October, Cadbury is summoned to the IBA's headquarters in Brompton Road and still stunned, like a Spanish fighting bull, he hears what the Authority has to say.

Later, the trade magazine *Broadcast* comes into possession of what it believes are the confidential minutes of that meeting and it publishes them on 10 November. Even if they are absolutely genuine, they do not make exciting reading – confidential minutes seldom do. There is, however, a subtle exercise of administrative power that can be detected in the body of the text. Cadbury has Andy Kerman, his solicitor, at his side throughout and at the end of the day, a very long one, Cadbury issues a weary statement:

> After discussions with the Authority, I have come to the conclusion that it would not be in the interests of the company to have another upheaval on the board at this time. I have therefore agreed that we will support a resolution to adjourn the meeting planned for 17th October *sine die*.

The Cadbury plan to virtually decimate the old board and replace it with a smaller group of 'television professionals' including John Hollowday, our erstwhile financial adviser, and Anne Whatley, is not acceptable to the IBA, presumably on the grounds that it so changes the structure of the company that was granted the original licence as to make it unrecognisable. Cadbury is shattered. He has to quit the fight. To bulldoze ahead with the shareholders' meeting on 17 October and carry out the threatened executions will be no more than a hollow victory. Its aftermath will be the certain loss of the licence.

As recently as ten months previously, Cadbury, Harris, Lisburne, Sir Robert Cooke, Anne Whatley and myself dined at the Alston Hall Hotel in Devon prior to a Plymouth board meeting. The atmosphere was genial, the food and wine exceptional. The two noble lords exchanged light banter; Harris was full of wickedly witty tales from Westminster; Cadbury was relaxed, charming. How, we asked ourselves, could such a closely-knit team possibly fail when the far distant franchise business came up for review?

Now the dream is shattered and Cadbury's sense of bitterness and betrayal is reaching Carthaginian proportions. Lord Harris notwithstanding, he is deeply hurt that Ronnie Perry, the Managing Director, should have sided with the 'rebels'. Ronnie owes much to Cadbury and his rise from Floor Manager to Managing Director has been, up until 14 July, one of Cadbury's best examples of promotion from within.

That evening we gather in the Chelsea penthouse to appraise the situation. I have received the news on my car telephone from a tearful Janie Cadbury earlier in the day.

'Harris has won,' she says.

Friends arrive quietly that night in Chelsea and when I see Peter Cadbury, he has aged ten years. His tan has faded and even the ferocious blue eyes are dimmed with exhaustion. There is desultory talk of fighting on, but it is no more than a ritual response to an already hopeless situation.

When I talk to my sales team the next day, there is genuine sadness that Cadbury's much-vaunted return to the throne has been thwarted. In spite of, possibly because of, his faults, they prefer his piratical style to that of the archetypal politician, John Harris. We resolve to apply ourselves to the work in hand. There is no other choice, the time for gestures and emotional sacrifices is finished.

Hindsight is not just a benefit, it is also a luxury that should be indulged in sparingly. Could the fiasco have been avoided?

27

Were there really such clear-cut villains and heroes? It's hard to be precise with years between then and now. Cadbury was a man of his time and his time and his style are forever gone. Perhaps with the Gadarene rush towards technological change and relentless respectability, his type have no place. If that is so, it is a cause for regret. He was a fabulous, larger than life figure and he brought colour and excitement to a small television station in the South West. He was also my mentor and supporter over the years and I will never be able to repay his kindnesses both to me and to my wife Carolyn.

Proust once said that each of us carries within ourselves the seeds of our own destruction. Cadbury had an imperviousness to criticism and that was perhaps his final vulnerability.

My 19 years with the man were packed with extraordinary events, a rich and varied tapestry that would, of itself, make compelling television. He was, when all was said and done, one of ITV's last true swashbucklers. But he gave me the encouragement I needed to build an extraordinary sales team and above all, he made it fun. I wouldn't have missed a minute of it for all the world.

Now in his eighties, but still vibrant, Cadbury was one of the key influences in my life. May he live to be 150.

The process of awarding television licences in the late 1970s defies rational analysis. The Independent Broadcasting Authority (the IBA) were charged by Parliament to carry out this task, and during the last days of Westward Television the Chairman of this august, remote and sometimes infuriating body was the redoubtable Lady Bridget Plowden, an educationalist whose demeanour often suggested Dame Edith Evans playing Lady Bracknell.

She was assisted, if that is the appropriate word, by her Director General, Sir Brian Young, himself an ex-headmaster of Charterhouse and a man whose classical education and fondness for Greek quotations made him uniquely unsuited to the role, at least in his early days. He later became a staunch supporter of the ITV companies and in particular the small regions.

After Westward had submitted its application for a renewal of its franchise – a weighty tome constructed under the whimsical editorship of Lord Harris – the entire board of Westward, minus of course its ousted founder Peter Cadbury, were summoned to appear at IBA headquarters in Brompton Road.

I recall sitting at the horseshoe-shaped table in the large boardroom with my Westward colleagues while facing us across the carpeted divide were the members of the Authority who were to seal our fate. They were then, and are today, even though the names have changed, a selection of men and women of middle-class style and appearance whose intimate knowledge of popular viewing tastes could be comfortably stored in a matchbox. Even as the litany of questions and answers passed across the room about our programme plans, our public service commitment, our financial structure and our staff hierarchy, I sensed a smell of death in the air.

At one stage a member of the Authority whose name eludes me, but who was almost certainly an ordained priest, asked a vague question about our commitment to religion. Lord Harris removed his spectacles with the usual flourish. 'I think,' he murmured, 'that is a matter for the Sales Director.' I am sure he had misheard the question – he must have done. Religion! A matter needing comment from a mere Sales Director – a rude mechanical tainted by trade and, moreover, the wearer of extravagant suede shoes. Surely not?

All eyes swivelled toward me as I struggled to find a suitable response. Should I comment airily on the importance we attached to the advertising of altar candles, cassocks and incense? Or was it a deliberate trick question? Fortunately, before I was able to utter and plunge the company into a black pit of ridicule and haughty disapproval, our Programme Controller, Terry Fleet, spoke up and made some splendidly non-committal remarks that seemed to satisfy the questioner.

After half an hour of icy politeness and stilted exchanges we all filed out into the corridor. I fell in step beside Terry.

'What do you think?' he whispered, for whispers seemed appropriate in that long, grey corridor.

'I think we're going to be comprehensively screwed,' I said. As history shows, this urbane observation was smack on target.

CHAPTER 2

Parish pump television – swearing priests and eccentric Etonians plus the mad airline venture and more ructions with authority.

In the early Westward days, the station provided programmes that reflected and celebrated the South-West. The daily flagship, *Westward Diary*, went out each evening fronted by the urbane and unflappable Ken McCloud who became a firm favourite with our viewers.

When TSW (Television South West) took over, the daily show was renamed *TSW Today*, but Ken still featured on a regular basis together with a new young presenter, Ruth Langsford, who has since been lured to the big city and has her own show with the BBC.

Another early 'star' was Judi Spiers, a local girl with a great knack for ad-libbing who briefly fronted the BBC's *Pebble Mill* from Birmingham. Both women, in my view, were infinitely better than many of the female presenters who decorate our screen today.

In keeping with other small regional stations, both Westward and TSW confined their locally-provided programmes to between 6.5 to 8 hours per week, the rest of the schedule, now over 100 hours, came from network or foreign sources.

Precluded from the glitzy show-biz-type programmes, the regional stations' strengths were in news and documentaries. Westward won an Emmy Award for its *Wyvern at War*, the story of the Wessex Division, and a brilliant series called *Walking Westward* in which reporter Clive Gunnel walked most of the coastline of the South-West peninsula with a camera crew, talking to local people and commenting on the abundance and variety of the local scenery. A smash hit locally, but of limited interest outside the region.

One of TSW's shows that did make the network was a series called *That's My Dog*, a kind of quiz for canines that was bought by Channel Four. Earlier in TSW's life, another series, the *Cut Price Comedy Show* also made the network. It was so excruciatingly bad that it became a cult show and people talk of it still with a mixture of awe and revulsion.

Both Westward and TSW had their share of trendy vicars who were required to appear in front of camera at *Epilogue* time. The religious slot was a requirement of the IBA and part of the contract or licence granted to regional broadcasters. While these worthy vignettes gave comfort late at night to a minority of viewers, I must confess I found them grindingly boring and most of the clerics about as charismatic as an undertaker with haemorrhoids. My fondest memory is of an Anglican priest walking off the set of Studio 2, tripping over a wire and hissing 'bollocks'. My only regret is that the cameras had stopped rolling.

It was perhaps inevitable that the sea, agriculture and tourism featured very strongly in West Country local programming – they were, after all, what the region was really about.

The audience of course enjoyed the big network shows like *Coronation Street*, variety spectaculars and smash-hit movies, but they were particularly fond of local programmes which showed familiar places and faces and addressed issues which touched their own lives.

Then as now, small regional companies relied almost entirely on advertising revenue, but less than 10 per cent of it was generated locally in the South-West. It was a hard slog introducing this new-fangled medium to very conservative shopkeepers and small businesses.

It was only in the late 1960s that local advertising agencies began to assert themselves. One of the pioneers was the splendid Harry Stillings from Exeter. Harry was a commercial artist who began to dabble in a small way in advertising from a converted shed in his garden. The production of television commercials outside of London was unheard of and when I first met Harry in his famous shed he was knocking out press ads for the local papers, designing posters, handbills and the like. Today, Harry Stillings's agency is one of the top operators in the South-West. They have campaigns on television and radio, and in magazines and newspapers. The company is still privately owned and since Harry died a few years back, it has been run by his daughter, Jenny Freer. Jenny has maintained a splendid West Country flavour with the agency and now has an impressive list of small clients who market their goods and services, in some cases well beyond the boundaries of the South-West.

While the West Country is unlikely ever to spawn a J. Walter Thompson or a Saatchis', it is a very attractive area for service industries and number of financial institutions, commercial banks, etc. have opened branch offices in Plymouth and Exeter and slowly an infrastructure of support businesses is growing up. In the early days, however, airtime sales were quite simply a retail business while representatives knocked on the doors of shopkeepers, ate ploughman's lunches in pubs and chased up on the small advertisements in the local newspapers.

In the mid-1960s the biggest single local advertiser, Millbay Laundry, spent less than £10,000 in a year. Local airtime selling was labour intensive and grindingly hard work. The local operation had been headed from day one by one of nature's great eccentrics, the delightful Henry Stracey. Henry had retained much of his boyish Etonian enthusiasm. After being invalided out of the Royal Air Force he lived a life of the rich dilettante, but had exhausted his generous inheritance by the time he reached his early thirties. His first marriage failed when his wife realised that the life of luxury and world travel was at an end and at an age when most men have long since settled into their career, Henry took his first job, as a jam salesman.

His commercial instincts (which were necessarily limited) were reinforced by an irresistible personality. Over six feet tall, he wore heavy tweed suits, thick-soled hiking shoes and

33

a dark green highwayman's cape that made him an unmistakable figure on his travels. He met his second wife, Jeltje, who was Dutch, when she was still a nurse and for the rest of their marriage, even to this day, he calls her 'Staff'.

Based in a pretty cottage in Buckland Monacorum, his forays into the region to sell airtime were usually very successful. He became a much-loved friend of dozens of our tiny retail customers. One particular instance will serve to indicate the sheer flavour of the man's personality.

For years a local restaurateur had booked a few local spots for transmission at Christmas time. One autumn when business was slack Henry arrived at this establishment only to be told by the proprietor that he would not be advertising that year. Downcast at the loss of an order worth every bit of £200, Henry sought solace by taking a glass of sherry with the proprietor's wife. She was so upset at her husband's decision and so entranced by Henry's persuasive charm that she uttered the following immortal words which, in my view, should be etched on Henry's tombstone, should the man ever be inconsiderate enough to die: 'Mr Stracey, I do not agree with my husband cancelling his campaign on Westward and I shall deny myself to him physically until he changes his mind.' The lady was 74 when the words were uttered.

Later in Henry's career we had a few brief altercations. I was by then Director of Sales in London and Henry had an irritating habit of submitting single expense sheets reclaiming 1s 9d for car-parking at Exeter's municipal car park. Once he telephoned me from a roadside booth near Tiverton claiming he needed to speak to me on a matter of great urgency. Even though I was in the middle of a board meeting I ran to my office to take the call. Was it possible, Henry asked, to purchase a powder-blue Ford Consul convertible as his company vehicle because it was not only a pretty colour, but would impress the clients with his sense of dash and style. It was hard to stay cross with Henry for very long.

I once gave him a small book on the history of Le Petomane. As every schoolboy knows, Le Petomane was a musical artist who, to put it delicately, could break wind in time to music.

He had so trained his sphincter muscles that a deep trumpeting noise would emerge from his pantaloons to the delight of his Victorian audience. Some years later a film was made of his life staring Leonard Rossiter. Henry, intrigued by the book, eagerly read the chapter which describes Le Petomane's special exercises. One of these involved crouching in a bath of warm soapy water, drawing the water into the back passage by the flexing of the sphincter muscles and then expelling the water in a fine jet against the tiled wall. Henry and Jeltje had tried unsuccessfully to perform this feat. I believe it was one of the great disappointments of his life.

He was assisted in the local sales office by another unusual fellow, Barney Camfield, who was a faith healer and a lay preacher in his spare time. It was not unknown for Barney to conduct a 'laying on of hands' ceremony if a client was hesitant over an order.

Eccentricity? Possibly. But life was never dull and strong characters like Henry and Barney helped stamp an indelible image of the station wherever they went.

The current vogue for numerate, grey, economics graduates with horn-rimmed glasses and Volvo saloons who call themselves sales executives leaves me less than tumescent with enthusiasm. But every age has its fashion and the 1990s was clearly to be the era of the bloodless, semi-invisible technocrat whose true love is a portable computer he or she can play with on his lap while travelling on an inter-city train to Milton Keynes.

It is worth remembering that much of Westward's pioneering work took place in the now famous 1960s, when youth (now known as yoof) was in the ascendancy and Britain was the epicentre of the universe. A curious social phenomenon manifested itself however, in the nature of the divide 'twixt London and Plymouth. That there was (and perhaps still is) a cultural and philosophical gap between the two cities is undeniable, one a metropolis of style and cynicism, great wealth and pace, the other an ancient seafaring port close to the great wilderness of Dartmoor, unfashionable, leisured in pace and conspicuously non-affluent.

In the 1960s the influence of Carnaby Street, the Beatles and the miniskirt took the Westward Sales Office by storm. Young women dressed like Barbie dolls – indeed never before or even since has there been such a feast of thighs and bottoms. Ah, the lost bird of youth has flown, etc., etc. The 'boys' (for even grown men of 30 were so described) dressed for their part in the *de rigueur* uniform of the time. Flared trousers that clung tenaciously to the hips, huge kipper ties and a cornucopia of hair. And what hair! Curly, greasy, frizzy. It mattered not a jot so long as it was worn *long*. Side-whiskers too, sprouted in awful profusion. I managed to force an uneven pair myself, and glancing through old photographs I have come to the considered opinion that I looked a complete and utter prat.

The age of the wine bar had arrived in London and every evening after work it was absolutely essential for salespeople to gather in one of these establishments and sip appalling plonk not entirely inconsistent with giraffe's urine while eyeing up the gorgeous young women perched on bar stools in their wonderful miniskirts. One of the most famous of the wine bars was situated in Pavilion Road just off Knightsbridge. It was called 'The Loose Box'. I do believe that more romances were started, more affairs terminated and more adulterous thrustings contemplated in The Loose Box than in any other establishment this side of paradise.

After a Friday night's sipping and flirting at The Loose Box the more affluent of the unattached would slope off to Luba's Bistro opposite Brompton Oratory for chicken-in-the-rough, chips, apple pie and thence, if they were really lucky, to some artfully decorated bedsit in Gloucester Road where they would engage in an activity known quaintly in those days as 'shafting'. It is a matter for social historians to debate whether the current word 'bonking' is worse, better or as obnoxious as the 1960s word. I remain silent on the issue, as any gentleman should.

Meanwhile in Plymouth, the stout-hearted Devonians resisted, or at least half resisted the fashion revolution. Even during a heatwave they favoured Fair Isle sweaters, anoraks and leather sandals. It is true that side-whiskers did appear. Great bushy things that could be seen from behind. The really curious fact is that they have remained, even to this day, along with the occasional kipper tie and faded pair of 1963 flares.

The average Plymothian is to high fashion what Rasputin was to needlework. During the 1960s, while London rocked and rolled and grew lots of hair and bopped at 'Samantha's' or 'Haddy's' in Earls Court, the Plymouth brigade still went to 'dinner dances' wearing white slingbacks and 'cardys' with hair tightly permed like a Brillo pad.

Even in the early 1960s, I was aware that Westward Television had aspirations to be a lot bigger than its 2.6 per cent of the network. Indeed from 1961 when it first began transmission, Peter Cadbury insisted that the Mendip transmitter which served Bristol, should be reallocated to Westward as it was, in Peter's view, a natural part of the West Country. The then IBA regarded these requests as no more than harmless public relations posturing, but Cadbury was serious and successive Director Generals eventually found his campaign a little too rich for their blood. Although sympathetic to his xenophobic enthusiasm, given that Cadbury's boyhood home was at Abott Lee, outside Bristol, they were compelled to issue a magisterial rebuke. Early in 1970s Sir Robert Fraser wrote to Cadbury as follows:

I think I must tell you that the Authority is increasingly embarrassed by the continuing agitation against its decision in the matter of the Mendip UHF transmitter station. There are some cases where the Authority found it difficult to decide the allocation of UHF stations, this was not one of them.

Having successfully applied for one contract area you have been seeking, by public agitation, to secure an important change in this contract in an effort to secure a major addition to your area at the cost of the neighbouring company.

Peace broke out, but not for long. In 1971, Westward was

37

ten years old and together with Cadbury's trusted PA, Rosemary Peacock, a formidable and talented lady, I helped organise a birthday party for the company at the Hyde Park Hotel. Various dignitaries were invited, including Jeremy Thorpe, leader of the Liberal Party and a Devon Member of Parliament. This was, of course, before Jeremy's downfall and the mysterious business of his friendship with peculiar men called Bunny. Not to mention the even more intriguing mystery of innocent puppy dogs that got riddled with bullets.

As a surprise at the party, Rosemary arranged for a huge cake to be made in the shape of the Westward transmission area. The plan was to have it wheeled in on a trolley immediately after the dinner and the formal speeches. I hit upon a brilliant wheeze, which later proved to be one of the more daft ideas I have ever conceived. In addition to the big cake, I arranged for the bewildered chef at the Hyde Park Hotel to make a smaller cake, suitably iced, in the shape of the Bristol area. With the benefit of hindsight, I realise that this was not likely to endear us to Lord Aylestone, Chairman of the IBA, one of the guests of honour.

Nonetheless, after a hearty meal and many rollicking speeches, cake number one rolled into view, Cadbury cut it and everybody belted down the champagne. Then, with what could only be described as a limp fanfare from the band, cake number two rattled up to the top table. Aylestone looked as if he had sat on a sharp stick, Cadbury bellowed with laughter and Jeremy Thorpe dashed off for a division in the House.

Much of what followed is a hazy memory, but another tiny black mark had been registered against the Westward name. The pessimistic among us (not including me) claimed that a nail had been driven into our coffin.

At the Westward annual general meeting in 1977, Cadbury punches out the same uncompromising message: 'We want Bristol! History and geography are on our side.'

'Why,' Cadbury asks me privately, 'don't the IBA pull their finger out over this issue?'

Minor explosives resound immediately after the AGM and Lord Harlech, Chairman of neighbouring HTV, demands and gets an apology from Cadbury. The IBA are even less enamoured and Sir Brian Young, now Director General, writes one of the sharpest letters ever sent to the Chairman of a television company. A brief extract is enough to give the flavour of the letter:

> It is not a question of your being asked by the IBA not to claim Bristol, it is a question of your having, on more than one occasion, given me a positive assurance that you would not. I cannot tell you how sick I am of this dreary running saga caused by your forgetfulness and indiscretion. The IBA should be able to rely on the Chairman of a company to behave responsibly and sensibly.

The letter does little, if anything, to ruffle Cadbury's feathers and reinforces his view that he is dealing with a bunch of amateur bureaucrats. The language he uses in describing them is trenchant and colourful, casting doubts on their collective parenthood and cerebral competence.

At this time we are possessed with a belief that the function of our independent television company is not only to reflect the life and interests of the West Country, but to actively promote them as well. We set up sponsorship deals with local businesses, we give cash and support to the arts and local theatres. We create a business initiative training scheme and the North Devon Economic Project is supported with programmes, training and technical advice. We establish Euro-Westward, a marketing consortium designed to promote tourism in the region. Over 1,000 local artists participate in our biennial open art exhibition (a number of fine watercolours from this period now hang in my home). At Exeter University we finance a series of Vice-Chancellor's lectures and a research project dealing with wind energy for farmers and horticulturists.

A sense of worthiness permeates all that we do – and we are still making handsome profits. We have the best, it seems, of all worlds. Until that is, the launch of Air Westward.

The plan is simple. Even robust. Cadbury, himself an extest pilot, wants to provide the region with its own airline with direct flights for businessmen on routes out of Exeter to Cardiff, Edinburgh, Paris and Brussels. The IBA reluctantly consent for us to use £1.3 million of our cash reserves to purchase two aeroplanes.

The money is swallowed up faster than you can say 'casino'. Restrictions on working hours for pilots mean that two pilots are needed on a 14-seat aircraft and many other hideously expensive snags are waiting to dog the enterprise.

We make a lovely TV commercial to promote the airline, but it produces very little in the way of increased business. Cadbury is a great enthusiast for the project, but it is tough going for those of us who are directors of Air Westward and who have little knowledge of commercial aviation. To our great chagrin, Air Westward only remains operational from May 1978 until April 1979.

Peter Cadbury is deeply disappointed. It has been his 'baby', after all, and now we've lost a hefty chunk of the television company's reserves. We all do our best to put a gloss on the failure of the enterprise and Cadbury, in his best pugnacious style writes to me on 12 April, 1979. He encloses a draft interim statement to be presented to shareholders, which will attempt to soften the blow. His letter to me is in typically upbeat, Cadburyesque language:

Dear Harry,

Attached is the new draft I typed tonight, which, as you see, dismisses the loss on Air Westward as minimal – it amounts to only about £150,000 after tax and quite a bit has been absorbed in the Levy. I will leave it to Roy [Baker, the Finance Director] to juggle the figures, as I agree with all that was said at the Board Meeting (apart from Roy's comments!). These half-yearly figures are more important than those we produce in December.

However, I am sorry Air Westward was not a success. I feel mainly responsible for introducing it in the first place, although, as everyone knows, the elements were against us in ways that we could not have anticipated. I

accept that it is more prudent to avoid publishing my
views on Exeter Airport, the County Council, the pilots,
et alia!

I hope this will reach you in time for you to let me
have any comments or amendments you want.

Yours sincerely,

Peter Cadbury

The explanation in the interim statement itself is brief and
uncompromising. It reads:

In May, 1978, we started Air Westward as a diversification after making comprehensive surveys, which showed
there to be a requirement for this new Airline. At the
same time, it was appreciated that it would be some years
before we could expect this new venture to be profitable
and when an offer was made by a competitor to purchase
Air Westward at a reasonable value, your Directors
decided to sell the Airline and use the cash for the development and expansion of our main interest, namely television and the making of programmes. Amongst the new
equipment we are acquiring is a Sony Outside Broadcast
Unit, which is the first of its kind in this Country, and
which we will put into operation this coming summer.

On current figures, I am confident that I will be able
to report another record year's trading as of July 31st. We
welcome two new Directors to our Company, namely Mr
Rodney Brimacombe and Lord Harris of Greenwich, who
until recently was the Minister of State at the Home
Office in charge of Broadcasting.

How elegant and optimistic it sounds even now, decades
later. The appointment of Lord Harris was seen by many to
be a master-stroke at the time!

CHAPTER 3

The ubiquitous Zionist who started the Montreux
Golden Rose Festival. Gauche posturing in the
South of France and Pearl & Dean's boss
displays cunning thrift.

Nobody who has worked as an on-screen personality for either
Westward or TSW has ever suffered from the 'star' syndrome.
This is not, as you might first suppose, because successive
programme directors have rigorously eschewed the cult of the
personality. Indeed the little station in the South-West has
spawned more than its fair whack of telly personalities: David
Vine, Judi Spiers, Angela Rippon, Brent Sadler (he of the
sand-drenched despatch from steaming war zones), Jan
Leeming – the list if not exactly endless, is undeniably impressive.

And why did such luminaries never succumb to the
overblown egotism so prevalent elsewhere? The answer is a
touch prosaic. They found it impossible to compete with the
station's unlovely rabbit who decorated our screen for nearly
30 years. His function was minimal, but utterly crucial. He
read out the birthdays of children in the South-West, regularly
every weekday, and some believe is likely to go on doing so
until the arrival of Armageddon. Starry-eyed housewives
whose fifth or sixth birthdays were once read out by the
ubiquitous bunny many years previously now clamour to have
their own children given the same treatment.

Now the life of a glove puppet is necessarily limited, at least
on screen. He has to be manipulated by a human presenter
whose primary task is to keep a straight face. I have been

asked on more than one occasion whether 'Gus Honeybun' is gay. 'No,' I invariably reply, 'just irrepressibly cheerful.' Others remark on the fact that his toothy features seem permanently cast in a mould of startled surprise. This is no wonder. If you spent most of your waking hours with somebody else's hand up your ass, you'd look surprised too.

When Westward Television lost its franchise to TSW, there were more letters expressing concern over the future of Gus Honeybun than for any other on-screen personality. I have never been sure whether this tells us more about our viewers than it does about our announcers. His future since TSW was blown out in the 1991 franchise debacle remains uncertain. Our successors, 'Westcountry', have yet to determine whether he is condemned to the cooking pot or is to enjoy yet another reincarnation as the children's favourite throughout the next decade.

When I realised in the early 1960s that television was my future, I had spent just under two years working in a dual capacity on the doomed *TV International* magazine. My primary role was that of Advertising Manager – a somewhat overblown title as I had no staff to manage. I was the entire 'department'. But necessity being the mother of invention, I found myself writing for the magazine too, a job I liked almost as much as selling.

The Editor, Margaret Cowan, a diminutive woman not unlike a brunette version of Dolly Parton, suggested I try my hand at what she described as 'celebrity interviews'. I was thrilled to be entrusted with such a prestigious assignment. My first was a landmark – for me at least. I was asked to interview Mr Melville Mark, the originator of the Montreux Television Festival. I knew little about the man and even less about interviewing techniques, but armed with the brass neck of confidence which 26-year-olds tend to possess, I flew direct to Geneva to set things in motion. Geneva is a clean, almost antiseptic city and its citizens unimpeachably respectable. I located Melville Mark at his apartment overlooking the lake and after a brief telephone conversation he agreed that we should meet there.

Mel Mark was then about 40 years old, an extraordinary

and charismatic man with a great fund of bubbling energy and a relentless torrent of ideas. He had conceived the Montreux Festival as means of creating a forum for world television leaders to come together, discuss their craft and market their wares. The Golden Rose Award was soon to be envied as the pinnacle of achievement for dedicated broadcasters.

Mel Mark, six feet, red haired, dressed in tasselled loafers and a shiny silk suit, exuded confidence and Old Testament Jewish wisdom. Born in Manchester of working-class Jewish parents, Mel worked as a journalist for the old *Manchester Guardian*, but before he was 30 was running his own successful public relations company. This was at a time when public relations was in its infancy and largely mistrusted by the business community, who thought it the last refuge of scoundrels and charlatans. Mel's skill as a superlative salesman was complemented by his ferocious charm.

During our interview, he paced up and down the living room of his large apartment, pouring out a stream of anecdotes, saws, blasphemies and wit, and I will confess I was awestruck. Here was a real internationalist. A Zionist also perhaps (indeed he had a spell in the Middle East with Israeli commandos in their struggle against the British in 1948). I had never met anybody quite like him before.

'No pockets in a shroud,' was one of his favourite pieces of advice. 'If the rabbi tells me I can't take it with me,' he would continue, 'then I'm not fucking well going!'

A great moralist, as well as an unashamed sensualist, in Mel the two things were not at odds. He would rant about the hypocrisy of the world in general: 'Walk into any boardroom,' he said, pointing an immaculately manicured finger at me, 'and put a revolver on the table. The assembled throng will smile nervously, realise that it's some kind of gimmick or joke, and then accept it. Walk into the same boardroom and take out your prick and lay it on the table – shock, horror, revulsion, calls for security guards to throw you out! Hypocrisy! A gun shoots death and a prick shoots *life*. We are so screwed up as a society we take offence at the one and accept the other. Pah! hypocrisy!'

That was Mel. Simplistic. Compelling and slightly loopy. I thought he was absolutely marvellous.

At the end of a couple of hours I had enough material for my piece and took my leave, but I was to see a great deal more of Mel Mark during the next ten years when he would visit London regularly and hold court in the Mayfair Hotel.

His public relations business flourished and he was retained by Sadruddin Khan (the Aly Khan's brother). His brief was to 'kill the playboy image' and promote young Sadruddin as a model of perspicacity and sober wisdom. Other clients, both corporate and personal, benefited from Mel's skills and charm, but if he had a flaw at all it was perhaps his inexperience of the financial side of big business. He made and lost a fortune – at least twice – and when I last saw him in London a few years ago he was a great deal less than rich and working out of humble offices in Soho. The Geneva apartment, the motor boat on the lake, the American saloon car, had all long since been sold. But Mel was a survivor. His kind – the charismatic hustler with a heart – is a dying breed, and the world will be a smaller place without such people. Sadly he died in 1997 and I miss him still.

In those halcyon days when commercial television was young and almost anything seemed possible, *Television International* magazine showed what city analysts might describe as 'early promise'. Advertising support was encouraging and subscription sales kicked off to a good start. We decided that the magazine should have a presence at the Screen Advertising World Association (SAWA) in Cannes where we not unreasonably assumed potential clients would gather in profusion.

I was therefore dispatched to the South of France in June 1961 and booked myself into the cheapest hotel I could find, which turned out to be very cheap indeed, except in price. The bulk of the delegates who had jetted in from America, Japan, the Argentine and Brazil or arrived by limousine from other parts of Europe were registered at the grand hotels along the fashionable Croisette, facing the Mediterranean.

Now the month of June in the South of France is famous

for its splendid weather, but I arrived wearing my only suit, a pinstriped creation from Burtons, which had been designed to withstand the ravages of the British summer. Walking on the Croisette at high noon on the first day drew fascinated stares from the locals who clearly thought this overdressed Englishman was on some kind of endurance test. I was armed with a typewritten list of the delegates and a bunch of rate-cards for the magazine. Supremely confident of my amazing powers of salesmanship I sauntered as casually as I could into the grandest of all the hotels; the Carlton.

Several of my key prospects, I was told by a faintly incredulous concierge, were at a cocktail party on the hotel terrace which was being given by Associated Television (ATV). I could not believe my luck. As a registered delegate myself I too had an invitation to the same party. I plucked it triumphantly from my black vinyl briefcase (Head Quarters and General Supplies, two quid). In a matter of minutes I would be there among the glitterati securing orders of such size as to rocket my magazine's advertising earnings beyond that of *Readers Digest*. I made my way past potted palm trees, over gleaming marble floors and out onto the terrace. Even as the waiter offered me a glass of champagne from a silver tray I knew I had made a fundamental mistake. Virtually everybody on the terrace, and there must have been a couple of hundred, appeared to be wearing white. There were dazzlingly beautiful women in glamorous white cocktail dresses and high-heeled sandals, cascades of shimmery hair tumbling over bare shoulders. I spotted Shirley Bassey wearing a white dress that had clearly been sprayed on. She looked impossibly glamorous. The men favoured silk shirts opened half way down the chest (remember this was 1961 when gold medallions had not yet become an item of derision). There was enough gold on display to have sunk Cleopatra's barge. The few suits that were being worn were of dazzling sharkskin or nearly transparent cotton. Everybody had lots of hair, everybody looked disgustingly healthy. I looked and felt like the nerd of the century.

Notwithstanding this culture shock, I found a small ballroom chair against the wall, sat down quickly and opened my briefcase. Then, armed with a ratecard, I ploughed into the fray having already identified the Managing Director of a production company in Soho, who I reasoned would be only too pleased to purchase a series of double page colour spreads in my magazine at £150 a throw. How could he refuse? Well, just how he could refuse was relatively simple. After my brief, earnest opening words he laughed and turned his back on me.

I now know what a grotesque figure I must have been, weaving among the beautiful people with a drink in one hand and an advertising ratecard in the other. I was baffled as I truthfully believed that delegates at a business conference were there to trade, to buy and to sell. After all I had to justify the cost of being there to my magazine and I had set myself a target of £1,000 worth of sales every day. Big deal. I had as much chance of achieving this as obtaining an O level in knitting.

After about an hour and a half of gauche fumbling and a battery of not so polite rebuffs I found myself on the ocean side of the terrace with the small of my back placed against a kind of parapet. 'Bastards,' I mused. 'Who needs them?' Well I did actually. I needed them badly and my failure to score was beginning to hurt. I began to consider my options.

Option one: I could wade in again and offer space in the magazine at cut prices. Good? No, lousy. They wouldn't want to know and even if they did, price cutting is not a good policy. It smacks of desperation. So was I desperate? No, I wasn't desperate. I'll tell you what I was. I was utterly paranoid.

Option two: give up. Go and drown myself in the Mediterranean.

Option three: get absolutely zonked on champagne and spend the rest of the day sunbathing.

Both options two and three were clearly the imperfect ramblings of a brain that was overheated with frustration. What else?

Option four: go and buy a white suit, a cheap medallion and some tasselled loafers, whack on a pair of wraparound

47

sunglasses and try the 'Mr Cool' approach – but not until *tomorrow*! I settled for option four.

I closed my briefcase with an authoritative snap and started to sidle away. A needle-sharp cold shower in my hutch-sized room at the 'Splendide' (these days the trades description boys would roast the hotel management's ass for naming the place so inappropriately) seemed the only thing to look forward to. Just as I reached the end of the terrace, an extraordinary figure blocked my exit. A man standing well over six feet wearing an impeccably cut midnight-blue silk suit was extending a hand in greeting.

'My name,' he said in a soft voice which only hinted at Irish ancestry, 'is Pat Henry.'

This simple statement had the same ground-breaking effect as Sean Connery's immortal words in *Dr No*, which for the brain dead, were 'My name is Bond, James Bond'.

Pat was the sales director of ATV and one of the most charismatic figures in British television at the time. He had negotiated a deal with his boss, Lew Grade, which involved commission payments based upon the airtime sales that he and his team were able to generate for this new, virtually untried medium.

In those early days very few commentators believed that ITV could survive, let alone become the phenomenal bonanza of the 1960s and 1970s. Shrewdly, Pat Henry, who had been a senior salesman at Hulton Press, had great faith in the medium and as a consequence his earnings in the 1960s had rocketed into the stratosphere. He had a Rolls-Royce and a yacht and the love of several good women and even more bad ones, and all of this was based upon his commission earnings as an airtime salesman. He was one of my heroes.

So there I was on the terrace of the Carlton, numb with champagne, having failed to sell as much as a one inch single, confronted by one of ITV's legendary figures. Pat Henry fixed me with a cool, but not unkind, gaze and said quietly, 'What the hell do you think you are doing?'

I mumbled something about selling space in this new magazine, *Television International*. A look of incredulity spread

48

over Pat Henry's face and he took me by the elbow and led me to a small table on the terrace.

'You are trying to sell advertising space here?' he said in tones which are frequently used by doctors when addressing mentally retarded patients.

'Well, yes,' I blurted, now even more conscious of my sweat-soaked, three-piece Burton's and my inevitably blood-shot eyes.

'And how much space have you sold?' he asked.

'Sod all,' I explained trying to sound nonchalant.

'Jesus,' Pat Henry said, signalling for a waiter to bring over two more glasses of champagne. There then followed one of the most unselfish and supportive acts in the history of our trade. With a cursory glance at my ratecard, Pat Henry agreed to buy a double-page spread, in full colour, in each of our first six issues.

'I would hate,' he said, placing an enormous hand on my shoulder, 'to go to bed tonight having turned a salesman away without an order. I wish you luck with the magazine, and for God's sake burn that fucking suit.'

Joy unconfined. I at once resolved to telephone my wife Carol and tell her that the purchase of a kitchen table, so long an object of anticipation and wistful dreaming, could now become a reality. Such orgasmic pleasures are hard to reproduce on paper, but believe me I was *spinning* with excitement. Pat Henry's act of kindness, for such it was, from one sales-man to another, remains a fond memory of those balmy times. I must here and now own that I have inherited from the late Pat Henry a kind of marshmallow softness towards any sales-man who is trying to pitch me. I *want* to be convinced. I *ache* to be persuaded that a set of encyclopedias of insect life in Honduras, 28 volumes bound in finest leatherene will be an indispensable addition to the quality of my life. Am I, for example, the only person on the face of the earth who has ever bought anything from one of those itinerant African boys who flog ivory elephants, beads and belts along the beaches of the Mediterranean? In my case I bought a little rhinoceros, nicely carved in teak, but promptly lost it on my way back to the hotel. It is of no importance. Losing it I mean. *Buying* it was *everything*.

Some years later I was strolling along the Croisette, properly attired this time in something white and flowing, when I chanced upon an extraordinary sight. In one of the side streets that leads up from the ocean promenade to the centre of town was a small grocery stores and outside it a queue of a dozen or so people. They were mostly French locals, women in summer dresses, young men in jeans and sweatshirts, but among them, close to the head of the queue, was the unmistakable figure of Ernie Pearl, Chairman of the cinema advertising group Pearl & Dean and one of the top honchos of SAWA. Now Ernie, a shrewd and very successful businessman was not without a few bob. Indeed by most people's standards he could be fairly described as rich. Yet here he was in a little queue outside a grocery store *clutching an empty half gallon plastic container*!

Curiosity has always been a weakness that I have been unable to suppress so I broke stride and sauntered over to Ernie.

'What,' I enquired, 'are you doing?'

Ernie gave me one of his famous grins.

'What do you *think* I am doing?' he said.

'You are queuing up, Ernie,' I said, quick as a flash, 'with an empty plastic bottle in your hand.'

Ernie nodded. 'You're sharp this morning boy,' he said, the Welsh lilt more pronounced. 'You got a mind like a bag of chisels.'

It was clear that Ernie was going to make me work my ticket so I ploughed on.

'You're staying at the Carlton aren't you Ernie?' I asked.

Ernie nodded again and moved a pace forward in the queue.

'Always do boy. Fine hotel. The best. Lovely room overlooking the sea.'

I glanced at my watch, noting that it was just before nine o'clock.

'Not breakfasting at the hotel?' I ventured.

'Yes,' said Ernie. 'Good grub. Best meal of the day.'

50

'Okay,' I said, 'I give up. What are you queuing *for*?'

'Orange juice,' said Ernie.

'Orange juice,' I repeated woodenly.

Had Ernie gone mad? Had the Carlton run dry of the precious fruit? Ernie had not gone mad. Ernie was far from mad. But Ernie Pearl, tycoon, top honcho at SAWA was *not* going to pay £6 a glass for orange juice in *any* hotel, however grand. Ernie would buy his *own* orange juice *wholesale* and take it back to the hotel and put it in his refrigerator. Now that's what I call shrewd. Not mean, because Ernie was the most generous of men, but streetwise, shrewd.

I left Ernie in the queue and resumed my stroll, ruminating on the fact that there were indeed sermons in stones and lessons in life that came upon you most unexpectedly. Later that day I tried to haggle over the price of a five quid gin and tonic – and lost.

CHAPTER 4

*TSW – the new franchise holder takes over led,
by a pocket-sized genius called Kevin. Uneasy
beginnings, board politics, high drama and
cheese rolls in Leicester Square.*

We must now fast-forward the tape a few years. It is 29
December, 1980 and my phone rings at 'Four Acres'. It is
the ubiquitous Lord Harris, his voice laden with suppressed
emotion.

'I am rather afraid,' he drawls, 'that I have some *disagreeable* news.'

Now the word disagreeable, when spoken by either Lord
Harris or Roy Jenkins from whom he frequently borrows
it, has cataclysmic connotations. For example, death is
'disagreeable'. So is having your testicles roasted over an open
fire. Aware of the Harris/Jenkins love of the word and the
context in which it is used, I naturally steel myself for some
horrendous piece of intelligence to be conveyed over my telephone. Well it certainly isn't *good* news.

'The IBA,' continues Lord Harris in sepulchral tones, 'doesn't like us any more. We've lost the franchise.'

My feelings are curiously a mixture of relief and disappointment. At least the tension and the uncertainty are now
over. A board meeting has been convened for Monday (the
following morning), and without hesitation I leapt into my car
to drive the 250 miles to Plymouth.

As I sail past the Bristol turn-off on the almost deserted M4,
I tune my radio to the local BBC station. An excited voice is
rattling off some stultifying local news which, as I imperfectly

recall, involved illegal activity with a crippled sheep, a ruthless landlord in St Pauls and a vicar who whistles 'Rule Britannia' through his nostrils. Underwhelmed by this timeless catalogue of human frailty, I am nonetheless quite unprepared for the news item that follows.

'Westward Television, ousted from its position as franchise holder for the South-West region is to be replaced by TSW, led by Mr Kevin Goldstein-Jackson.'

With an involuntary groan from the depths of my soul, I nearly swerve onto the hard shoulder. *TSW*. Surely not. There must be some mistake. I brake. I tuck myself into a picnic area and gather my shattered wits. TSW? But all the smart money was on West Country TV. Or WCTV as it is laughingly referred to. This consortium is packed with worthy notables from the West Country. It is led by a wealthy local businessman, Mr Simon Day, a Bertie Woosterish character with a loud voice and considerable connections in the region. He has managed to recruit a small core of television professionals to give his bid credibility, including an ex-Managing Director of Harlech Television, Tony Gorard. Gorard is an accountant and about as charismatic as double glazing, but he at least has a track record. It is this group, *WCTV* who are favourites to replace Westward, who are suffering the effects of their now notorious internal strife.

When I have recovered my composure I try to remember what little I know about the surprise victors, TSW. Goldstein-Jackson is a relatively junior producer at Anglia Television where he has been involved in the network series *Tales Of The Unexpected*. Certainly his winning a franchise while still in his early thirties is spectacularly 'unexpected'.

I drive on to Plymouth, eat a solitary meal at the Holiday Inn and go to bed in sombre mood. My television career, it seems, is about to grind to a halt. I am nearly 45 and I have given 18 years of my life to Westward. What lies ahead? I am not poor, but huge wealth has somehow passed me by. I dream of tropical islands and beachcombing in ragged shorts. When I wake, at six in the morning, it is pouring down with a ferocity unmatched anywhere except perhaps

53

in the Brazilian rain forests. I think I am just starting a cold.

Time moves on and it is now January in Sloane Square and I am gazing down at the traffic as it snakes past Peter Jones and into Sloane Street. The sky is blue and outside it is crisp and pleasant. Today is an important one. The Westward London staff are to be introduced to their new bosses. Brian Bailey, TSW's Chairman, Peter Battle, the Joint Managing Director, and of course the strange and relatively obscure Kevin Goldstein-Jackson, who couples being Joint Managing Director with the role of Director of Programmes.

The mood of the London staff, mostly sales people, is restive. They have watched their company chopping itself to pieces in the daily press during the Harris-Cadbury gladiatorial and the loss of franchise is a kind of Neroesque thumbs down from the IBA.

At the appointed hour, staff assemble in the small boardroom at Sloane Square. Cigarettes are lit like so many pilgrims' candles and a nervous receptionist telephones me in my office just before I leave to join the troops.

'There is a man in reception,' says dear Lynn, ever polite and cautious, 'who *claims* to be the new Chief Executive.'

'*Claims* to be,' I repeat, a touch mystified. 'What does he look like?'

Lynn pauses and I know she is struggling with her natural instinct to be kind to everybody with whom she comes into contact.

'Well,' she says very softly, clearly not wishing to be overheard by her visitor. 'Mr Turner, he looks like the window cleaner.'

This clinches it for me. Kevin Goldstein-Jackson, single-handed founder of TSW and franchise winner, it surely is.

'Kev', as I am later to discover, is a complex character with as many protective layers as an onion. He is also a mass of contradictions and wildly fluctuating moods, making him a particularly hard man to get close to. His intellect is undeniably brilliant and he has a capacity for absorbing detail

54

and mastering technical intricacies that is breathtaking. His beginnings look ordinary enough, even humdrum.

The son of a maintenance engineer, he fails to win a place at grammar school and has to be content with the proletarian ambience of a secondary modern in Buckinghamshire. Even here the headmaster, unimpressed no doubt by 'Kev's' crumpled, owlish demeanour writes the boy off as a failure. Undaunted, our Woody Allen look-alike fights his way to Reading University and gains a BA in philosophy and sociology. His sharp mind and the obstinate tenacity so common in the diminutive of stature spur him to even greater efforts and he chalks up an M.Phil degree in law after spare-time study at Southampton University. Already the complexity of his character is forming. The more knowledge he crams into his fertile brain the more like an unpressed bag of laundry he looks in personal appearance. This not only doesn't worry him, he positively revels in it. (Let the tall and handsome fret over clothes and grooming – he will dazzle the world with his dishevelment.)

Onward he plunges, ferret-like in his endeavours. In 1970 he wins a Time-Life Award for Journalism writing articles in such diverse publications as the *Solicitors' Journal* and *New Society*. Each new challenge absorbs him and, still in his twenties, he lands a prestige job as an assistant producer at HK TVB in Hong Kong and then, after soaking up as much experience as he can, he departs for the Middle East to become Head of Film for the Dhofar Region TV Service in the Sultanate of Oman.

In 1977 he is back in England – still in the wrinkled horse blanket that pretends it's a suit – and he persuades the aristocratic Anglia Television to take him on as an Assistant to the Head of Drama. His mentor is the egocentric Sir John Wolfe, who among other things, collects strange artefacts. Still restless, his too-large spectacles steaming with unfulfilled ambition, Kev writes 11 books – some of them quite unreadable, including a mysterious tome called *Experiments With Everyday Objects*. By now he is married to a tiny Chinese girl, Jenny Mei Leng, the daughter of a former Malaysian diplomat, and they are soon to have a daughter Jenkev (yes, *really*).

But in the frontal lobes of his unusual brain a burning ambition stirs. Soon the ITV franchises are coming up for grabs, and Kev is hungry for a slice of the action. He perfects his image with care. The baggy clothes, the studied air of scruffy casualness – open-neck shirt, occasionally a bow tie. Never a briefcase, *far* too middle class – instead he adopts as his trademark a plastic shopping bag (usually Tesco's) in which vital documents are crammed. A latent aestheticism asserts itself too. No smoking, no drinking, a diet of white fish or cheese rolls will be his source of nourishment, although his physique screams out for a good steak and a soupçon of exercise. He shuns materialism, yet lusts for power and influence. It is a devastating cocktail which will surprise all those with whom he is about to make contact. His industry is prodigious and with a young artist, Jonathan Harvey (later TSW's Arts Consultant) he forms his fledgling TV consortium, writes the prospectus himself, raises the money, recruits the board, and persuades the IBA to hand over the licence for the South-West of England – previously the 20-year fief of Westward Television. It is a modern fairy story, but without Prince Charming – Kev is clever, but he is to personal magnetism what Margaret Thatcher is to nude rollerskating.

It is this strange and fascinating man who shuffles into the Sloane Square boardroom at noon to address the sales staff and introduce them to the brave new world of TSW. The assembled throng are young, ambitious and streetwise, one could even describe them as forerunners of the yuppie. Now they face their new bosses with a calmness that might be mistaken for insouciance.

Brian Bailey (later Sir Brian), TSW's Chairman, introduces Kev and 'Pete' as 'our sparkling Managing Directors'. My heart sinks like a stone. Kev and Pete are giving out about as much sparkle as a pair of raw parsnips and Kev in particular looks as if he has just received a blow on the head. What follows is a low-key monotone of underwhelming significance.

'This is a new regime,' we are told. 'Belts will have to be tightened,' we are warned. 'Gone are the patrician ways of Cadbury, Harris, Lisburne, *et al*.'

Clearly the noble struggle ahead is to be punctuated by a virtually alcohol-free boardroom: 'I found a case of white Chablis in Ronnie Perry's office,' says Kev in a voice dripping with horror, disdain and loathing. 'I *dumped* it,' he adds, menacingly.

The tone of TSW's early days has been set and the decades of lotus-eating, Dom Perignon-sipping, caviar-guzzling hedonism are to be superseded by spartan ethics and a retreat from style.

Ah, *style*. The one thing that has marked Westward's progress over the years. I recall with a stab of remorse Cadbury's words in a previous life: 'You can get away with almost anything if you do it with *style*.'

But this is no time for maudlin reminiscence. Kev is in full cry and even Pete (Peter Battle, a decent and honourable man, Sancho Panza to Kev's Quixote) has perked up a shade. He is to oversee the sales operation while Kev the creative guru will concentrate on programmes and our infrastructure in Plymouth.

The speeches end and we all shuffle back to our desks in a leaden silence. There is no way I will fit into this new team. I feel 'weightless', out of time, superfluous. I phone Carol and have a little moan. She reassures me that being unemployed at 45 is not necessarily the end of the world. I am marginally uplifted by this, but still convinced that the end of my career is looming. Then my internal phone jangles. It is Brian Bailey: can I 'slip down to the boardroom' for a chat?

I tidy my desk, straighten my silk tie (surely a frippery Kev will disapprove of) and prepare to meet my fate. This will be a civilised affair if Brian Bailey is in the chair. He is a wise man, experienced in the ways of the world. His *coup de grâce* will be gently administered and softened further no doubt by a handsome cash settlement.

I enter the boardroom and there the three of them sit. It is the economy version of the last supper: 'Sorry squire, I know you ordered twelve disciples, but times are hard.' Brian is seated at the table's head, flanked by Kev and Pete. Brian, instantly direct and without any verbal fencing, offers me the job of TSW's Sales Director.

57

I am flattered as this is an unprecedented move – directors of ITV companies that lose their franchises usually get dumped at the same time and are not offered unbroken employment opportunities. The reputation of my sales team – easily the most enthusiastic on the network – has been a key determinant in Brian Bailey's decision to take me aboard. I accept and the atmosphere relaxes a shade. There is, however, a slight problem. Nothing earth-shattering, a mere bagatelle even: will I accept a pay cut of £7,000 a year? The reason, Brian Bailey explains, is that both Kev and Pete have restricted themselves in the first year of TSW's operations to salaries of £25,000.

I do a swift bit of mental arithmetic, and my finely-honed brain concludes that if I accept a pay cut of £7,000 a year I will be £7,000 worse off! Astounded at my own razor-sharp logic, I further assume that if I *refuse* the offer I shall be £25,000 a year worse off. I accept.

Celebratory coffees are poured and while not exactly chinking cups, we at least exchange promises of fidelity, love and toil. I return to my department and call a meeting of my senior sales managers, who are delighted that the team is not to be broken up and I am to remain at the helm.

Later that week I receive dozens of supportive letters and phone calls from clients, ad agencies and friends, who seem as pleased as I am with the turnout of events. At home Carol thinks it is a mixed blessing. She's happy that I am happy, but nonetheless wistful about what might have been if I had said no. Gardening? Raffia work? Hang-gliding? Senility? Foaming insanity? All five perhaps?

We dine at Pennyhill Park in Bagshot and I drink three-quarters of a bottle of Moet. Suddenly we *both* agree that continuous employment, even at seven grand less, is preferable to gardening, raffia, etc. After dinner I smoke my usual Monte Cristo and reflect on what I have committed myself to.

I am to become a Director of a virtually unknown and untried company led by a lifelong trade union official (Brian), a middle-ranking sales manager from Southern Television (Pete) and a wildly unpredictable but outstandingly clever scruff with tiny feet (Kev). Have I done the right thing? Will I be able to adjust my style to the new environment? Is the Pope a Catholic? Do bears crap in the woods? Alternatively, is the bear a Catholic and does the Pope – no, the prospect is unthinkable. I *have* made the right decision. Whatever else it is, the new job will be challenging.

A few days pass and I receive a most welcome phone call from Brian.

'Don't worry too much about the salary,' he says, 'once we're up and running and the cash register is ringing, we'll review the situation.'

Not for the last time, Brian has displayed his sense of timing and shrewd judgement. I am later to call on it during one of the many mini-crises of TSW's early years, and as usual Brian rises to the occasion. Come to think of it, I've *never* seen the man in a state of agitation, regardless of the pressure or the awfulness of the situation. Tranquilliser manufacturers would go bust if they relied on the Brian Bailey's of this world for their business.

Sadly, it is not long before I find myself in disagreement with Peter Battle, to whom I am required to report. Peter is conscientious, but his measured, low-key style is not what my sales team are used to. He writes thoughtful, but over-long memos and seems a trifle disconcerted by my own methods of operation. To say that our respective techniques differ in terms of how a sales operation should be run is to state the obvious. I am not, and never have been, obsessed by detail or minutiae. Being naturally lazy I work extremely hard to mask the fact and specialise in the 'broad canvas' or, to coin an even more excruciating cliché, 'the big picture'. Pete on the other hand, is concerned with the number, length and thickness of the bristles on the brush! Thus, while I am planning spectacular sales presentations with bells, whistles, jugglers and Handel's Water Music, Peter is agonising over the cost of stationery and paperclips. (I'm not saying he was wrong, he probably wasn't – but he was different.)

A kind of uneasy truce exists between us in those early months, and I do try to bottle up my more extravagant impulses. For me, an inevitable crossroads is reached when, over lunch in Langan's (a meeting-place sternly disapproved of by Pete and Kev), we try to discuss the venue for my next sales conference. A sales conference is, or should be, an emotional watershed. Forget all the rubbish about sales graphs and targets (oh, they are part of it *too*, but *not* as the main event). A sales conference is a gathering of the faithful, an occasion for body warmth, passion, conviction, energy. It is also a catharsis for people who have been at the sharp end of the market for 12 months and need their batteries jump-started by mega-volts.

Enthusiasm is a vital ingredient in any sales team and whatever other failings I may possess I do claim to be of an enthusiastic disposition. This is, or can be, infectious. I explain all this to Pete who, while expressing sympathy, looks pained. I think he assumes I am an arrogant son of a bitch with a little too much flash. He is right, of course, but I cannot change. Neither can he. We are both honourable men. There needs to be a solution and only one man in my view can find it. The ubiquitous Brian Bailey.

After the Langan's lunch, which solves nothing, we have a few more meetings and exchange self-justifying memos and I eventually ask Brian Bailey for an urgent meeting at his NALGO (National Association of Local Government Officers) headquarters in Taunton. I am prompted to do this as it is clear that unless some resolution of our different styles is found, the company's operation will suffer.

On the drive to Taunton I have convinced myself that the only action for me to take is to offer my resignation. As the miles roll by this decision becomes something of an obsession. I have a mild accident just south of Bristol which creates the first dent on my splendid new bronze Mercedes.

I arrive tense and hot, with tiny but mechanically significant bits dropping from the underside of my car, at the Taunton headquarters of NALGO. Once in Brian's office and with two cups of tea inside me, my previous 'suicide' frame of mind is settled and I explain the situation to Brian.

60

'We really cannot work together,' I conclude, referring of course to the lovely Pete.

Brian shrewdly makes no instant decision, but promises to consult the board. After less than an hour the meeting is over and I drive the crippled Mercedes onwards to Plymouth.

It is instructive to note just how Brian handles this knotty problem. He is, after all, the Chairman of a new company scarcely two years into its franchise and already one of its Directors is claiming that he can't work with a founder member of the team. Telephone consultations take place with all of the non-executive Directors. Charles Ansell, the epitome of a solid and reliable Devon countryman, asks Brian who is wrong and who is right in the dispute. Brian displays his usual cunning and replies, 'It is not a matter of who is right or who is wrong, it is who can the company afford to lose?'

It is upon this fulcrum, therefore, that the decision turns. Well, as history shows, I am still here. Pete remains for a few months more as a Director of the Company, but finally moves on to join Ulster Television as Director of Sales. I am genuinely pleased that he makes an immediate and considerable success of this new job.

If I assume that my worries are over I am in for a further rude awakening. I am now to report directly to the enigmatic Kev, with unforeseen circumstances. I try hard to get close to the man and in truth we do strike up a reasonable working relationship. He is, however, very mercurial and his moods swing between a benign ambience and the ferocity of a Rottweiler which has recently been stung by a wasp, twice, on each buttock.

I suspect that his agile and inquiring mind is not suited to the mundane business of actually running a television station and he hankers after the excitement and challenge he experienced during the fight for the franchise. This demonstrates to me one of the fundamental flaws of the franchise award system. The special skills you need to set up a consortium, write the prospectus and go through a beauty parade in front of ITV, bear no relationship to the 'hands on', day-to-day grind of regional television life. And Kev's eccentricity, while fascinating in the early days, soon palls.

That autumn, ITV sales directors stage a major presentation at London's Talk of the Town restaurant. It is a showcase for the winter schedule and is designed to impress 350 agency buyers who turn up in tuxedos to eat, drink, be entertained and sold to. I am one of the presenters and I have rehearsed my pitch for two weeks.

Managing Directors have been invited, as have Programme Directors. It's going to be a glitzy, pushy evening. All the ITV top honchos are designated to host a table. Even though I am a speaker, I have 12 guests from agencies on my table near the stage.

When Kev shows up, he is wearing a lounge suit and a string tie. This is as formal as he gets. All the smooth agency executives in their designer shirts, Italian shoes and shiny dinner jackets gaze at Kev in disbelief as he announces in his 'quiet' voice that he won't eat the food on the set menu. He insists on either cheese rolls or white fish. The steak, the prawn avocado, the wine, all will be untouched. Gilly Hartley, my PA, dressed to kill in an off-the-shoulder number, senses an impending crisis and volunteers to go out into Leicester Square and obtain the necessary grub to suit the fastidious Kev.

She vanishes minutes before I am due to mount the platform and do my stuff, and as the house lights go down I ponder briefly on whether a pretty woman in evening dress punting around Leicester Square for cheese rolls and boiled fish on a wet Thursday night will be considered unusual. Happily she returns, unscathed, loaded with nutritious scoff and Kev relaxes at the table to enjoy the show. But it is clear that running a small TV station has become boring to him.

Not long after this, he leaves TSW and sets up as a financial advisor. This extraordinarily clever man soon makes a success of it and even writes an erudite column for the *Financial Times*.

62

CHAPTER 5

*Selling the West Country to big business. Harry
Secombe nearly vanishes over a cliffside and
our reporter makes an admiral blush.*

Goldstein-Jackson's departure left the company rudderless – it
was 1985 and TSW was in mid-franchise. The first board
meeting after Kev's departure was a sombre affair. Who from
our ranks would replace him? Who indeed *could* replace him?

Not me, for sure, even though I was the senior Executive
Director in the company. My role was clear. I was a salesman
not an administrator and the prospect of moving to Plymouth
(Anorak City) had little appeal. A compromise was reached –
uneasily. We would find a person from outside who would be
Joint Managing Director and I would be the other half of this
Siamese twin, based in London.

Sir Brian Bailey and I were charged with the responsibility
of briefing a head-hunter to locate my 'other half'. He or she
would run the Plymouth end of the operation while I would
remain exclusively in charge of sales. The Joint Managing
Director title was really to mollify my presumed feelings of
displacement if a new, sole Chief Executive had been hired.

After briefing a laconic head-hunter in Mayfair with dandruff and a gold watch chain, Sir Brian and I took coffee in
the Richoux Café on Piccadilly.

'It won't work you know Harry,' said Sir Brian. 'It didn't
with Kev and Pete.'

I was inclined to agree. But what was to be done?

'You'll have to take on the whole job yourself' said Brian,
without conspicuous enthusiasm.

My hesitation was in no way due to false modesty, but

63

based on a cold assessment of just what the job would entail. As a London-based Sales Director, I enjoyed an excellent lifestyle and my bonuses had pushed my earnings close to £100,000 per year. I was familiar with the cut and thrust of media negotiations and derived great pleasure from working with a young, enthusiastic sales team. I entertained clients in fine West End restaurants, I threw parties for them at my house in Surrey and at Henley Regatta, and my day-to-day interface was with people who were, by and large, metropolitan in outlook and ambitious.

Plymouth would be different, the pace provincial, the challenges unfamiliar. I would have to become an administrator, deal with trade union problems, dine with Lord Mayors and other local dignitaries, change my lifestyle and become an integral part of the regional scene. I expressed these doubts to Brian and told him that the only aspect of the Managing Director's role that really appealed to me was the chance to work with creative programme makers and journalists.

His response was the usual mixture of sphinx-like inscrutability and Somerset cunning. 'I'll talk to the board,' he said.

We met again a week later on a blustery March day and it was agreed that I could do the job from London, but I would have to spend two or three days a week in Plymouth. The company would supply me with a flat and my loss of sales bonus would be reflected in a healthy salary hike. I was still reluctant and said I would sleep on the offer and discuss it with my wife. She, as always, was supportive and said, 'Go for it on your terms.'

Later that night at home in Surrey, I received a phone call from a TSW shop steward in Plymouth. 'If we've got to have another boss,' he said, 'we'd rather an old Westward hand like you than some total stranger. The staff here want you to be the Managing Director.'

That, as they say, clinched it. I phoned Brian and said yes. Two days later in Plymouth, a month after my fiftieth birthday, I was formally appointed Chief Executive of TSW Holdings and its main subsidiary, TSW itself.

The announcement in the trade press that I would be

London based caused no more than a minor ripple at the IBA who often made a fuss about 'absentee landlords'. But I was determined to tackle the job in my own way. To begin with, I had seen executives from London arrive in Plymouth, neatly costumed in designer suits, mobile phones quivering, adrenalin foaming through their veins, only to observe them six months later arriving for work in anoraks, with string vests glowing through the fabric of their 1970's drip-dry nylon shirts.

Like most ITV Chief Executives I clearly needed to be in London regularly for industry meetings anyway. So I reversed the process and still operated effectively in Plymouth for one, two or three days a week. (Life without a regular fix of 'San Lorenzo' in Beauchamp Place would have been unbearable).

The highest priority I set myself was to create an atmosphere within the company where my Executive Directors could pursue excellence and exercise their own skills to the maximum of their ability. One of television's most distinguished executives, Sir Paul Fox, told an amusing anecdote at the 1991 annual dinner for the Society of Television Lighting Directors in the medieval splendour of Great Fosters Tithe Barn. When he was first appointed Managing Director of Yorkshire Television in the 1970s he was living at Mill Hill in London. A colleague suggested that 'as he was running Yorkshire would he be moving north?' 'Yes,' replied Paul and bought a house in Radlett a few miles beyond Mill Hill.

Sir Paul Fox, doyen of our trade, made some of his most effective decisions from the Garrick Club in London's West End. Nobody can say he didn't run a very successful company!

Clive Leach, who took over from Paul as Managing Director at Yorkshire is, like me, an ex-Sales Director. His style is dramatically different from his predecessor, being very hands-on, very detail-orientated and very Yorkshire based. There are clearly more ways to kill a cat than to choke it with cream.

The world is shrinking and with the advent of the fax machine and the car telephone, busy executives can operate from almost any place in the world they choose. This is not to rubbish the value of personal contact, which is still an essential ingredient and one to which I attach high priority, but it is no longer *de rigueur* to operate entirely from a fixed point on the compass.

While I spent a great deal of time on public platforms extolling the values of federalism and the regional system, I have been, I think, scrupulous in not confusing regionalism with provincialism. The word 'provincial' of course, is a cheeky little soubriquet for 'dull', 'safe' and 'boring'. This may sound like élitist metropolitan claptrap, but it is close to the perceived truth. However much we believe in the rich diversity that regionalism brings to our television screens the dividing line between it (regionalism) and twee parochialism is wafer thin.

In the early days of ITV, locally produced programmes carried an indelible stamp of amateurism about them. Grinning jackanapes would gaze at the wrong camera while wearing pullovers of excruciating design. This ham-fisted, forced jollity was never so apparent as in locally-made commercials, where presenters with more rows of teeth than could conceivably be human would shout slogans of mind-watering banality at the bewildered viewer: 'Tregunners of Middle Trollop offer twenty per cent off all anoraks in stock. *Yes* twenty per cent!' The final incredulous repetition of 'twenty per cent', prefixed by a triumphant 'yes' served no purpose other than to irritate people. It was as if the presenter had uncovered some ancient truth which he could no longer keep to himself and had to share with the gawping millions sitting out there on the edge of their sofas in tumescent anticipation.

A local car salesman in the West Country once made a commercial in which he insisted his wife starred. It was a grisly experience made all the more awful by the fact that at the time we really needed his money. His 'good lady' as he constantly referred to her was a person of resounding enthusiasm, but little talent. She had once played 'Elvira' in Noel Coward's *Blithe Spirit* at some local amateur drama group and one can only guess at her interpretation of such a role. She bellowed

66

her lines in a strident monotone directly to camera and as my memory serves, the sales pitch climaxed with the immortal slogan: 'Our used cars have *everything* you want in a family motor – and much, much more besides!' I have for years grappled with the intellectual conundrum these triumphal words have posed. 'And much, much more besides'. Besides what? And if her cars had *everything* you wanted what were these mysterious extras promised in the ad? Draught champagne on tap? Square wheels? Flock wallpaper in the boot? The lady herself? A not considerable prize when I tell you she was of a flawless, peachy complexion, but abundant in the haunch and buttock department. Indeed her quivering flesh seemed to overflow from the screen during her final, yelled peroration.

On another memorable occasion a local tailor, in demonstrating the thornproof quality of his tweed suitings, drove a six-inch nail into the palm of his hand, live on camera. To give him credit he finished his sales pitch with blood spurting over his trousers which were, happily, out of sight. Many viewers at home must have wondered why, in extolling the virtues of Irish open weave, his voice shot up two octaves and a crescent of perspiration formed on his upper lip.

Programmes could be funny too. During the filming of a TSW *Highway* with Harry Secombe, the director, John Bartlett, decided he'd like to have Harry singing 'Eternal Father Strong To Save' while standing at the end of Portland Bill. The crew were positioned in the Portland Bill lighthouse from which vantage point dramatic pictures of Harry in full bellow could be taken. Harry likes to perform to a playback for the final verse, but on this occasion the sound engineer inadvertently played back the whole hymn. As the cameraman pulled back to take in a long shot of the fabulous Dorset coastline a violent wind sprang up, precursor to a really majestic storm. Harry Secombe was almost lifted off the ground, his hymn book catching the wind like a sail. I often wonder what the viewers would have thought if Harry had vanished over the edge, still singing.

During the filming of *Village Action* we had enormous difficulties with the outside broadcast vehicle. At one stage while we were filming, engineers were underneath reconstructing the vehicle's gearbox. Further mechanics were replacing the radiator while two more were trying to repair two of the tyres which had punctured. We made good use of the time by recording a promotion with Michael Bentine, saying how peaceful the countryside was!

On another occasion, we had set up outside a school to show pupils being collected by their parents. Since it was midday, we were short of parents and engaged the Series Adviser, Brian McLaughlin, as an additional parent. Unfortunately, no child attached itself to Brian, who was left looking like a dirty old man outside the school, until one of the cameramen (Geoff Miles) appeared around the corner of the school with his trousers rolled up, yelling 'Daddy! Daddy! Here I am!'

Tom Goodison, our Head of Education, also reminds me of the time we filmed the famous floating flower market in Amsterdam with an inexperienced new presenter, Sue Phillips. She proceeded to do her first piece to camera which was abruptly ended by the director, Derek Fairhead, swinging open the door of the outside broadcast vehicle and yelling 'That was utter crap, Sue!'

Sue turned quietly to Tom Goodison and said, 'Do you know that's the first piece of directorial advice I've had from Derek Fairhead.'

In the early 1980s TSW received a commission from Channel Four to make a low budget 'fantasy' drama. The script *Someday Man* was about West Indians, and as the writer, Barbara Angell, hadn't indicated any specific location we decided to set it in Plymouth. I have to tell you that when we deposited a coachload of black actors in the city centre for a location sequence, two charming ladies rushed up and begged for autographs because they thought we had produced the West Indian cricket team.

My favourite programme story was when we were making a film abut the future of the navy and how cuts in manpower might effect employment prospects in Plymouth and Devonport. The Admiral, who must remain nameless, had agreed to be interviewed on the deck of his warship. There were blue skies overhead, a light, choppy sea and a few seagulls wheeling above the mast. The Admiral however, tough old sea dog that he was, found talking to camera somewhat intimidating.

Jilly Carter, a lady of impish good humour, who was to conduct the interview, decided that the Admiral needed to be put at his ease. Smiling sweetly she said, 'I suppose being away at sea for months on end, one of the things you most miss is a good fuck.'

The Admiral's reply has never been recorded.

CHAPTER 6

*A nasty encounter on the Orient Express to
Venice, plus the Monte Carlo caper and a
polite brush with the Japanese in Tokyo.*

It is nine-thirty on a warm June evening and the fabled Orient
Express is snaking its way through sleepy vineyard country,
towards the Swiss border *en route* for Venice. In the piano bar
the wall lamps are glowing softly behind silk shades and the
buzz of conversation is punctuated by the discreet popping of
champagne corks and the tinkle of ice in Waterford crystal.

Men and women cluster around the pianist as he runs his
fingers lazily over the ivories, producing with apparently no
serious effort a marvellous and lilting version of Cole Porter's
'Night and Day'. The men are wearing dinner jackets and
black ties, the women long silky dresses, their hair shining,
their diamonds sending out sharp reflections as they move
their hands to light cigarettes.

From the open door which leads beyond this elegant salon
drifts the merest hint of rich food. Tantalisingly it mingles
with the exotic perfumes and cigar smoke around the bar. A
young waiter glides between the crowded sofas, balancing a
silver tray laden with champagne. Past the gleaming reflections on satiny wood panelling and through the big picture
windows, darkening countryside flashes by. We see the stripe
of a distant river, copper-coloured in the pale moonlight, and
a huge forest crouching like a massed army on the curved hill-
side.

I observe this most pleasing scenario from my corner seat
by the piano. The Dom Perignon '72 is ice cold and I am pondering on whether to start dinner with chilled soup or smoked

salmon and caviare. At this precise moment an outlandish figure appears in the doorway from the sleeping compartments. He wears bright pink golfing slacks, white shoes and a flimsy cotton shirt, unbuttoned to the navel, exposing a hairy paunch. A gold chain thicker than a child's finger dangles from his throat. His hair, although white, is elaborately waved and arranged carefully, but unsuccessfully, to conceal a bald pate. He is obviously American.

Impervious to the ridiculous sight he presents among all these elegant people, he goes to the bar and orders something unpleasant with cherries in it. The barman, trained to within an inch of his life, winces discreetly, but serves the confection as if he is handling a live grenade.

The man in pink trousers downs the drink with a single gulp and lights a pale green cigar which looks, without a soupçon of exaggeration, just like a smouldering cucumber. He then moves towards a group of people with their backs to him and I hear him vainly try to insinuate himself into their company.

'Hi. I'm Al. Hell of a train isn't it?'

The group nods politely, but by a subtle display of body language indicates that he is unwelcome in their presence.

He shuffles to another group, who briefly succumb to his empty charm, but then their eyes glaze over and he tries his luck on a tall blonde with earrings the size of ducks' eggs. She is momentarily trapped, but rescue comes in the form of an Iranian businessman who leads the woman away.

Al is undaunted. He circulates on the outer fringe of the salon like a persistent wasp. I strain to catch what he is saying, but only snatches are audible. He produces a wallet from which visiting cards appear as if by magic. A dreadful realisation begins to steal over me. This awful man is a salesman. He is actually trying to pitch the people in the bar – oblivious to the fact that they regard him as an intrusive buffoon, with all the subtlety of an inflamed wart.

It occurs to me with dawning horror that it is only a matter of time before he gets round to my corner of the bar and turns his attentions to me. If I let slip that I too am a member of the selling trade I will be doomed.

71

I visualise the explosion of delight that will wreathe his bland features. A bangled, Neanderthal arm will encircle my shoulders as he recognises a fellow huckster! Drinks will be purchased – frothy creations with improbable names like 'Cowpuncher's Tonic' or 'Cleveland Chainsaw'. He will cling limpet-like to my wife and me at dinner, winking and grimacing with a grotesque intimacy that chills the soul. Information about his family will be offered in Byzantine detail.

We will hear of his split-level, ranch-style pagoda in Philadelphia. His voice will drop an octave or two as he provides us with a blow-by-blow account of his recent vasectomy, his tendency to mild haemorrhoids, his plucky battle with gum rot, the fraught web of his personal relationships, his meaningful dialogue with his analyst – inevitably a Hungarian immigrant with a leatherette couch. We will learn of his struggle with 'sexual identity problems at this moment in time'.

By the time coffee is served we will be soul mates. He will have extracted information from me like a dentist hacking out a dead molar with a cold chisel. Desperately, in self-defence I will deflect the conversation away from my own family history and he will spring into the void with devout enthusiasm.

As razor-thin chocolate mints are consumed and more coffee poured, he will sketch in his views on premature ejaculation, socialised medicine, the Reagan administration, cocaine sniffing in California and the British royal family. Eventually he will proffer his business card revealing his true colours as either an insurance salesman or a vendor of real estate in the Florida swamplands.

A naked panic engulfs me, but mercifully I am spared. His attention has been lassoed by a vast Canadian widow in a tent-like evening dress studded with rhinestones. He homes in like an Exocet missile and they lock together in a conversation of immediate and deep sincerity.

Later, in my elegant *couchette*, I lie awake as the train rackets through unseen tunnels and past sleeping farmland, pondering on the foolishness of the dreadful Al. Cold canvassing on the Orient Express is not to my taste exactly, but if it has to be done at all it seems vital that the salesperson blends into the surroundings.

I doubt if Al made a single sale of whatever it was he was hawking, although I concede I could be wrong. To aspiring sales stars I would only offer this advice: unless you have the hide of a rhinoceros and the discretion of a wounded buffalo you should try and anticipate the style and the surroundings of your intended prospects. To sell successfully is to gain people's confidence and this is not achieved by jarring their sensibilities with a sledgehammer.

There is a sequel to the story. Many months later I met a real estate salesman in a Soho restaurant and we got chatting about how to identify new opportunities and avoid selling to 'brick-wall clients' who are hostile to commercial persuasion. Unprompted, he revealed that he travelled regularly on the Orient Express from London to Venice and found it a rich hunting ground for his high-priced real-estate propositions. Unlike the unfortunate Al, my friend becomes part of the stylish crowd on the train, always taking his wife and only hinting in the most gentle fashion imaginable that he sells land in Swiss ski resorts and vineyards in Tuscany. He understands the secret of good salesmanship: the customer has to believe he or she is making the decision to buy and the salesperson is merely there to provide information. In reality, of course, this particular real-estate man was exerting immense pressure on his potential clients, but it was subtle, restrained, brilliantly conceived and patiently executed. I'll wager that pink-trousered Al wouldn't have recognised him as a fellow salesman in a thousand years.

In some situations the 'belt-it-to-them-between-the-eyes' routine actually works. Selling sheep in an Australian market, for example. Subtle nuances of style would be lost in such a maelstrom of sweaty turbulence. Only a nose-picking, beer-swilling, all-belching, all-scratching swaggerer is going to catch anybody's attention.

Likewise the activities on the floor of one of the City of London's money markets, where well-dressed men with carnations in their buttonholes scream and bellow like maddened bull elephants.

73

On my first visit to Japan I had listened carefully to wise counsels about the intricate nature of the Tokyo business scene. I knew that the smash-and-grab approach would be a disaster and that I had to observe the rituals so beloved of my important hosts. Written appointments had been made and I had prepared brief presentations to give to each client I called on.

One morning at the Regency Hyatt Hotel, as I sipped coffee overlooking the city's Manhattan-like skyline, the phone rang. It was the secretary of a client I was due to see later that day. She confirmed the time of the meeting – 11.30 a.m. – and then asked me how long exactly my presentation would take. Twenty-eight minutes, I told her, having rehearsed it to the second over the previous weeks at home. After breakfast I caught a cab to the Ginza, Tokyo's business and shopping area – a vast web of boulevards, fabulous department stores and narrow side streets crammed with boutiques, restaurants, showrooms and curio shops.

My client was located in a skyscraper of awesome proportions. The lobby was a symphony of grained marble and soaring glass panels. Fountains of pink water bubbled in a huge circular mosaic and from the central cupola depended a modern chandelier like a vast melting toffee of bronze fibreglass.

I caught the elevator and was rocketed 25 floors to an elegant suite of offices and greeted by a pretty Japanese girl in Christian Dior clothes. She showed me into a circular boardroom, panelled in dark oak and dominated by an enormous table surrounded by 30 chairs. At the top end of this gleaming slice of African teak sat a half circle of six sombre Japanese men in identical grey suits. They rose as I entered and we went through the bowing and smiling routine. Introductions over, I opened my flip charts and placed them on the table. At previous presentations I had used slides and tapes, but today was rather more basic. I launched into my act, speaking carefully lest my enthusiasm blur the compelling nature of my pitch and I was received with rapt and polite attention.

I was through in 27 minutes, just ahead of schedule and was

74

about to invite questions when the boardroom door opened and the Japanese girl appeared carrying a tiny gong. This she struck with an even tinier padded hammer. The effect was instantaneous. The six Japanese rose to their feet, smiling, hands were extended for me to shake and I was shown out of the room.

At first I was perturbed. The smooth finality of the proceedings seemed odd and I wondered whether I had committed some ghastly social blunder. I certainly hadn't mentioned Pearl Harbor or the Burma Railway, as far as I could recall. The mystery was soon cleared up, however, when the youngest of the six men reappeared, still smiling, and offered me tea.

His board colleagues, he explained, were at an all-day annual meeting, but had broken off for half an hour specifically because I had asked to give them a presentation. It was a privilege to have them interrupt their important deliberations to hear my little speech, and I told him so.

The incident with the gong was even more interesting. If I had been over-running my 30 minutes, interrupting me verbally would have been discourteous, but by sending in the secretary with gong and hammer any rudeness was prevented and we all responded like boxers breaking at the sound of the bell.

During my years as Sales Director for Westward Television, that charismatic buccaneer, Peter Cadbury, dreamed up a scheme which he believed would further enrich the company's fortunes and as an incidental bonus, give us a bit of fun *en route*. We were to provide Monaco-based Tele-Monte Carlo with an hour of English language television programmes each week and in return I would sell hundreds of thousands of pounds' worth of airtime to international advertisers anxious to address themselves to the rich cosmopolitan audience strung out like a glittering necklace along the coast of the French Riviera.

The Monte Carlo caper, as Peter Cadbury and I dubbed it, more or less paid for itself and we had some stupendous times flying into Nice in Peter's private aircraft and talking to Bulgarian princes, Jewish financiers from Edgware and canny

75

Monegasques who spent more time in the casino than at their desks.

One day I was preparing to check out of the Hotel de Paris in Monte Carlo after a two-day sales visit, when the concierge rang my room and informed me that there was a lady in reception who wanted to see me. Her name, I was informed in halting English, was Fiona Leigh-Smith.

Normally I will see anybody who is selling. My sympathy for kindred spirits, I suppose. But my plane was due to leave in two hours and I was anxious to get back to England.

'I'll see her on my way out,' I explained brusquely and continued packing.

Now the French Riviera in general and Monte Carlo in particular is notorious for pedlars of get-rich-quick schemes and I had met more than a few in my frequent visits to the principality. Nevertheless I rang for a porter, lit a Davidoff cigar and descended in the ornate lift to the stunning baroque foyer of the hotel.

There, sitting demurely in a skin-tight pink trouser suit, was a strikingly attractive redhead, clutching a wedge of files on her lap. Not unnaturally I strolled over and introduced myself. Yes, she was Fiona Leigh-Smith and she did have a proposition for me. Monte Carlo is a place where dreams come true, but on this occasion the lady had very serious intentions. She worked, it transpired, for a Middle-Eastern billionaire in Cannes who was well connected with the Saudi Arabian royal family. His name was Mr Mouffak Al Midani.

Her husband, whom I met much later, was not only the skipper of the tycoon's yacht, but also – and are you ready for this – the godson of a previous Pope! After I had digested this mind-bending intelligence I suggested a light breakfast and a discreet bottle of champagne. Over the scrambled eggs and '68 Krug, Fiona unfolded her proposition. Would I like to set up a commercial television operation for the Saudis?

Her boss had expressed an interest in such a scheme and if it were properly presented he could sell it to the King. Now it is fair to record that at this stage the scheme was largely the brainchild of Fiona – an energetic and vivacious lady who found working on a $3 million-yacht for a fabulously wealthy foreigner fun, but less than totally fulfilling. The lady was thinking laterally, trying hard to be original and creative and to inject her own life with a little bezazz!

There were, Fiona told me, some 30,000 British expatriates resident in the desert kingdom and one of their most persistent enemies was boredom. Most of them were in Saudi on contracts which ranged from two to five years and their prime motivation for being there in the first place was money. Large, tax-free incomes, plus free housing, servants and Mercedes motor cars were the sort of lures that drew engineers, chemists and quantity surveyors from the security of Surbiton and Leeds to the land of sand, oil and sunshine.

Fiona's boss, Midani, a very shrewd international businessman with considerable contacts, believed that an English language television service, aimed at the Brits and possibly the Americans and supported by high quality advertising, would achieve two vital objectives: it would make the Saudi posting more attractive to those technicians and advisers upon whom the kingdom's economic future depended and it would also enable native Saudis to learn the high-tech skills of running a television operation for themselves.

Clearly what was needed was a complete package – an entrepreneurial person or persons to put the whole thing together, costed, researched, resourced and viable. As I sipped my champagne and ate my scrambled eggs, I entertained visions of wealth and prestige on a scale undreamt of even by Aladdin after he had snaffled the magic lamp.

It was but a moment's work to cancel my flight from Nice and re-book on a different airline later that day. I was gripped with an overwhelming sense of certainty. My company had the skills and the resources to set such an enterprise rolling. At a later date, I mused, we might need additional funding, but that, of course, would come from the Saudi Arabian treasury. Our involvement would be as contractors for the whole deal. We would provide the management skills, the marketing expertise, the programme know-how, the motivation. What at first appeared to be a very small operation covering at most

100,000 English-speaking foreign residents would surely grow until we were instrumental in setting up – for colossal managed fees, of course – a whole Arabian television network for the Saudis themselves. Our commissions from the sale of international advertising would run into millions of pounds alone. It is of such stuff that dreams are made. And frustrations.

Fiona and I strolled through the fabulous tropical gardens near the casino, talking earnestly about this great idea. Finally at noon we parted, she to return to Midani's yacht in Cannes, I to Nice airport to catch a plane to London. On arriving home I set about writing a preliminary plan of action. Research and costings, together with perhaps a feasibility study would come shortly afterwards. Speed was essential. Once it was known that a man in the King's confidence was being pitched for a major television scheme in Saudi Arabia, all manner of keen adventurers would throw in rival bids. The Americans with their vast resources could probably drown us, but if Fiona was right – and I believed she was – the key was getting the King's approval. This would come via her employer, who was trusted implicitly by the royal family.

At this stage of the narrative you may well be asking, why me? How come the delectable Fiona had chanced upon me when she could have contacted any of the world's major network companies like ABC, NBC, Thames or Granada? Simple, really. During the hour of English language television my company was providing each week on the Riviera I had appeared regularly in a series of promotional ads. My face was now well-known and my company was clearly familiar with how to set up English programmes in a foreign environment.

On the following Monday I met with Peter Cadbury and his reaction was typical and generous.

'It sounds as if it's worth a shot. You put the package together, research it and sell the concept to this mysterious financier and I'll see that we find the necessary start-up resources. If you blow it, you'll just have to abort and pick up the pieces.'

I lunched that day with a client of international standing at

San Lorenzo in Knightsbridge. Over chicken Béarnaise and a bottle of chilled Frascati I sketched out my ideas about a full-service television operation in the Middle East. My client listened in fascination. Should such a venture come to fruition, he said, his company would certainly support it with advertising. They had a line of luxurious products in the games and leisure market that would suit expatriate Britons far away from home. He had in fact already advertised with us during our Monte Carlo caper and was just the sort of adventurous businessman we needed to attract.

Later that day I received another visitor in my office in Sloane Square, an advertising agent who had influence over several million pounds' worth of international business – a man who had already created a market for design and printing in the Middle East for one of his specialist clients. He gave me further encouragement. I was now excited by the prospects and impatient to get the whole show on the road.

Working at high speed I spent the weekend at my desk in Surrey and wrote a complete position paper for the project. Before I could translate advertiser promises into hard cash I knew many hurdles would need to be overcome. The first priority, however, was to sell myself to 'Mr Fixit', Fiona's boss, as the man most likely to succeed in such an extravagant enterprise.

A week later I flew again to Nice and took the short helicopter journey from the airport to Monte Carlo. The chopper skimmed along the coastline, past Cap Ferrat and a series of mouth-watering mansions belonging to the rich and powerful. It was only after I checked into the Hotel de Paris that I began to realise that actually meeting this critically important billionaire was going to be difficult. This proved to be the understatement of the century.

His yacht, roughly the size of Harrods, was anchored in Monaco. He however, was in Rome, but was expected back within 24 hours. Thirty-six hours later he flew in from Italy in his private Lear jet, only to telephone from 30,000 feet above the Alps to have his yacht meet him in Cannes. I drove along the Côte d'Azur through traffic-choked Nice in order to

79

clinch my appointment. By the time I had parked in Port Canto he was aboard, but incommunicado.

Fiona was in Cannes, but not actually on the yacht. A huge man in a T-shirt, with muscles like Atlas, politely turned me away. Later Fiona phoned me after I had dejectedly driven back to Monte Carlo. Her boss, she explained, was an extremely busy man and it might make more sense if I went to Paris in a fortnight's time to see him at his office there. With hopes still relatively undimmed I returned to London and wrote a long introductory letter, explaining the outline of my proposal. I had three copies made and posted: one to the yacht in Cannes, one to a poste restante in Paris and one to his 'occasional' house in London (a pitifully small 12-bedroom job, valued at £1.5 million).

There was no reply.

With the recklessness born of misplaced optimism, I decided to fly to Paris unheralded and tackle the situation head-on. If I just showed up, I reasoned, my amazing powers of persuasion would surely transfix him and the deal would be on, if not exactly clinched. One tiny problem presented itself. His forwarding address in Paris was a secret. Even Fiona, whom I telephoned, didn't know it.

'I've mentioned the idea to him,' she explained, 'but the only way to sell him anything is to see him face to face.'

I remember laughing like a hyena at this remark, having spent the best part of a month trying to chase a shadow.

A touch of detective work and 200 francs to the bellboy at L'Hotel in Rue des Beaux Arts revealed the following intelligence. An Arab businessman of stupendous wealth had taken an entire floor at the Plaza Athenee. Rolls-Royces by the dozen clogged the hotel forecourt and there were rumours of the man from Cartier arriving with a trunk full of samples twice a day.

My man, obviously.

I caught a cab from the Left Bank to the Plaza Athenee and sauntered into the fabulous lobby. There were more Arabs lounging about than the cast of Lawrence of Arabia. I selected one in Savile Row suit and asked politely if Mr Mouffak Al

Midani was in the hotel. At this point I should confess that my pronunciation of complicated Arab names left a little to be desired and it is not unknown for several Middle Eastern gentlemen to have similar-sounding names, although Midani, on reflection, was not one with which I anticipated any difficulty.

On the fifth floor I was met by two more Arabs in full Rudolph Valentino costume. One of them appeared to have a diamond stuck up his left nostril. Either that or he was having trouble with his Vick inhaler. I was shown into a sort of ante-room, devoid of furniture save for a velvet *chaise-longue*. Another man with a vivid scar on his cheek gave me a glass of orange juice and a copy of *Time* magazine. Half an hour later I was taken into another room, which looked like a converted bedroom, with a desk, chairs, telex machines, several telephones and a map of the world pinned to the silk wallpaper. Four men in immaculate English suits were drinking tea. None of them was my billionaire. I introduced myself. They smiled. What were my credentials? they asked with old-world politeness.

Credentials?

Could I prove I was British? Yes. I showed them my passport. Did I have the authority to act on behalf of my corporation? Of course I did. I was a director of a public company. I gave them one of my business cards. They read it as if it were the *Kama Sutra* and slid it back across the table. The card, they explained apologetically, was not sufficient evidence that I was a bona fide courier.

I thought, 'What the hell is going on here?' But said (with a grace to equal their own), 'Gentlemen, I have been trying to meet Mr Midani' (I pronounced his name with exaggerated care), 'for several weeks now. A senior employee of his, based in the South of France has already appraised him of my intentions. All I ask is a chance to meet him man to man and discuss my proposals, which incidentally were sent to his yacht and his London house as well as his forwarding address here in Paris.'

One of the suits frowned and picked up my business card again.

'Mr Turner,' he said slowly, as if addressing an idiot of unpredictable temperament. 'Mr Midani has neither a yacht nor a residence in London.'

While I absorbed this neat little whiff of grapeshot, one of his colleagues produced a tin of lozenges and offered me one. I refused. Never take sweets from a stranger.

'Furthermore,' said the first man, adjusting what looked suspiciously like an MCC tie, 'we cannot fathom the connection between your television company and our request for written tenders associated with an animal health project in our country for cattle serum and sheep inoculations.'

'Funny you should say that,' said I, closing my briefcase with an authoritative snap. 'I do believe we've been talking at cross purposes.'

We shook hands solemnly and I left. To this very day I am convinced they believed I was an eccentric sensation seeker with mad designs to steal sand from the Sahara, using the television story as a cover.

Shortly after this Kafkaesque charade Fiona left the employment of the real Mr Midani and went to America. I dropped all plans ever to locate him and filed my position paper among the unread novels of Sir Walter Scott. The moral of this cautionary tale is clear. If you can't talk directly with the man who has the power to say 'Yes', then you may well end up wasting your time and energy talking to men with diamonds up their noses in Paris hotel bedrooms.

Not every jaunt into Europe was quite so abortive. In 1982 I received an unexpected phone call on a rain-slashed February morning that immeasurably brightened my day.

Imagine if you can the jolting lift of the following conversation: 'Allo – my name is Rita Majocchi. You are 'Arry Turnere?'

There was little to be gained by frenzied denials even though my subconscious was riffling through a card index of awful horrors committed abroad over the past 20 years. Was it perhaps the proprietor of that tiny italian bistro off West 42nd St in New York whose lasagne I once dared to criticise? Worse, was it the Istanbul hotelier who, through ignorance and

82

an excess of red wine, had cocked up the machinery provided by American Express 12 years ago and was now claiming his £300 plus compound interest?

Happily it was neither. Rita Majocchi, it turned out, was the General Manager of FincomRadiovideo Pubblicita in Milan. It had fallen to her to organise a 'television conference' in Venice in March to which I was invited, with my wife, all expenses paid, to deliver a speech on 'the effect and value of local television on the political, economic and social structure of the country'. The seminar ran for two days over a kind of elongated weekend and I agreed instantly. Later I asked myself, would I have accepted with such magnanimous alacrity had the venue been Macclesfield or Grimethorpe? Who knows? Maybe their canals are a thing of undiscovered wonder. Who am I to act as Solomon in judgement? Venice, however, is the most magical of all the European cities and my regular visits over the years have only increased my addiction to its charms.

Rita Majocchi's brief was, well, brief. I was to talk for 45 minutes, preferably without visual aids, and extol the micro-economic benefits of our federal ITV structure. That evening I dashed off what I thought was a fairly racy piece, full of ringing phrases like 'community enhancement' and 'the vigour of the free market-place'.

It's amazing how Churchillian one becomes after three brandies and a Monte Cristo cigar. I rehearsed my speech a couple of times in front of my wife and as she didn't exactly collapse laughing in a heap I got it typed the next day and placed it in my 'Foreign Pending Adventures' file.

On 19 March we arrived in a Venice of azure blue skies and sharp, brilliant sunshine. The Hotel Monaco, into which we were booked, was situated magnificently on the Grand Canal with a view over the shimmering lagoon towards the island of San Giorgio. It was in the magnificent Fondazione Giorgio Cini on this island that the actual conference would take place. Probably the most splendidly exotic setting for any business meeting I've ever attended.

We had a couple of hours free before our 'briefing' meeting at 6 p.m. with Rita Majocchi, where we would be introduced to the other international speakers from America and Germany. Not unnaturally we filled that two-hour period in the only way that any civilised person can: coffee at Florian's in St Mark's Square, a stroll over the Rialto Bridge, a soupçon of shopping, the calm of the church of Maria de Giglio with its fabulous baroque façade and huge organ above the altar. Then back to the hotel for a hot bath and a vital phone call to Harry's Bar for a dinner reservation later that night. We were saving the Gritti Palace for our second evening – one should never snatch at one's pleasure!

Just before six I was hanging round in the lobby waiting for Rita Majocchi to manifest herself when I encountered Leslie Halliwell looking like Monty Woolley in *The Man Who Came To Dinner*. We chatted and he revealed that he too was scheduled to speak, on his favourite subject: movies for television. This was good news for there is no greater expert or enthusiast than Leslie. He did, however, confess slight bafflement as to what the conference was really all about.

Suddenly Rita Majocchi appeared – a tiny, ebullient figure clutching a huge wad of files and a reporter's handbook. We were briskly organised around a table in the bar and Rita started the briefing. At first confusion reigned. In spite of her enormous enthusiasm and clear dedication I realised that my brilliantly prepared speech would need to undergo certain revisions.

Could I, for example, explain just how regional television helped the 'ordinary' people – the 'proletariat'? Could I slant my comments in such a way that would reveal the vast 'community benefits' showered upon the yeomen of Devon and Cornwall from the cornucopia that was Television South-West? For a mad moment I contemplated standing up in the great, vaulted conference room delivering an avuncular diatribe, hands in pockets, the apple-cheeked man of the people, telling how local peasants broke off from dancing round the maypole and rushed to their television sets, weeping gratefully, whenever our local programmes began transmission.

84

We were joined by a droll and charming American, Bill Copperfield of Hubbard Television, who was also asked to 'heavy up' on the 'benefits to the ordinary folk' routine. It became apparent that we were part of a gentle propaganda exercise being skilfully orchestrated by the splendid Rita.

Finally satisfied that we were imbued with her philosophy, Rita ordered us a round of drinks with a theatrical flourish and grinned. She was, I thought, a miniaturised Sylvana Magnani and earth mother rolled into one.

Bill Copperfield was of the opinion that he and I were no less than vanguards in the cause of capitalism, Italy having more than its fair share of communists, extreme lefties, pinkos and Wedgwood Benn's. Certainly, the future of Italian television was the subject of continuous and heated debate between the exponents of free enterprise and those forces who believe that paradise can only be attained through state control. The conference of which we were part was another arena for this long-running duel.

The other speakers were pretty impressive. Professor Roberto Grandi of the University of Bologna, who was to comment on sociological matters and the effects of television on people's behaviour patterns. Alfredo Valletti, a government minister with special responsibility for broadcasting. Guiseppe Orlando, the President of Confocommercio, Dr Maurd Volf also from the University of Bologna and Giovanni Girone from the University of Bari. Simultaneous translations would be provided by a team of young lady linguists who were to be crammed into a glass booth at the end of the great vaulted conference room next to the Chiostri dei Cipressi.

After drinks we were, in Rita's immortal words, 'free to tinker as you will in this most nice town'. Assisted by a glass or three of Dom Perignon I reshaped my speech and practised my most 'sociologically aware' facial expressions. This vital work complete we walked the few yards to Harry's Bar for a meal of stunning opulence.

The next day a launch, all gleaming brass and polished woodwork, whisked us over the glassy surface of the lagoon to Isola San Giorgio and we walked through eighteenth-

85

century formal gardens and courtyards to Fondanzione Giorgio Cini.

The conference – like all conferences – had its fair share of droning bores and the English translation, I am bound to say, proved to be less than spectacular: 'We believe social justice musta be served not only to be seen in the context of the television situation and so forth, but no effort musta be spared to achieve these aims of such importance to the technology of the country as a whole and to the people whose lives issa affected.'

What, I asked myself, does it all mean?

At set moments during each speech, the dynamic Rita, barely visible behind a refectory table of gigantic proportions around which it was possible to imagine the Last Supper, would leap to her feet and call for questions from the floor. However, nobody in Italy asks questions – they simply make speeches.

These interruptions somewhat lengthened the proceedings so that when Bill Copperfield and I were scheduled to do our bit for freedom, the holy dollar and the pragmatic pound, Rita told us, with a charming smile, 'You cutta to twenty minutes each, please.'

This we did, Bill Copperfield by crossing out some of his more stirring phrases and me by talking faster. This, however, caused a sort of mild revolution in the glass booth where the hard-pressed translators were sweating like horses trying to keep up with me. Rita waved a hand to signal that I had 'lost' the translators so I slammed on the brakes and finished my speech, sounding a bit like Archbishop Carey on a programme for the hard of hearing – all carefully articulated vowel sounds and meaningless ecclesiastical pauses. It was however received with considerable applause – my wife said 'relief' most likely – and we mingled with the audience. However, such unstructured lounging about was not part of the Rita Majocchi plan.

'We meet at seven in the hotel to go at once to the reception,' she ordered daintily.

'What reception?' I asked, seeing my anticipated dinner

86

at the Gritti Palace replaced by vol-au-vents and cooking sherry.

'The Mayor of Venice will be our host,' she said, 'at the Palazzo Ca Farsett.'

At seven sharp Rita Majocchi had us all mustered in the lobby of the Hotel Monaco and we were led at a brisk march through the fabulous Venice dusk beyond St Marks, across serpentine bridges and dark, limpid canals until we arrived, tingling, at the great brooding piazza near Rialto. Inside we were led over a beautiful stone-flagged inner courtyard, up a grand marbled staircase and into a vast and exquisite reception room. Tall windows looked out over the purple waters of the canal and towards the open lagoon, glittering under a pale moon. Two dark-suited stewards stood behind a table on which were massed a regiment of drinks, tiny snacks, pickles and what looked like dwarf pizzas. But the two men politely refused to serve anybody with a drink.

'We have arrived ahead of our host,' Rita explained.

After a 15-minute, drink-less wait the Mayor showed up to greet his 50 or so guests. He was, I suppose, a sort of Italian Ken Livingstone and he shook us all by the hand. He gave me the distinct impression that our views on the way television should develop throughout the world were at best slightly incompatible. The old concept that television should inform, educate and entertain seemed as far from his heart as the concept of objectivity was to Citizen Kane in Orson Welles' immortal movie.

The reception lasted for another 40 minutes and it was with considerable relief that I realised our dinner at the Gritti Palace was still on. Having done my bit for the enterprise and hopefully the future of Italian television, we surrendered ourselves entirely to the grape and pasta, the splendour of which can only be fully appreciated after enjoying them both in the magnificent dining room of the Gritti Palace Hotel.

If I get really lucky again in 2002 I suppose my phone could ring, say in mid-November, and an exotic voice could ask me to extol the virtues of independent television in Peru, Latvia or possibly Katmandu. I live in a state of delicious anticipation!

CHAPTER 7

I'm the boss at last. A trip to the South American Jungle and the launch of the Astra Satellite, plus a visit to an American ship in the Mediterranean.

When I became Managing Director, I resisted falling into the 'acquisition' trap. There is a belief still fashionable, and in my view foolhardy, that argues that growth by acquisition is the only route to progress and increased profits. While this is something of a 'Holy Grail' in the city of London, I believed that a vital prerequisite is to promote organic growth within your own organisation first. It is seductive and relatively easy for cash-rich companies to mask sluggish performance by embarking on the take-over trail. In the short term, take-overs fatten the balance sheet, enhance the share price and make exciting upward curves on the sales graph. But when things slow down, as they always do (all businesses are cyclical, there are no exceptions), the predator seeks new victims to consume, further obscuring their own internal performance.

Of course, it can work well if all factors conspire to maintain a healthy business climate, but too often the predator suffers a nasty bout of indigestion. The ITV companies' record on diversification and take-overs is not overwhelmingly impressive. At the time of writing, commercial cannibalism is rife, the minnows are being consumed by bigger fish and with no perceptible improvement in programme quality. As television professionals, we saw no logic in trying to manage other businesses in markets with which we were unfamiliar.

Notwithstanding all the above, when an opportunity arose to become an investor in the Astra Satellite venture by acquiring a shareholding in SES Luxembourg, we took it. Astra, now hovering 22,500 miles above the earth's crust and not visible from the gardens of Budleigh Salterton even on a starry night, is a miracle of technology and human ingenuity. It has 16 transponders all capable of beaming television signals into Europe and all of them, at the time of writing, have been leased to international broadcasters, the most famous of whom is Rupert Murdoch. His Sky channel was one of Astra's first customers.

Some months after we had made the decision to invest, I received the sort of 'out of the blue' invitation that one usually only dreams of. Would I like to fly to South America as a shareholder of SES Luxembourg and watch the launch of the Ariane Hecke rocket which would carry the Astra satellite? As TSW had £500,000 riding on the venture I accepted the invitation at once. I could not help reflecting at the time that life in ITV could be a tapestry of great surprises. The plan was simple, but undeniably glamorous – I was to fly from Paris in a privately chartered Concorde among an impressive passenger list of French and English army generals, civilian VIPs and a handful of journalists.

As we gathered in the Concorde lounge for pre-flight champagne, stories were swapped about the many and varied health precautions we had endured, from malaria pills to a range of jabs for swamp fever, hoof rot, yellow jaundice, swine rash, housemaids knee, tennis elbow, athletes groin and degeneration of the pancreas. We were, after all, bound for French Guyana which nestles at the top of the South American continent adjacent to Brazil. We had been warned of its ferociously humid climate, the snakes, crocodiles and spiders as big as your fist, which infest its every nook and clearing. Why Guyana? I asked myself as I settled into the surprisingly spartan interior of the Air France Concorde. Would I survive? If the crawling, stinging, biting, sucking things didn't get me, it was abundantly clear that the Indians with their blowpipes from the depths of the rain forest would. These thoughts warmed me until we made a fuelling stop at Dakar on the edge of the Sahara.

Here I had time to make the acquaintance of some of my

distinguished fellow travellers, among them Sir Peter Anson, Chairman of Marconi Space Systems, Captain Appleyard-List, Chief Signal Officer, Ministry of Defence, Richard Dunn of Thames (who are 10 per cent shareholders in SES/Astra, and of course our host Pierre Meyrat, Director General of the Société Européenne des Satellites. For Pierre's company, the first private enterprise group to finance and launch a satellite, this was a crucial trip. The high risks involved and the massive investment incurred meant an atmosphere of excitement and anticipation throughout the visit.

Day One, launch day, was wet and humid and we started early on a tour of the facilities, built quite literally on the edge of the jungle. We were briefed in the Guyanan Space Centre optics room and shown film of the complex preparation of the Ariane rocket. This would have been more reassuring had the film *and* the slides not broken down, which they both did.

The launch site stands at 5.2 degrees north, near the equator, which enables the launcher to obtain a transfer orbit without complicated manoeuvres, thus making a fuel saving on the payload equivalent of 15 per cent of the satellite mass. The technology surrounding the project is awesome. The launch platform contains 12,000 tons of cement and the rocket itself is powered by 150 tons of liquid oxygen and hydrogen and two solid propellant boosters delivering a thrust of 650 tons on lift-off.

In the event we were in for a day of high drama and nail-biting suspense. The vast rocket was wheeled out on tracks and secured at the launching pad to await the magic hour of 9 p.m. We were coached to the Toucan observation field which afforded a splendid view of the site and we waited. And we waited some more. Finally came the drama of the countdown – well within the six-minute computer controlled final sequence – and then (a heart-stopping moment) something wasn't right. The firing was aborted. The disappointment was palpable and we had to wait another hour before being told that there was a problem with one of the tracking stations and the launch would be postponed for 24 hours!

On the Saturday the waiting was made bearable by a boat trip to Devil's Island, of Papillon fame, where we swam in a palm-fringed cove alongside giant turtles and contemplated the beach where Dreyfus spent his lonely exile in 1895. I found myself in conversation with a pleasant young man in jeans and sneakers who turned out to be His Royal Highness Prince Guillaume of Luxembourg. It was that kind of day.

Later, at nightfall, with a star-studded sky above us, we assembled again at the Toucan field. Luminous fireflies and bats swooped through the gloaming making a spectacular backdrop. There was one false start and then, after an agonising half hour, we were into the final countdown.

The sight of that mighty rocket rising majestically in to the heavens is one I'll never forget.

The human skills and perseverance behind it are beyond praise – everyone on the site was filled with wonder and admiration, so I lit a cigar.

'Who would have thought,' I mused, 'when I joined ITV in 1962 to flog airtime, that twenty-six years later I'd be sitting on the edge of the South American jungle watching half a million quid's worth of TSW's money roaring into the stratosphere *and* be happy about it!'

1988 was one of those years crowded with incident. In addition to the remarkable jaunt to South America, only a few months earlier, in April, I was a delegate at the MIP COM Festival in Cannes. Normally this five-day event follows a traditional pattern. Television programmes are viewed, bought and sold. Prodigious lunches are consumed in outrageously expensive cafés and enough champagne is swilled to float a sizeable aircraft carrier. However, perhaps not enough to float the particular aircraft carrier that I was invited to visit during my stay.

The Palais des Festivals in Cannes squats toad-like in all its concrete awfulness alongside the old port where expensive and mouth-wateringly beautiful yachts bob in the swell. A few hundred yards out to sea the ocean falls away sharply and can accommodate vessels of huge size. It just happened that 1988 was the twenty-fifth anniversary of this particular festival and it coincided with a visit to Cannes of USS *Dwight D. Eisenhower* of the United States 6th Fleet.

When I first caught a glimpse of this incredible hulk anchored half a mile out to sea I thought perhaps that there had been a subterranean explosion deep on the ocean bed which had thrown up a volcanic mass bigger than the Isle of Wight. The exaggeration is forgivable when I tell you that the USS *Dwight D. Eisenhower* is the second biggest warship and aircraft carrier in the world. Awesome though it was viewed from the terrace of the Palais des Festivals, this was merely a foretaste of what was yet to come.

On the Tuesday of Cannes week I received a glossy invitation from Rear Admiral R. G. Guilbualt, Commander Battleforce 6th Fleet, together with Captain G. L. Beck, Commanding Officer of the USS *Dwight D. Eisenhower* and Edmund van Gilder, Consul General of the United States, to join them at a reception on board. I can only assume that this brace of Yankee sea dogs and their Consul General had quickly scanned the delegates' list and invited the most senior representatives from each of the companies present at the festival.

Promptly at 7.00 p.m. on the Friday I joined a bunch of dinner jacketed television professionals on a US navy boat which took us out to the *Dwight D. Eisenhower*. Imagine, if you can, the impact of a vessel one-sixth of a mile long, with a flight deck covering four and a half acres housing 100 combat planes. Further, try and picture such a vessel standing in the water, taller than a six-storey building, with a crew of 6,000 men. The USS *Dwight D. Eisenhower* was all of these things, and more. Half as big again as the *QE2*, this incredible monster was packed with nuclear weapons, Phoenix long-range missiles and twin nuclear reactors. Armour-plated and virtually impenetrable by conventional shell fire, the *Eisenhower*, with all her bulk of steel, can attain a speed of 30 knots. She was built in 1969 at a cost of £200 million. Naturally, being a Yankee ship, she also has a cinema, several libraries, saunas, and would you believe, an ice-cream parlour!

It was into this fabulous world that I stepped as a guest of the Rear Admiral of the US 6th Fleet and his Consul General.

To say that I was mildly impressed would be something of an understatement. The immaculate, white uniformed officers aboard the *Eisenhower*, all intensely proud of their ship, seemed to possess an encyclopedic knowledge of their floating home.

'Do you realise,' said a young Lieutenant within minutes of my getting aboard, 'that the kitchens are stocked with twenty-two thousand, five hundred frozen chickens?'

I told him that it was not a piece of information that I normally associated with a US fighting ship. He looked mildly shocked.

'Not only that,' he continued, 'we have ten thousand pecan pies, fifty thousand doughnuts...'

As the litany of food unfolded, my eyes must have started to glaze over, because he suddenly grinned and said, 'But I'm sure you want to see the rest of the ship.'

I did, and staggering was the word that sprang to mind as we were conducted through its huge, echoing, steel-clad interior.

'More fire-power on this tub,' said one young sailor, 'than the entire French army had in World War II.'

'What about security?' I said. 'Do you ever get stowaways?' I might as well have suggested that the Pope was Jewish.

'This is a secure ship,' said an officer with a fierce ginger crewcut. 'We are on constant alert.'

He indicated with his thumb towards an upper deck. Two marines, built like Rambo, stood splay-legged at an observation post. They appeared to be carrying, around their necks and waistbelts, more fire power than the entire British Home Guard during World War II!

As we roamed around the ship the torrent of statistics flowed unceasingly. Every plate, rivet, floor sheet, gun emplacement, deck angle and thickness of the steaks served in the officers' mess was lovingly revealed. I could tell by looking around the carrier that it was a very young crew indeed. There was a lot of heavy manual work being done – the lifting of machinery, humping steel plates, hauling wheeled trolleys across the huge decks. I asked an officer to

give me a run-down on the composition of the ship's personnel and he whipped a typewritten sheet from his immaculately
starched breast pocket. Unsurprisingly, 75 per cent of the
enlisted people were aged from 17 to 25. Among the officers
only a handful, including the top rankers, were over 40. This
was a *young* ship. Seventy-seven of the enlisted personnel
were white, 16 per cent black and the rest Hispanic or Asian.
A regular stewpot that fairly reflected many average American
cities. Over a third of the sailors were married, conjuring up
images of weeping wives on the quayside every time the carrier sailed on one of its long missions. Another unsurprising
statistic was that those states with the highest unemployment
rates provided the most recruits.

One of many impressions that has stayed with me vividly
was the old-world politeness of both officers and men on this
amazing ship. The visitors were addressed as 'sir' or 'madam'
and no request for information was dealt with other than cour-
teously. In many ways the *esprit des corps* was reminiscent of
my own army days way back in the 1950s. Everybody was
proud of their role and keen to do their best.

After the tour we were treated to a display of gun drill and
marching on the upper deck. To arrive on this deck we were
gathered *by the dozens* on a vast steel platform as big as half
a football pitch and the whole thing was raised hydraulically
until we were 'up top'.

The closely-packed ranks of jet fighters with folded back
wings gleamed menacingly in the late evening sun. A hundred
planes, all capable of flying at staggering airspeeds and delivering death and destruction the while. I found this display of
naked power quite unsettling.

After the marching and the gun drill a podium was wheeled
out on deck and Rear Admiral R. G. Guilbualt, Commander
Battleforce 6th Fleet, stepped up to say a few words. I have
to tell you that whatever else you may hear, John Wayne lives.
The Admiral, his face hewn from teak, spoke in a lazy drawl,
his speech peppered with cracker barrel philosophy and thinly
veiled macho warnings to 'any would-be aggressors' who
might be listening. We all glanced nervously at the persons

sitting next to us. Could that elegantly dressed Chinese lady with the Gucci scarf really be a commie agent? Or that overweight television producer whom I vaguely recognised from the Carlton beach be a Russian navy spy? Fortunately, no enemies surfaced during the Admiral's speech thus depriving him of the need to nuke them into a pile of smouldering ash. Then, as the shadow of the great ship lengthened over the gleaming, glassy calm of the Mediterranean we took our leave of the officers and men. We had been aboard for two and half hours and all of us, without exception, had been deeply impressed by what we had seen.

In the launch that took us back to the old port there was an excited buzz of conversation. Some were clearly hostile. 'Yankee warmongers, waste of resources when half the world is starving,' etc. Others, like me, took I believe, a more sanguine view. The world is a wicked as well as wonderful place and the price of freedom is, as always, eternal vigilance.

Much later that evening a group of us dined at a small restaurant in the old port. Sailors from the *Eisenhower* drifted past, caps tucked under their shoulder straps, gawping at the glitter of Cannes, whistling at the girls. It was a reassuringly human end to a quite remarkable day.

CHAPTER 8

*To Russia with love. The ITN news team perform
feats above and beyond the call of duty.*

In 1990 I spent four days in Russia, but it seemed longer, shall
we say about a year and a half? The first two days in Moscow
were not entirely without incident, mostly awful, but at least
we got to the Bolshoi twice. Once to see a sumptuous production of *Giselle* and again to see an obscure opera the name
of which eludes me.

Our hotel, the Cosmos, a 3,000 bedroom job, lacked
elegance and comfort. But it was warm. So warm in fact you
found your shoes curling up like Turkish slippers if you left
them within a foot of the unswitchable-off radiators. But we
knew that the Soviets were not yet into luxury so we shrugged
and told ourselves that after the long journey from Gatwick
at least we would get a hot meal. What we got in fact was
nothing like a hot meal. Any resemblance to food was purely
coincidental. And it was cold. The meat had clearly been
hacked by chisel from the flanks of a diseased and probably
muscle-bound yak. The pint of vodka that I consumed later
did however kill some of the pain.

Day two was bathed in bright sunshine. Our spirits lifted a
shade. My itinerary was straightforward – I was to telephone
ITN's Moscow bureau and fix a meeting with their team there
– Robin Staniforth, Tim Ewart and Penny Marshall. They in
turn would arrange an appointment for me to meet Valentin
Lazutkin, the Head of Soviet television.

Let me state quite plainly that making a telephone call from
a Russian hotel may *sound* simple, but it is a ferociously complicated affair. To start with getting a free outside line takes

at least 15 minutes. Then there is the time-honoured and deeply traditional 'wrong number ritual'. This swallows up another 10. When you finally reach your goal (in my case the ITN bureau number), you are faced with the language problem.

'Can I speak with Mr Staniforth?' I asked, not unreasonably I thought.

'*Nyet*,' came the reply. Then the click as we were cut off. Clearly an extended part of the time-honoured tradition. After three further fruitless attempts to persuade the Russian operator to put me through I gave up and said to my wife, 'We'll just catch a cab. We have the address. The ITN boys expect us at 10 a.m. anyway.'

I should explain that we had been warned about the taxi 'problem' in Moscow. It can be summarised thus: nobody knows where anything is. We selected a taxi driver who looked reasonably bright. He was in his twenties, cheerful, fur-hatted and (what a mercy) he spoke a little English. We showed him the ITN address: Ul. Marksistskaya, Corpus I. Simple enough? No problem he said, it's near the latest Moscow landmark, 'McDonald's'.

There followed a nightmare journey in a cab so battered, so soiled and so smelly as to beggar further description. The driver had not the smallest notion of where we were supposed to be going – and neither of course did we. I exaggerate not a *jot* when I declare that we were in that cab for two hours and five minutes in traffic that would have made Istanbul seem like Shangri-La. We bumped and rattled through featureless streets, past huge tenements and empty shops, alongside vast stadiums and tiny kiosks selling cakes – these of course were distinguished by the queues of human misery standing in mute crocodile outside them.

At length, frustrated and bewildered (the driver's English, by the way, turned out to be limited to the phrase 'not here, sorry'), we instructed him to bring us back to the hotel. By this time my wife was slumped against me in a state of advanced travel sickness. Back in our room a dozen or so more phone calls finally connected me with ITN, who by now

98

had assumed, not entirely without cause, that I had disappeared into the wastes of Siberia. A car and driver was despatched to the Cosmos and lo and behold only another half hour passed before I was at the ITN Moscow bureau.

I am able to confirm, as a non-Executive Director of ITN, that the small staff of four people there did not reside in anything that could be remotely described as luxury. The operation, in point of fact, was conducted from a high-rise slum that bore an uncanny resemblance to a 1950s council estate in Accrington.

After a brief pause for tea I was given a conducted tour of the facilities, which took all of five minutes. Then as we discussed the current situation in London (I was to reassure Tim Ewart that the demise of ITN into insolvency had been averted), a freelance American cameraman arrived with his Russian interpreter. They had just conducted some 'vox pop' interviews with ordinary Muscovites in the local supermarket and were anxious to show me the unedited tape. Seldom have I seen such an angry crowd. The shelves of the market were almost empty and the few items of food that did exist were of poor quality. A huge queue had been waiting for three hours for a delivery of bread, but none had come and none was now expected. The ITN reporter spoke to several customers and asked them what they thought of Mr Gorbachov. The replies were explosive.

'He may be a world statesman, but he can't put bread on our table!' cried one middle-aged woman. 'Glasnost?' another spat contemptuously, 'we are in chaos here. We are *serfs!*' One tired looking man in shabby overalls told the interviewer that he was a shift worker who had not slept for 36 hours and had been waiting at the market for two hours hoping to buy bread and eggs for his four children. He left empty-handed and all in all it was a chilling confirmation of how state communism has brought the Soviet economy to its knees and how freedom, briefly tasted, is heady wine indeed.

As my visit was private and we were due to fly to Leningrad the following day, strenuous attempts were made to fix the meeting with Valentin Lazutkin – but alas he was in Georgia, unexpectedly delayed, and I had to be content with a brief chat with a minor Soviet television official, Rudolph Galtzin, who while courteous and charming, clearly was no top banana in the Soviet television hierarchy. I gave him a few tapes of TSW's local programmes which were eagerly accepted and a Gus Honeybun for his grandchildren. Thus, Plymouth made its weighty contribution to *perestroika*!

After making my farewells to the ITN team their driver shipped me back through the dreadful traffic to the Cosmos Hotel. A party of Finns were arriving by coach as I alighted from the car and the vast lobby of the hotel was swarming with visitors from other parts of the Soviet empire.

The decor of the Cosmos could be charitably described as bleak. From the ceiling of the lobby hangs a grotesque metal sculpture that is mysteriously entitled 'The Space Bicycle'. The hotel receptionist however had another name for it, popular among the locals. They call it Gorbachov's brain. Another curiosity. Free enterprise flourishes in all the hotel lobbies in Moscow. Young men are always lurking by the swing doors ready to offer black-market tickets for the Bolshoi at hugely inflated prices (£25 for an eight-rouble seat), or tins of dubious caviar at £10. They also offer fur hats with CCCP badges (one of which I purchased for two quid and a cigar). Nobody wants roubles. Everybody wants 'hard' currency, dollars or pounds being the favourites. Inflation is raging and the rationing of bread, petrol, cigarettes and meat is imminent. The hotel also sported another unusual extra. A profusion of fur-coated prostitutes whose method of soliciting is bold to say the least. Barter is popular too. If you are short on sterling or American currency, English cigarettes or Cadbury's chocolate will do nicely thank you. My wife had packed about half a ton of chocolate in our luggage as we had been fore-warned of this unusual means of exchange before we left London, but as the hotel food was unfit for human consumption we had eaten most of the chocolate by day two.

The evening, by contrast with my harrowing day, was enchanting. The Bolshoi Theatre is superb and the acoustics magnificent. It is wise however, not to anticipate refreshment

100

during the interval. Bars do exist, but it is part of the obstinate Slav tradition to disdain service and make customers feel as unwanted as possible. We settled for ice-cream, and it wasn't as bad as we had expected. The obscure opera was pleasant but not uplifting. Our real treat would come on the following evening when we would return to the Bolshoi for a performance of *Giselle*.

On Wednesday morning we toured the great armoury inside the Kremlin, marvelling at the spectacular state coaches, robes, jewels and weapons on display, all of them remnants of the Czars of Russia before the revolution. We lunched at Slavinsky's Bazaar, a bustling Moscow restaurant housed in a crumbling old mansion just off Red Square. It had been recommended by an Intourist guide who described it as 'typical'. It was a vast, echoing chamber with high ceilings and lots of flaking gold paintwork. At the door a stern matron barred our way and demanded two roubles entrance fee (about 20 pence). All the waitresses were middle-aged, and surprisingly for Moscow, quite cheerful. An awful band scraped out Glen Miller music very badly from a raised platform at one end of the huge room and we were given a small table (there were four of us) in the centre. The menu being incomprehensible we asked our gold-toothed waitress for a typical Russian meal. She nodded agreement and proceeded to serve us with an extraordinary range of food. Caviar, smoked salmon, raw white fish marinated in vinegar, black bread, potato salad, bowls of hot, spicy borsch covered with lids of soft dough, a kind of goulash with onions and leeks, cake and tea. The whole lot came to £12. For *four* people. It was the only meal in Russia that I enjoyed without a sense of impending amoebic dysentery.

That evening, prior to the flight to Leningrad, we returned to the Bolshoi for *Giselle* and it was quite magical, the sets and the staging on a monumental scale and the dancing spectacular.

The 11.50 plane from Moscow to Leningrad is a popular one although the domestic airport from which it leaves bears a close resemblance to a disused knacker's yard. Aeroflot, however, managed to take off on time and we arrived in Leningrad an hour later. Tired by now, we were bundled into a waiting coach and subjected to a long, bumpy ride through wide, bleak streets to our hotel, the 'Moscow'.

Like the Cosmos it was vast, hideous, shabby and impersonal. And like every other hotel in Russia, room service was a luxury that could not, under any possible circumstance, be tolerated. The very idea! Food in your room! Utter depravity, Western corruption! And the room? Would you believe a monk's cell in a high-rise monastery whose order was dedicated to the worship of plastic furniture, dead flies and dwarf's beds? No plugs in the bathroom of course, and when my wife ran some water by means of an experiment it burst from the tap in a glutinous brown sludge. We had also been warned not only *not* to drink the water, but to avoid cleaning our teeth with it as well. The smuggled plastic bottle of Evian was to earn its keep over the next 48 hours!

But dawn brought a bright, cold, sunny morning, and from our room a view over the Neva River. A city tour had been arranged, by coach, and after a breakfast of cheese (hard), cream buns (rancid) and coffee (urinal) we set off eagerly with cameras loaded and dollars and pounds lining our pockets.

St Petersburg, as I prefer to call it, is one of the most sumptuously beautiful cities I have ever seen, and that includes Venice, Paris, Florence and Vienna. Built on a series of islands and connected by superb eighteenth-century bridges, its buildings are truly fabulous. The Winter Palace is heart-stopping, an extravaganza of architectural splendour that overlooks the River Neva. And elsewhere a cornucopia of cathedrals, churches, gold-topped onion domes, huge garden squares, classical government buildings, scientific institutes, palaces (and *such* palaces), beyond belief, some of them. And in the centre of the city no high-rises, no ugliness of any kind. If the Soviets ever get their act together, St Petersburg will become the thinking tourist's most popular destination.

CHAPTER 9

Hollywood eat your heart out. Our big movie is rejected by the network but I get to entertain film stars on a yacht in Cannes and I meet my old fencing partner, Fiona Fullerton.

There are a number of hazards and temptations strewn in the path of a small regional television station, although at first glance the very nature of an ITV franchise suggests that expansion beyond one's geographical boundaries is virtually impossible. However, the trap into which some fall, namely growth by acquisition, has been dealt with elsewhere in this book and history is littered with examples of ambitious enterprises that not only failed, but very nearly destroyed their parent company with them.

It would be churlish to dwell in gloating detail on the misfortunes of colleagues, but as a matter of historical record it was the ill-advised TVS purchase of the Mary Tyler Moore studio in Hollywood that dealt the company a crippling financial blow and cost Chief Executive James Gatward his job into the bargain. My other neighbour, HTV, had an equally embarrassing time when they acquired a company that published diaries. Instead of a steady stream of profits to underpin the television operation, what did they get? They got financial grief and a lot of flak from their shareholders. Somewhat earlier in the history of ITV the Yorkshire/ Tyne Tees conglomerate (Trident) suffered a rush of blood to the head and decided to buy the Windsor Safari Park. Just what qualifications a bunch of television executives had which made them capable of mucking out Bengal tigers and exercising dolphins will remain an unanswered conundrum of our time.

Well, we all know that divine providence punishes corporate greed in the end. But what about corporate ego? This can be almost as dangerous and has been known to afflict all manner of television companies. Including TSW. What happened was this.

In the mid-1980s, British television was considered to be pretty much a global leader in quality. Indeed, in a famous phrase, the distinguished Canadian television critic Milton Shulman said it was 'the least worst television in the world'. Excited by this somewhat spurious accolade a number of larger companies began to accelerate their sales efforts in the USA. Thames in particular did rather well, as did Granada with their acclaimed *Jewel in the Crown* and LWT with *Upstairs, Downstairs*. The Americans loved these shows and it seemed that the transatlantic market was insatiable. If it was British it meant 'quality', and to the producers (Thames, Granada, LWT etc.) it meant big bucks *and* international prestige.

But the American market is a jungle full of predators waiting to gobble up the unwary and it is a 'high risk' market too, with fierce competition from indigenous producers who know how to fight dirty and hard. To run with the pack in America you need to be well resourced, aggressive, talented and streetwise.

Traditionally, the small regional companies in Great Britain have concentrated on their core business, providing fine local programmes to their own familiar audiences. But from time to time they succumb to the seductive glitter of Hollywood. They find themselves drawn into a vortex of co-production deals, 'packaging' and 'bartering' in a world where a sucker is born every minute. And the temptation to play with the really big boys can be mesmerising and appallingly magnetic.

Once upon a time we found it irresistible too.

One fine morning in Plymouth when the rain had stopped and the Hoe glistened with a thousand sparkling drops and the Barbican cobblestones gleamed like polished glass, my

104

Director of Programmes, Michael Reinhold, burst into my office with a high-pitched, keening cry, almost imperceptible to the human ear (in fact it may well have been audible largely to dogs, but I cannot recall exactly whether a chorus of barking broke out after his first ululation). Michael had been in discussion with a writer called Ian Scrivens and an American producer, Larry de Way, who had developed an outline treatment for a one-hour drama which, in Michael's words, 'looked hot' and probably 'had legs'. Now to the simple lay reader, when a Director of Programmes says a show has 'legs' he means that it has the potential to run into a series.

Scrivens, the writer, was a young, owlish gentleman with a penchant for yellow neckties and an addiction to mobile telephones. The mid-1980s saw the zenith of yuppie-style aspiration, so his constant yelling into the mouthpiece to mysterious 'contacts' was considered acceptable behaviour. One or two of us however found it a pain in the ass, particularly as Scrivens seemed inordinately fond of conversing excitedly with a number of people, many of whom were called Nigel.

To be fair, however, Ian Scrivens also had the ability to charm and persuade and he had a perfectly respectable track record as a television script writer, having contributed to the hugely successful *Crossroads* series and other blockbusting extravaganzas that bring a lump to the throat and a tear to the eye when recalled in moments of maudlin introspection.

The concept that had been dangled before Michael Reinhold was tempting enough. We would co-produce with Larry de Way's Silverwold Productions a one-hour pilot entitled *Where There's A Will*. The storyline was amusing and the plot promised a fast-paced tale of love, lust, greed and chicanery within a firm of West Country solicitors. The story involved a stunning American heiress, and there would be London locations too, to add a touch of glamour and sex. Lots of fine West Country scenery, gnarled Devonian 'characters', comic policemen, bucolic local gents, a car chase, a significant number of trousers falling down and sufficient impetus to develop into at least 13 half-hour episodes. Quite frankly it sounded not unreasonable.

'How much will it cost TSW?' I asked Michael.

Now Michael Reinhold was and still is a charming and talented man who had been Westward Television's distinguished Head of Education. A former journalist, he possessed great enthusiasm for the project, and suggested that our exposure would be of the order of £150,000 to £200,000 – or 50 per cent of the pilot costs.

'What about its sales potential?' I asked, sounding more like an accountant than I dared admit.

'Fabulous,' said Michael with his usual circumspection. 'We'll make a bomb if it goes well,' he yelled cautiously.

Now it is one of the quirks of television that nobody – I repeat, *nobody* – knows for sure what the ingredients are for a hit show. If we did we'd only *make* hit shows. What you do is use that curious thing called 'judgement'. Do the component parts look good? Is the script pacey? Will it appeal to a wide audience? Can big international stars be persuaded to appear in it? Will we get a 'name' director to kick the whole thing into shape?

With these questions still unanswered, I took home the first of many draft scripts to read in my bath. And I liked it. Scrivens had knocked together a fair piece of work, rough at the edges of course, but definitely promising.

There are those who believe that a Chief Executive of a television station should be a rock of caution in an ocean of frothing uncertainty. He should avoid engaging his emotions when churning through the decision-making process. He should take no unnecessary chances and always play it safe. I will confess that I am not by nature or inclination a cautious man. Television is a peripheral and gossamer medium at the best of times and I've always believed that creative talent should be encouraged to experiment, to probe, to expand horizons. To deny writers and producers the right to just occasionally fail and to insist only on 'safe' options would, I fear, result in grey and excruciatingly boring television.

Warmed by my bath and reinforced by these profound thoughts (and let it be said, a half bottle of Moët et Chandon), I decided to give Michael Reinhold the nod. We would embark

106

on TSW's first venture into serious film-making with an eye on the international market.

It's easy now, with the benefit of hindsight, to argue that we allowed our hearts to rule our heads, but at the time Michael's enthusiasm was infectious and in the early months of the project much seemed to be going our way.

The ingredients looked appetising, and frankly still do. The mix was right, the time was 'now' (or *then* it was *now* if you catch my drift) and we had big-name stars. Wow, how could we fail? How could we?

The production had been specifically designed for the international market-place and contained elements that we hoped would make it of particular interest for screening in the United States, Australia, West Germany, Italy, France and Canada. The format of *Where There's A Will* was ideally suited for development into a long-running series and it was estimated that each episode would fall within a $700,000 US budget taking approximately four weeks to complete. Each episode was to be shot entirely on location both in the UK and overseas, with possible guest appearances by internationally-known artistes.

Essentially we were looking for an organisation that had access, directly or indirectly, to at least one major distribution or broadcast/cable outlet and could secure the necessary production funding and exposure. Division of all worldwide territories was negotiable as was the form of the co-production, although a 50:50 share split of all costs in return for an equal share of all receipts was preferred. How simple it all sounds now!

We secured the services of a top actor, Patrick MacNee, to play the lead. Patrick was known internationally for his personification of the suave secret agent John Steed in the popular and long-running series *The Avengers*. From his first major theatrical role as Laurie in *Little Women* in 1941, Patrick had been continuously employed in a staggering variety of roles covering all aspects of the entertainment industry. Demand for his talents meant frequent commuting between the United States, Britain and Canada to fulfil film and theatrical commitments too numerous to list. Patrick, we thought, would bring to the role of Charles Crow-Ffinch the experience and style that would ensure worldwide interest in *Where There's A Will*.

An American actress, Louan Gideon was to play the part of Cavatina Andretti, the wickedly attractive, extremely wealthy, high-flying businesswoman who was president of the US-based Andretti Corporation. Louan's credits included a recently-completed three-year run as Liza Sentell, one of the lead roles in NBC's daytime drama *Search For Tomorrow*. In addition to her television experience, Louan had a large number of theatrical credits including Beauty in *Everyman* and Roxanne in *Cyrano de Bergerac* for the Casa Mariana at Fort Worth. Between television and theatrical appearances, Louan had exercised her talents as a singer with lead billings at Bally's Park Place, Atlantic City; The MGM Grand, Reno; the Sahara Tahoe, Las Vegas and the Shangri-La Hotel, Singapore.

Michael Howe was to be Rupert Crow-Ffinch, a handsome, successful British lawyer, employed by the Andretti Corporation and with whom Cavatina was hopelessly in love. As well as his many television roles, Michael was an accomplished actor in the world of theatre. He had been in the West End production of *Chess* and had also starred in *42nd Street*, *Grease* and *Cats*.

English actress Amanda Burton was scheduled for Alice Freemantle, desperately in love with Rupert Crow-Ffinch and secretary to Charles Crow-Ffinch. In 1982, Amanda had been chosen to play Heather, one of the lead roles in the serial *Brookside* – a ratings winner in the early years of Channel Four.

Where There's A Will was also the television debut for the costume design talents of Jacqueline Mills. Although television costume design was new to her, she was well-established as a designer of individual day and evening wear for members of the aristocracy, the horse racing fraternity and the entertainment industry. Jacqueline's stunning and individualistic designs for *Where There's A Will* were to play a major part in enhancing Cavatina's character and reflected

108

Gus takes the chair

The West Country's favourite presenter - Ken Mcleod

Open Days at the Westward studios attract thousands of visitors - as well as making a useful contribution to the industry's own charity, the CTBF. Here a young visitor is somewhat overawed by Sports Editor Chris Fear and Gus Honeybun.

With Gordon Honeycombe at ITN in the 70s

At the Colombe D'Or Hotel in St Paul de Vence, South of France

On the 'SS' Hedonist in Cannes

On the 'SS' Hedonist in Cannes with actor Micheal Howe (left) and Ian Scrivens (producer)

APRIL 1986

A CRAIN PUBLICATION

media**WORLD**

THE UK's No. 1 MEDIA MAGAZINE

HARRY TURNER ON TSW –
HOW'S HE FARED ONE YEAR ON?

**PAN-EUROPEAN
TELEVISION –
THE LANGUAGE BARRIER**

**HOW TO PLACE YOUR
PRODUCT IN THE MOVIES**

**MEDIA BY TELEVISION
REGION – ULSTER**

With Michael Rheinhold, TSW's director of programmes

Aboard the 'Orient Express' bound for Venice

Riding in Hyde Park

Carolyn and I meet the Princess Royal

Meeting the Duchess of York

A woman is just a woman remember - but a cigar is a damn good smoke (Anon)

The bronze - by Mary Saxe-Falstein

With Gilly Hartley - the world's best P.A.

Two TSW productions of the 90's

Drama - 'Where There's a Will' showing prize winning costumes by Jaqueline Mills

Co-production of 'Mother Goose' series with Jim Henson of 'Muppets' fame

With Lord Thompson, Chairman of the IBA

With Richard Luce, Minister for the Arts (A business sponsorship Award)

TV news fear

From Mr Harry E. Turner

Sir, I understand that ITV may be planning to cut the news budget for ITN to fund more down-market games shows and comedies and thus improve the ratings.

Such a money-driven agenda would be a direct result of the notorious Broadcasting Act of 1990 which forced ITV companies to compete in an auction for their TV licences. ITV used to be a commercial service which was proud of its commitment to quality. Now it is a playground for chartered accountants and men with the creative instincts of snake-oil salesmen.

Yours faithfully,
HARRY TURNER
(Managing Director,
Television South West, 1985-92),
Four Acres,
Lake Road, Deepcut, Surrey.

Financial Times

Feb 6 1992

Fighting on: Harry Turner, pictured at the High Court yesterday, said TSW's stance had been totally vindicated

Arriving to deliver the 'Bid' at the ITC Headquarters. Sir Brian Bailey (left) Ivor Stolliday (right)

With Carolyn at 'Four Acres'

Bruce Gyngell, Managing Director TV AM   H.T.   Clive Leach, MD Yorkshire TV

I perform onerous duties as President of The National Advertising Benevelent Society 1997
Centre: Dominic Proctor, J Walter Thompson's whizz-kid M.D.

Facing the Iron Lady

Relaxing in Cuba with a friend after finishing this book

Jacqueline's enthusiasm for 'characterisation through costume', a concept, although true, that would now sit well in *Private Eye*'s 'Pseuds' Corner'.

Baz Taylor was the director, a man synonymous with the most popular programmes to come out of British television in recent years. The first series of ITV's *Auf Wiedersehen Pet* had been directed by Baz, as were a number of programmes in the *Dempsey and Makepeace* series. His 29 episodes of *Shine on Harvey Moon* were the longest ever British television drama series by one director. In addition, he had directed *Lovejoy* for the BBC and the Victoria Wood trilogy of *Talent, Nearly A Happy Ending* and *Since I Met You*.

After the fourth, or was it the fifth rewrite of the script, we were ready to fix a shooting schedule. Locations would be scouted in London and the West Country and in order to maintain a regional profile, one of our own Plymouth crews would work under Baz Taylor's direction. The first shooting was based in and around Plymouth and everything, to me at least, seemed to be kicking off to a brisk, well ordered start.

Baz Taylor is a large, grizzly bear of a man with a sharp metropolitan sense of humour and a very keen eye for detail. On the evening of the second day's shoot I was having dinner with Michael Reinhold and Patrick MacNee in the Artillery Tower Restaurant at Devil's Point overlooking the ocean when Taylor telephoned. He'd just viewed the 'dailies' and wanted to speak with Michael urgently. While he was taking the call I chatted amiably with Patrick, who after an initial coldness became relaxed and anecdotal. He has an 'actorish' way of making conversation and one senses that he is listening carefully to the resonance of his own voice. Pudding was served – something huge and Plymouthy that squatted in a puddle of excrutiatingly sweet, bright yellow custard. No sooner had I raised a loaded spoonful to my lips than Michael returned to the table, his face like a clenched fist.

'Problems?' I enquired.

Michael nodded and toyed disconsolately with a fragment of drenched pudding. 'The first two days are unusable,' he said.

109

MacNee pricked up his ears. 'Trouble at the mill?' he asked unhelpfully.

'Nothing we can't fix,' I bluffed desperately, and led Michael to another table.

'Baz says the footage is total shit. Out of focus. We can't use it.'

I was mentally calculating what two lost days would cost the company. No change out of £80,000.

'What went wrong?' I asked.

Michael shrugged. 'Our cameraman was so nervous he just couldn't cut it. He's never worked on a feature film before. A bit overawed I suppose.'

'But he's usually very good,' I said.

Michael agreed. 'Yes, but this is a whole new thing for him. He's only been doing documentaries and lots of studio work. I think Baz works so fast on location that it's thrown him.'

We finished our meal without telling MacNee the alarming news, and later that night I spoke to Baz. As ever the complete professional, Baz filled me in with the details.

'I want to do a good job for you,' he explained. 'But I need a cameraman who *anticipates* my requirements. You *could* use what we've shot, at a pinch, but it won't be top quality and I'm not happy to put my name to less than top quality pictures.'

The next day we pulled our cameraman off the job and between them Michael and Baz secured the services of a guy who had been second unit cameraman on a recent James Bond movie. A total pro. But at such short notice he didn't come cheap. By now my budget of £200,000 looked like ending up at £300,000. £300,000? Who was I kidding, I decided to create a contingency of £50,000 making a total of £350,000. I felt better immediately. What was £350,000 against the millions we were going to make when the show went into a series?

The following day I saw our young cameraman who had behaved impeccably on the two-day shoot.

'I'm sorry Harry,' he said, 'I know I've let you down.'

In fact he had asked to be dropped from the team when he

110

realised his experience wasn't up to what Baz needed. I told him he had nothing to be ashamed about and it was our fault for pitching him into something he wasn't ready for. The experience itself, he admitted, had been valuable, if a little painful.

I left for London the next day and didn't reconnect with the production until they came up from Plymouth to shoot the London exteriors. This was some weeks later. Coincidentally they chose Bathurst Stables in West London where I regularly hired a horse to ride in nearby Hyde Park. The shooting went smoothly and I was introduced to our female star from America, Louan Gideon. Tallish, dark and very Los Angeles, Louan was perfect for the part of the glamorous Cavatina. We laughed a lot and got on famously. MacNee meanwhile was holed up at the Plymouth Holiday Inn where he waited for the next phase of work to be shot in the West Country.

As the weeks rolled on the budget moved up a few notches, but I calmed the board as best I could. Baz worked like a demon and at last the job was complete. All that remained was the painstaking business of editing, laying down the music tracks, titling, etc. Now we had to sell the damn thing. Michael had been priming his programme director colleagues on the network that TSW was about to deliver something 'hot'. Their reaction, as it always is to small companies who show delusions of grandeur, was cool and neutral. A combination of 'we'll let you know' and 'fuck off'.

No matter. We knew we had a good product. It was only a matter of time before we would have a network series running in peak. The network controllers would surely recognise a hit show when they saw it. Wouldn't they? Would they bollocks. A stone wall is what we got. With barbed wire on top. But we were not dispirited. We picked ourselves up, dusted ourselves down and decided to take the pilot when completed to MIP, the programme market which takes place in Cannes in the South of France.

The plan was pretty straightforward. Charter a yacht. Moor it in Cannes' old harbour. Print a colour brochure. Fly MacNee and Louan over from Los Angeles, bring the other star,

Michael Howe, from London where he had been playing the lead in *Chess*. Throw in Baz Taylor, Scrivens, costume designer Jacqueline Mills and lawyer Douglas Stewart and then make an assault on the many American companies who were represented in Cannes.

It was here that I learnt an important fact about Hollywood television moguls. They are all full of shit. It matters not a jot if they are independents, solo producers, money men, network honchos or station owners. They are all *full* of it. Up to *here*. And then some.

Michael Reinhold worked his socks off setting up meetings on the yacht (the *Hedonist* – a good name as it transpired) with a stream of 'could be' partners, distributors and co-producers. Men who looked like refugees from a *Godfather* movie filed up the gangplank to sip our champagne and eat our canapés and open discussions with Michael and Scrivens, who by now was behaving like Michael's deputy. The panelled cabin of the *Hedonist* rang with showbiz mogul-speak.

'We'd like to get into bed with you over this one, but we can't put any money up front.' 'I'm excited about the project, but maybe the storyline needs jacking up.' 'We could pick this up and run with it for you. Give us sixty grand development money and we'll slide it up the flagpole and see who salutes it.' 'If you could pick up my expenses I'll introduce you to some hot guys who run cable. I won't rip you off. Give me twenty grand.' 'Give me fifty grand.' 'Let's be partners. You produce the show at your expense and I'll sell it and we'll split seventy:thirty, thirty for you. Michael why are you crying?' 'Give me eighty grand.' 'Are those *Havana* cigars? Jesus Christ I'm in spasms. You don't mind if I take a handful?' 'Give me ninety grand.' 'Together we can make this thing get up and run, just give me a hundred grand.'

And so on.

The meetings were strong on hype, but weak on anything that remotely resembled action. Word soon spread that TSW had a yacht anchored in the harbour and before long all manner of adventurers and hucksters came trooping aboard. They came, not to talk about *Where There's A Will*, but to try and sell *us* things. Post-production packages, wonderful new editing equipment, duff programmes from Japan, partnership deals where we put up the money (naturally) and 'they' supplied the 'intellectual input'.

In the end we had to beat them off with sticks. One man from London, who for the sake of argument we shall call Irving, demonstrated that sheer persistence coupled with a skin like a rhinoceros always gets you listened to. Irving stuck to us like a limpet until we agreed to talk about his specialised titling company called 'Scores'. As it happens, Irving does great work and I'm convinced he could get it on merit without all this ballsaching, headbutting chutzpah. Everybody at the Cannes programme market tries too hard. The air is thick with wild promises, ridiculous claims, mega projections. Every two-bit actor in every half-assed series is described as 'a major new talent'. Every co-production deal is 'breaking new ground'.

But we had fun too. The skipper of our yacht, Brian, an Englishman, made us very comfortable and his staff provided a standard of cuisine that no hotel along the Croisette could have matched. Louan and Michael Howe hit it off perfectly, Baz Taylor kept us supplied with a series of fabulous, very rude jokes and Jacqueline Mills wore a one-piece bathing suit the size of a child's handkerchief.

My PA, the lovely Gilly Hartley, 'mothered' our little delegation and provided the framework of disciplines and time-tables we needed to stop us from going native.

Patrick MacNee became expansive, even volatile and suggested we eat one evening at a little 'manoir' he knew of near St Paul de Vence. It turned out to be a rather showy place with flaming braziers over the arched entrance and a menu that read like a chef's memoirs. The meal was good, if not spectacular, and just as I was about to thank Patrick for his generosity the waiter gave me the bill and Patrick smiled like a Cheshire cat.

'Most kind, dear boy,' he murmured.

And I paid.

Before leaving however, Ian Scrivens, now displaying all the symptoms of a man who had recently suffered a blow to

113

the head rushed into the restaurant foyer to phone for 'limousines' to take our stars back to Cap d'Antibes where they were staying. I bottled down the urge to cut Scrivens's throat and explained that our budget didn't run to such extravagances and taxis would have to suffice. He looked crestfallen, like a little boy who has been told he can't have another ice-cream.

The next day on the yacht I had further cause to exchange words with dear Ian – who, let it be said, is capable of charm when he tries, but can be infuriating when he is on one of his hyperactive, yuppie-phone-using-screaming-jumping-up-and-down binges. I overheard him persuading Michael Reinhold that 'the only way to "move" Where There's A Will' would be for both of then to fly almost immediately to Los Angeles, book into the Beverly Hills Hotel and hoof it around town to show the pilot to whoever would give them an audience. At a rough calculation this little trip would probably cost TSW another £10,000. And this on top of feeding and watering our group in Cannes, Patrick MacNee's and Louan's return fares from America, yacht hire, champagne, oysters, brochures, phone calls, faxes and hotel bills. I could see our budget rising to the level of the Nicaraguan national debt and I told Michael to cancel the trip, in spite of the fact that his PA in Plymouth had already been phoned and asked to make the bookings.

Scrivens requested a 'private' meeting with me, and we took ourselves onto the prow deck where we could talk alone. He was in a highly emotional state, near to tears in fact. I explained as best I could that my intervention was not intended as a personal slight, but I simply could not condone expenditure on the scale proposed. He calmed down a little, but I think he believed I was being harsh and hard-nosed, which of course I was.

Towards the end of our five days in Cannes Louan got violently sick (probably due to one of Michael Reinhold's bloody oysters which he insisted on providing, and she lay in her darkened cabin moaning and shivering for the best part of a day. When she emerged she looked pale and mysterious, wearing a Garbo-like outfit that fitted her like an unpressed nun's habit.

114

We finally said goodbye to the *Hedonist* and flew our separate ways, our hopes still high for the success of our venture in spite of all the hype and negative hustle we had endured.

Fast-forward to England. It is raining. Everybody who has been in Cannes seems to have developed a cold. London is tolerable and there is always San Lorenzo, the Royal Opera House, pretty girls to lunch with and horse riding in Hyde Park. Plymouth by contrast is giving off negative vibes. Everybody is wearing anoraks. The rain is heavier. Reality in all its awful majesty is setting in and thoughts of Hollywood and aspirations for success are fading.

There is much to attend to in London however and my ITV colleagues at Council ask politely how our 'project' is going. Stupendous. I say. But they know I am jesting. The prospect of TSW *not* having a hit series cheers most of them up more than a champagne enema. I am reminded of the words of David Merrick the American impresario, 'It is not enough to succeed – others must fail.'

Back in Plymouth Michael Reinhold follows up the 'leads' we made in France. Nothing much happens for a few weeks and then I agree that Michael should go to Los Angeles alone, and Scrivenless, to try and get things moving. While he is away I receive a phone call at home from Herb Liebovitz in New Jersey. Herb is an old friend from when he ran Britannia Records in London ten years earlier. Does he want to finance a series based on *Where There's A Will*? No, he doesn't want to finance a series even if it's based on the *Kama Sutra*. What he wants is to start a bagel factory in North London, and will I be his partner? I tell him to weave his bagels into the shape of a pyramid and stick them up his ass. But good naturedly.

Michael returns from Hollywood with a pair of new brown shoes which go with nothing he had in his wardrobe, but no television deal.

I decided a little more shove is needed and I ask Gilly to arrange a fashion show in our admittedly sumptuous Knightsbridge offices where Jacqueline's splendid costumes for Cavatina in *Where There's A Will* can be displayed. The

115

press come in droves, drink champagne and admire both the costumes and the girls wearing them.

The actress Fiona Fullerton turns up. She lives in an apartment just across the road from the office, and she greets me warmly with the words 'Hello Sir Toby.' There are surprised looks from Gilly and other TSW staff at this unusual remark, but I am able to explain, not without a touch of blasé understatement, that some years earlier when Fiona was a pupil at the Elmhurst Ballet School in Camberley, I was invited to play Sir Toby Belch in the school's production of *Twelfth Night* by William Shakespeare. Fiona, as Viola, had in one scene to be disguised as a boy, the usual nonsense in a Shakespeare play, and as the rubicund, boozy Sir Toby, I was required to draw my sword and fence briefly with her. Even since then, 25 years on, wherever I see Fiona Fullerton in restaurants or theatre foyers or in the street, I am hailed as 'Sir Toby!' A kind of fame I suppose.

I amuse guests by introducing Jacqueline as a frockmaker from Newbury and the *Sunday Express* gives both the frocks and our programme a bit of coverage the following weekend.

I lunch with Michael Howe at San Lorenzo and he presses me on when we are 'going to start producing the series'. Probably never, I tell him, but he takes this news philosophically. Six months on and still not a flicker of interest. I let Malcolm Vaughan of Fox view the pilot and Malcolm, an old and trusted friend, says the following: 'It's too much like all the rest of the stuff on offer. MacNee's fame as Steed in the *Avengers* is fading just a bit and the script could be sharper.'

I decide to stop throwing money at the project which has now cost over half a million pounds and we all get on with running a small regional television company. The Hollywood dream has faded, we are all sadder and wiser, but life continues.

Over a year and a half later the UK network finally agree to buy *Where There's A Will* and it is played at different times around the country, to not very spectacular acclaim. But at least it's been screened and we've clawed *some* money back.

116

Not much. Not very much at all in fact. But we put the whole thing down to experience.

The major lessons in all this for me? First, small ITV companies shouldn't believe they can take Hollywood by storm. Second, don't even take the camera out of the case unless you have a pre-sale agreement and a guaranteed distribution deal scrutinised by eight lawyers, ten accountants, a bishop and a fortune-teller. Failing that, why not open a bacon factory in Israel?

CHAPTER 10

On overpaid Thespians, rude presenters and a brush with modern art.

Working with actors during the filming of *Where There's A Will* got me thinking about their role in our culture. No other profession rewards its successful members so lavishly, heaps them with such admiration or invests them with such awesome importance.

Now it is beyond dispute that acting on television requires a different technique from that employed on the stage or in movies. This said however, the quality of acting on British television is not high. The demand for actors to fill the humdrum soaps and noisy docu-dramas means that even third-rate performers get a chance to appear on the box.

We used to joke that the BBC ran a special 'school for shouting' that most actors graduated from. It is certainly true that a great deal of BBC drama consists of men and women delivering their lines at maximum volume. Yelling always seems a substitute for technique.

If you think about *The Bill*, London's Burning, *EastEnders* or any of the other contemporary dramas on television, you will see and hear men and women bellowing until they are red in the face. This is probably because producers of modern TV believe that that subtlety would be lost on a mass audience.

The television presenter is a horse of an entirely different colour and a late twentieth-century phenomenon. Here are a breed of young people who can neither sing, dance, act, play musical instruments or in some cases string a sentence together without electronic prompting. A few of them, almost entirely devoid of any shred of talent, become as rich as maharajahs and their off-screen utterances are seized upon as pearls of erudition. The whole thing is faintly ridiculous, but the salaries of these 'icons of the little box' continue to balloon at an alarming rate. As mother used to say, it will probably end in tears.

I once tried to obtain the services of a young disc jockey to perform a simple presenting job on TSW. He was moderately well-known on radio and popular with young audiences. His agent, however, was something of a pit bull terrier who yelled down the phone at me when I refused to increase the proposed fee from £3,000. That was £3,000 for half a day's work. In 1985! When it was obvious that I wouldn't budge, the agent tried another tactic.

'My boy will agree to a grand,' he shouted magnanimously, 'but he wants a limo to and from Plymouth airport and a suite at the Holiday Inn, champagne and *company*. Know what I mean?'

I knew what he meant and told him, very politely, to fuck off. That, as they say, is show business.

Colleagues at the big ITV companies and at the BBC will almost certainly disagree with my sentiments, but in their heart of hearts, they know that unless there is some sensible new approach to how we pay our leading performers, the spiralling costs will continue until they reach obscene levels. Then perhaps the balloon will burst.

If all the aforementioned sounds like a blanket condemnation of all TV presenters, it isn't. There is a largish minority who are first rate, in particular those trained journalists who become newscasters or front the best current affairs programmes. My real despair is directed at the 'celebrity' presenters of daytime broadcasting and the trendy incompetents who dominate children's programming.

One of the most dramatic changes in television over the past 30 years has been in the way that political interviews are conducted. In the 1960s, ministers of the crown and even humble MP's were questioned by journalists in a non-confrontational way. The exchanges were usually polite and the interviewee was allowed to complete each of his sentences without rude

119

interruption. These interviews were, in truth, too bland and the politicians frequently got away with evasive waffle and even bare-faced lying. Clearly there was a need to sharpen up the whole procedure.

Men like John Freeman, himself an ex-minister, and the brilliant Sir Robin Day, introduced the intelligent, forensic-style of questioning that put politicians on their mettle. They were never rude, and they and their producers never forgot that it was the politician the viewers wished to hear opinions from, not the interviewer. It was all a question of balance.

Now the scales have tipped too far in the opposite direction. The interviewer is the star. The whole 'show' is based on he or she bullying, humiliating or insulting the interviewee. The questions asked are frequently obtuse, designed to trick or baffle the victim who sits in front of those studio lights like a prisoner in some quasi-judicial courtroom.

The inflated egos and sheer arrogance of some of our current interrogators is little short of disgraceful. The research that fuels their questions is often skewed to show the 'victim' in the worst possible light.

But politicians are fair game, are they not? Certainly, but surely the *objective* of the political interview is not *just* to prove the interviewee is a mendacious, lying bastard, but also to elicit information from him or her that will increase the viewer's understanding of the political process and how the politicians are handling it.

And all current political interviews start, it seem to me, from a left-wing, liberal standpoint. I'm sure this is not always intentional, but I've yet to see an interview conducted with a politician were the interviewer doesn't automatically assume that any political stance right of centre is somehow reprehensible.

Modern television producers for the main part are 'sixties' children, weaned on faintly leftish, trendy values. They seem to share a common hatred of anybody or anything that could be described as middle-class, although they themselves with their large salaries and comfortable lifestyles fit perfectly into this category.

120

The plague of 'political correctness', itself an insidious invention of the left, now taints almost all current affairs programmes. This bias *must* be wrong, and in a democracy, it's vital that broadcasters should demonstrate even-handed impartiality when dealing with political matters. I would hold to this view even if the current bias were clearly to the right, which it probably was in the 1950s. It's hard to get the balance right, but today's producers are failing in their duty when they allow the lazy trend of partiality to continue.

As part of our 'involvement' with the region, we sponsored an open art exhibition in Plymouth in the late 1980s and young artists from across the West Country were invited to contribute.

I took a camera crew onto the Hoe to view some of the work that had been specifically designed to be accessible to the general public in an urban environment. If you think a pile of bricks in the Tate Gallery was bizarre, you would have been astonished, nay flabbergasted, at what we found silhouetted against the waters of Plymouth Sound. One large ball of string sprayed with orange paint and mounted on a pram without wheels. An admittedly monumental hunk of cement with holes in the side, like an immense grey cheese.

More was to come. One particularly enterprising young artist, a black art student from Exeter, had created his 'piece' by utilising a disused air-raid shelter close to the Hoe. What you did was walk in darkness through a long tunnel to the accompaniment of cymbals and distant trumpets. Then you emerged into daylight at the other end of the tunnel. That was it. 'Action art' or some such cute name.

Unable to appreciate or understand what it was all about, and afraid of being labelled a philistine in a pin-striped suit by my cameraman colleagues, I offered no opinion of the work. A wise decision under the circumstances.

Later my PA, Gilly Hartley, and I were driven in a jeep to a small wood outside the city. We were promised an artistic treat. A veritable banquet of creativity. Here among the ash trees and silver birches, a young artist had created a surreal 'experience'. Several TV monitors, mounted on plinths, were arranged in a circle all facing inwards. Each monitor was playing a continuous loop of tape consisting of still photographs of dead insects in close up. Nothing else. On the trunks of various trees surrounding this weird scene and apparently placed at random, were little wooden shrines containing photographs, dead flowers and the claws of tiny animals.

As I struggled to absorb all this creative magnificence, two young artists appeared from behind the trees and greeted me warmly.

'Great isn't it?' they chimed.

Even though diplomacy is not my forte, I managed a 'Jolly unusual.'

'Yes,' said one of them earnestly, 'the *whole* point however, is that nobody comes to see this – you're the first.'

'I see,' I said, nodding foolishly.

'The thing is this,' the artist continued, 'it's a happening in the woods, and it goes on day after day, *all on its own*. The monitors keep rolling the tapes, all at the same speed. They all face inwards so anybody approaching cannot see what they're playing. Fabulous isn't it?'

Later back at the studio, I opened a half bottle of champagne and drank it in one swallow. And no, my favourite work of art is not the Chinese woman with the green face, or the Monarch of the Glen. But come on, give me a break, TV sets playing to nobody in the forest!

When I told my daughter Jane, who has a BA in fine art, about it she smiled enigmatically and said, 'It's a generation thing, Dad, you'll never understand.'

And I still don't.

CHAPTER 11

*The ITV system: Byzantine or what? I get hugged
by the Duchess of York and a stiff talking to from
Jeremy Isaacs.*

ITV has, in the recent past, been criticised for its overmanning, its excessive profits and its low productivity. The
famous Thatcher taunt that ITV was 'the last bastion of
restrictive practices' still rankles with some.

The truth is somewhat different now. The companies are
leaner and fitter and the omnipotence of the trade unions has
been diluted. Competition looms like Banquo's ghost and the
apocalyptic effects of the dreaded 'sealed bid' have all taken
their toll.

One area of activity, however, remains sacrosanct: that
gleaming monument to bureaucracy, the ITV committee. In
few other spheres of human endeavour have so many committees, working parties and study groups developed, with the
possible exception of Her Majesty's civil service.

It is a curious contradiction, but ITV's committee structure
is both a bane and a strength. A bane certainly, because it
drains energy away from the core activity of programme making and turns creative men and women into clerks. Its strength
lies in the pooled resources, knowledge and experience of 15
companies scattered widely across the United Kingdom. That
said, to get 15 companies, all of whom are fiercely independent, to agree on anything, even the time of day, may sound
difficult, but what genuinely amazes is the range of issues on
which there *is* general consensus.

Part of the reason is protective. The BBC is a unitary system, a great monolith that can swing resources into play with-

123

out having to dance to the tunes of 15 sovereign states. But with a sense of almost primeval self-preservation ITV knows that on certain issues it *must* act collectively. Perhaps the most obvious and fundamental area for such collective action is the network schedule. That there are arguments about how it is constructed and just who contributes to it is undeniable. But every Managing Director and Programme Controller knows that without a strong schedule none of us, including giants like Thames or Granada, could survive in the rating war against the BBC for very long.

Now, more than ever, ITV needs a strong, centrally constructed schedule. If it falls away from this principle and fragments, then the competition will tear it to shreds. I believe this as one who has also consistently advocated the importance of regionalism – and let me say at once that believing in a strong network schedule *and* regionalism is not a contradiction in terms. Provided there are reasonable 'windows' in the schedule for each region to do its own thing, then the two objectives can sit side by side quite comfortably.

Notwithstanding all the above, I do reluctantly accept that committees are here to stay and in spite of my taunts and the terminal boredom they induce whenever I sit down at the table, some very sound work and robust principles have emerged from them over the years, many of which will serve the industry well for some considerable time to come.

If I have a *serious* point to make – and my desire to make serious points is not overwhelming and never has been – it is this.

Too much time and energy is spent by talented men and women inside ITV discussing the *mechanics* of the system instead of concentrating on the vital topics of creativity and marketing. Cut to the bone ITV is about programmes and money. All the rest is rock and roll and an exercise in ego-polishing. A degree of bureaucracy is inevitable of course, in a £2 billion a year industry that is the hunting ground for consumer protection agencies, anti-advertising fanatics, broadcasting complaints commissions, minority rights groups, gay liberationists, weights and measures officers (yes really) the

124

RSPCA, the NSPCC, Mary Whitehouse, Lord Longford, Norman Tebbitt, the Lord's Day Observance Society, the Office of Fair Trading and the bewildering thicket of European legislators.

What then are the qualities that make a good ITV Managing Director? Creativity? Engineering expertise? A passion for the television medium? Numeracy? Statesmanship? Well, all of these things help of course and among ITV's chieftains past and present there can be found an abundance of these qualities, although in the 1980s the shift towards ex-accountants became somewhat marked. In the 1990s, and as far as I am able to judge through to the next century, the real stuff of which a Chief Executive needs to be made can be summarised as follows:

1   An exceptionally *low* boredom threshold.
2   Tactical cunning and the ability to dissect any subject, however obscure, down to its essentials.
3   A love of abstract principles.
4   A knowledge of the more esoteric reaches of creative accountancy.
5   A willingness to learn the culture of committee and how to become part of it (outside of the committee there is no reality, no substance, only chaos).

I won't go as far as to paraphrase *Othello* and say I would rather be a toad and live on the vapour of the dungeon, but if I never sit in another committee room watching 20 middle-aged men in suits droning on about NETCO, central scheduling, cross subsidies, ITFC budgets, mezzanine finance, statutory instruments, MAC directives, electronic transmission logs and the unauthorised use of BARB data, no opalescent tear of remorse will decorate my cheek.

Observers more astute than I have suggested that the awesome burden of responsibility carried by an ITV Managing Director soon grinds down to a fine powder any pretensions they may have had towards gaiety or a love of things carnal. A somewhat harsh verdict perhaps, but the atmosphere at most committee meetings of the ITVA is not marked by the robust skirmishing of egotistical tycoons dedicated to the entertainment medium. The prevailing climate is of ordered calm. People use words like 'interregnum' and 'moratorium' and even 'illustrative formulae'. The effect this has on individual personalities is fascinating.

The late Richard Dunn, Managing Director of Thames Television, was in his very early forties when he succeeded Brian 'Ginger' Cowgill, the man who lost his job because he broke a gentleman's agreement and purchased *Dallas* for ITV from under the BBC's nose. *Dallas* of course was never shown on ITV and Cowgill was damned to the ultimate hell: working for Robert Maxwell.

Richard Dunn however, was a role model for ITV Chief Executives. Handsome, prematurely grey, tall and slim, he was just the sort of man producers would cast in that very part were they making a drama about television. In reality, he was not a typical ITV bureaucrat, having sprung from a production background where he once worked for Swindon Cable. There is a curious video of him actually appearing on it during his younger days, albeit with a silly haircut.

When he became Thames' top man, Richard underwent a metamorphosis. As one colleague at the ITVA Council put it, from boy wonder to elder statesman in one huge leap. The ex-Chairman of ITVA Council, and once chairman of ITN, Richard carved out an important role for himself until fate struck him with two hideous blows. The first when Thames lost their TV franchise to Carlton in 1991 and the second when he died tragically young at age 54.

A television programme, when it is finally transmitted, is the sum total of many complex parts. A raw, unformed idea, a writer's words, a director's vision, a cameraman or lighting director's technique, an editor's skill. When a programme is referred to at committee, it ceases to be this magical, complicated thing and is at once drained of all meaning to become an item, a product, a fragment of merchandise. While this may be inevitable, it is undeniably sad.

Some Chief Executives not only *never* watch television, but

126

actively dislike it. But a soupçon more warmth towards the medium from which they earn their livings wouldn't go amiss.

A few exceptional examples disprove the rule. Sir Paul Fox, gruff, opinionated, utterly impervious to the whingeing of accountants, is passionate about television. Brian Tesler, urbane and smooth (so smooth in fact that it was once said if you grabbed him in a vice, he would slide elegantly from its grip with a debonair smile), also loved the medium. He also had a tendency to nod off at council meetings, a technique to be admired and even emulated, like learning to yawn with your mouth shut. Michael Grade, carrying the name of his famous uncle with pride, but not arrogance. Probably the sharpest scheduler in the business with a showman's eye for new talent and the courage to occasionally take a chance, now of course running First Leisure Ltd, a family concern.

The combative Jeremy Isaacs, ex-Director-General of the Royal Opera House whose tenure as Chief Executive of Channel Four from its fledgling days was a landmark in television history. He took over the role of performer when he quit the opera house, fronting the cerebral *Face-to-Face* programme made famous 20 years ago by John Freeman. A small, articulate man, Jeremy believes attack is always the best form of defence and his sometimes brutal style ruffles many feathers. He and Greg Dyke of LWT could form a double act, 'The Lack of Tact Brothers'.

I was at a ceremony at the National Theatre early in 1991 to receive an award on behalf of TSW from the Duchess of York. It was for the company's business sponsorship of the arts and we were in distinguished company. Jeremy Isaacs spotted me at the pre-ceremony drinks and chose the moment to attack me for not having sponsored The Royal Ballet's recent visit to Plymouth. I thought it was a curiously inappropriate time and venue to raise such an issue, but Jeremy is famous for his outbursts. Curiously enough at that ceremony, Fergie not only shook my hand when giving me the award, but gave me a brief hug. Perhaps I looked in need of it after Isaacs's bollocking.

And of course there are the great 'characters' like Brum

Henderson who for many years was Chief Executive and then Chairman of tiny Ulster Television. Brum didn't so much as engage you in conversation as subject you to a Niagara of words. He had views on everything and was possessed with a driving desire to impart them to whoever happened to be within earshot. A marvellous man and a brilliant television professional. In today's climate, he'd be too rich for a lot of people's taste.

HTV's Ron Wordley, an ex-Sales Director, ran the Welsh station like an infantry regiment billeted in Khartoum. Known affectionately as 'Boomer', Ron's voice could penetrate inch-thick concrete at 50 paces.

Then more recently Greg Dyke, BBC Director General designate who succeeded Brian Tesler at LWT, demonstrated that the maverick tradition still lingers on. Greg, like Jeremy Isaacs, has a way of expressing disagreement which could best be described as explosive. I once wrote to him during a mild dispute between his company and TSW and told him that 'he was to diplomacy what Ghengis Khan was to flower arranging'. His spell at the BBC should be a performance to relish!

As part of the grooming process before he took over the helm at LWT, Greg spent some months at Harvard Business School. This process is usually enough to squeeze the juice out of anybody leaving behind a flavourless husk of corporate conformity. It has left no visible mark on Greg. He remains what he is. Clever. Rude. Streetwise and short-fused. Perhaps this is inevitable for a man whose earliest claim to fame was introducing the world to Roland Rat on morning television during his time as head of programmes for TVAM.

All these men have at one time or another sat on various committees of the ITVA. I have avoided listing all the sub-committees as to do so would probably make this book too heavy to pick up without the aid of a fork-lift truck. A short summary may be enlightening, however. There is the Council, the supreme decision-making body. Membership consists of all ITV Managing Directors. Under no circumstances are television programmes ever discussed at this committee. To even mention a television programme is punishable by castration.

128

The main topics are money, networking and how the fuck did TVAM get away with it for so long? There is also the Marketing Committee which consists of all the Sales Directors, the Research Committee, itself a sub-committee of Marketing and the Programme Controllers Committee which ought to be vitally crucial to the whole operation of ITV, but somehow instead gives off the vibrations of a raffish gentleman's club at the turn of the century.

Then there is NIRC (or the Network Industrial Relations Committee) which exists to translate the gibberish of agreements between the ITV companies, the Musician's Union, ACTT, EPTU, NUS, etc., into language human beings with a good degree in psychology might just conceivably understand.

There is the Copy Committee, a kind of filter, or drain, through which all television commercial scripts have to pass before transmission. This function, delegated to the ITV companies by the ITC, is to ensure that television adverts conform with ITC rules and regulations. For example, the Copy Committee will pounce on all pharmaceutical scripts to make doubly certain that neither Anadin nor Nurofen sneak in claims that hint at cures for premature ejaculation, baldness or swine fever.

So much for the selection. Even as you read these words other committees may well be springing up like mushrooms in a dank basement. Just writing about them makes my gums ache, my bowels shrivel and my scrotum retract so I will merely list the rest without further comment:

Agency Recognition Committee
SCC (Standing Consultative Committee) (with the ITC)
Chairman's Committee
Rights Committee
Technical Development Board
ITVGR Working Group
Oracle Board
ITSC
Business Administration Committee
International Relations Committee

Business Development Committee
Broadcasters Audience Research Board (jointly with BBC)
Broadcasters Audience Research Board Finance Committee
Broadcasters Audience Research Board AMMC
Broadcasters Audience Research Board AAMC Technical Sub-Committee
Technical Committee

Whatever else happens to Channel Three, Four, Five etc., whoever survives or perishes, whatever apocalyptic changes are wrought by hostile governments of the future, one thing will remain constant. Nay, will grow, probably in glorious profusion. The ITV committee system. Omnipotent, magisterial, long-winded, time-consuming, indestructible.

CHAPTER 12

*The ITN saga. A great news organisation
undergoes radical surgery.*

By 1990, TSW had established a reputation as a keen supporter of the arts, a tradition inherited from the previous contractor, Westward. I collected an award from Richard Luce,
the Minister for the Arts, for TSW's sponsorship of the
International Animation Festival in Bristol during 1989. Later
in 1990, I received a trophy from the Duchess of York for our
Business Sponsorship of The Arts – we were one of the smallest companies to receive one, most of the others being major
corporations and international conglomerates. Things were
looking good and at the time we had not the slightest doubt
that our future as a regional broadcaster was secure.

Our boardroom in Plymouth was hung with some fine
eighteenth-century West Country prints and as I was a
Director of the Prince of Wales Youth Business Trust, I com-
missioned two young art students to paint a large mural on the
wall of the studio's first floor. I also arranged for a brilliant
sculptress, Mary Saxe-Falstein, to model Sir Brian Bailey's
head in bronze. Mary, a strikingly attractive Indian lady had
established a reputation in London for specialising in sculpt-
ing media personalities.

Towards the end of 1991 as the ITC's day of decision
approached, there were rumblings about the cost of the mural
(£10,000) and Sir Brian's bronze bust (£3,500), but it wasn't
the first time I had been accused of extravagance. I preferred
to think of it as a profitable company celebrating its success
in stylish and appropriate fashion.

1991, which media historians will undoubtedly describe as

'franchise year', was peculiar in many other ways too. It was a year of recession, false election fever and a retreat from the rigid principles of Thatcherism. It was also the year when ITN (Independent Television News) underwent a painful and traumatic metamorphosis. Long the new jewel in ITV's crown, it had, by the nature of its structure and its funding been artificially protected from the harsh winds of competition and commercial reality.

I joined the Board of ITN as a non-executive Director in 1989, replacing Alex Mair of Grampian to represent the 'Small Five' ITV stations who were all shareholders in the news service. Even that long ago other non-executive board members, notably Leslie Hill of Central Television and Brian Tesler of LWT were asking for the heavy journalist bias in management to be leavened by the appointment of a commercial Chief Executive or at least a business manager who *wasn't* a journalist. This never happened and the financial disciplines and strict cost controls that ITN clearly needed were put off, delayed, placed on the back burner and perhaps most damagingly, ignored.

Non-Executive Directors must take some of the responsibility for this inaction, but ITN was no ordinary company. Its shareholders (the 15 ITV companies) were also its core customers. Its funding is by way of subscriptions from these customers and its need to earn its own living had never been tested. The customer/shareholders, by the way, had *no choice* in whether they funded ITN or not. Each of them had signed a contract with the then IBA agreeing to maintain a prestigious international news service as part of their franchise obligations. Running a huge, volatile news service is no picnic and, let it be stated plainly, very few if any television news services in the world actually run at a profit. ITN was no exception.

But back in 1989, or even later, nobody could foresee what a mess this financial leviathan would get into under the multiple pressures of inflation, a property slump and an unprecedented series of international news stories that simply had to be covered: Tiananmen Square, near-revolution in China,

132

Eastern Europe in turmoil, Russia in upheaval, the collapse of the Berlin Wall, the Gulf War. All these things, plus the dreaded ingredient of slack financial management, combined to create a cocktail of nearly lethal effect on the giant news company.

In January 1991 Sir David Nicholas, ITN's Chairman, a Welsh journalist of passion and distinction, phoned me at home on a Sunday evening, the day prior to an ITN board meeting. He had been contacting all board members to tell them that the company had uncovered an *overspend* of £7.6 million for ITN's past financial year. I was, not unnaturally, a touch baffled by this revelation. We were already trying to swallow the implications of a £2 million overspend incurred during ITN's move to new premises in Gray's Inn Road. The old headquarters in Wells Street had been cramped, antiquated and unsuitable, located as they were in the middle of London's garment district. Access was difficult, the streets were narrow and congested and there was always the danger that a television news crew hurrying back to ITN might be run over by a van containing ladies' frocks and sequinned knickers. Gray's Inn Road was the site of the old *Sunday Times* building, now replaced by a state of the art media palace which had been designed and purpose-built for ITN's own use.

I gulped at the prospect of a combined £9.5 million-plus overrun, but Sir David said we could thrash out a plan of action, or even reaction, at Monday's board. He sounded weary and downcast, as well he might.

Only one thing emerged with any clarity at the Monday meeting. ITN's financial controls were virtually non-existent and urgent remedial action, possibly of Draconian proportions was now urgent. ITN had been unfortunate to fall foul of the property market during their ill-fated move to the lavish glass and concrete emporium of Gray's Inn Road. Costing in excess of £46 million it remained empty of other tenants even though ITN needed to let out over 50 per cent of the space to meet the budgets agreed for the move. The anticipated income from letting was over £5 million annually. By mid-1991 there was still not a single other tenant.

133

It was also apparent that ITN's ability to stem further flows of cash from its treasury was seriously under question. A few months earlier, in 1990, the government's desire, expressed in its 1988 White Paper and subsequently in its Broadcasting Act, that ITN should acquire *outside* shareholders for 51 per cent of its equity, led to an acrimonious row between colleagues and friends at Wells Street. The doyen of newscasters, Sir Alistair Burnett, friend of royalty, prime ministers and other movers and shakers within government, openly clashed with his fellow Directors on the board of ITN over this issue. He had made his dislike of the regional companies' involvement at ITN patently obvious. He wanted 'outside' shareholders to replace the existing ITV companies so that ITN could be 'properly' funded. He suggested that we had starved ITN of cash. Ye gods and little fishes! After a £9.5 million overspend!

I argued with Sir Alistair quite sharply, and our differences were pounced on by the press. I thought then, and I think still, that a Director who publicly criticises his owners (i.e. the ITV shareholders) is well out of order. But shortly after this row Sir Alistair resigned as a Director, remaining however as a newscaster and the highest paid employee in the company.

'Relations between ITN and its parent ITV companies reached rock bottom', wrote Andrew Davidson in *The Sunday Times* in June 1991. He was right. The situation was hideous and getting worse. Subsequent ITN board meetings in 1991 became a litany of despair. Money had been gushing out at an alarming rate and showed scant sign of being staunched. Sir Alistair expressed no regrets. The big international news stories of the day cost serious money if they were to be covered properly and he repeated his attacks on ITV.

Just who he thought existed in the outside world who would pick up the tab for ITN if the ITV shareholders divested themselves of 51 per cent he never made clear. ICI? Polly Peck? Father Christmas?

Early in 1991 ITN appointed Bob Phillis as Chief Executive and he set about cleaning the Augean stables. The consummate professional, Phillis had been Managing Director of

Central Television and more recently the Group Chief Executive Officer for Michael Green's Carlton Communications. Seizing the poisoned chalice he tried to rationalise ITN's Byzantine accounting systems.

Overseas journalists in places as far afield as Moscow, Peking or Delhi have to spend money, not just to exist, but to pursue, film and send back stories. Helicopters, taxis, hire cars, hotel bills, cash payments to sources, international faxing and phoning eat up pound notes like a furnace, particularly when you consider how many ITN bureaus and stringers there are spread across the globe. Board meetings were exclusively devoted to examining ways of turning ITN round. Tempers flared regularly – but briefly. Greg Dyke of LWT, who had inherited his board seat from Brian Tesler, was particularly outspoken.

'The place is a bloody shambles,' he once said. 'Practically insolvent.' One wonders if he will say the same about the BBC! Nobody really disagreed, but a British sense of aplomb and morbid fatality usually dominated by the end of each rollicking board session.

An audit committee was set up after Richard Dunn, Thames's mature beyond his years Managing Director, was appointed non-Executive Deputy Chairman. Sir David, clearly a rattled man, now took something of a back seat with only a year to run before his retirement. Leslie Hill of Central, an ex-accountant, sat on the audit committee, complaining that much of the trouble had sprung from lack of information. Management letters from Cooper's & Lybrand Deloitte, one of Britain's blue chip accountancy firms, which warned of flaky financial control, were never tabled at the board. We were, quite frankly, virtually in the dark until it was almost too late to do anything except throw our hands up in despair and then go back to our own companies for extra cash. All this at a time when advertising income was plummeting. There were a lot of unhappy Finance Directors in ITV during those dreadful months.

Staff cuts followed and Bob Phillis took a tough line on expenses and made line managers much more 'cash aware'

135

and accountable. It was a painful time, and the scars may take years to heal. Daringly, Bob also led the assault on the TVAM breakfast franchise, forming a consortium with the *Daily Telegraph*, NBC, MAI, Taylor Woodrow and Carlton. Sir Paul Fox, ex-Managing Director of Yorkshire and BBC Television was appointed Chairman. Critics groaned audibly. How could ITN contemplate a bid for another franchise when it was almost bust itself and up to its neck in administrative mire? Bob, however, saw the breakfast franchise as a hugely lucrative lifebelt and in my view was right to go for it. This in spite of my great admiration for Aussie Bruce Gyngell who had turned TVAM into a huge money-spinner. But life is like that. Business is business and in television in the 1990s dog really did eat dog.

At the official opening in May 1991 of the Gray's Inn Road media palace an atmosphere of heady unreality prevailed. ITN personnel, already angry at staff cuts, were calling for management sacrifices too. The shop stewards wrote to me saying 'the management got us into this mess, why shouldn't there be an equality of suffering?' Newcasters' six-figure salaries were openly criticised and the press, sniffing a rival in trouble, had a field day.

Her Majesty the Queen, together with the Duke of Edinburgh performed the opening ceremony and I still wonder if they realised what passions and despair lurked below the surface of jollity and celebration on that historic day. The Queen looked tired, I thought, and after asking me 'How many ITV companies actually *are* there?' turned her attention to the sausage rolls. Clearly the grub at the Palace wasn't up to snuff because I was treated to the spectacle of the Sovereign enjoying the cold buffet with all the enthusiasm of a schoolgirl. At least the caterers felt that their efforts had been appreciated.

Much was to follow in the battle to put ITN on stronger foundations. The size of the board was to be reduced and it was agreed some 'outside' directors would be recruited. The audit committee took an active and critical role in the company's affairs and the staff numbers were further trimmed.

There was pain, even anguish, but even this was preferable to the stark alternative of a great institution in its death throes.

It is something of a miracle that throughout all these upheavals, right back to 1988 and 1989, the quality of news provision never faltered. It is to the considerable credit of the journalists, editors, camera crews and technicians that this should have been so. It would be easy to point the finger in an attempt to find scapegoats. Sir David Nicholas for example *was*, it is true, Chief Executive at the time the accounting horrors were uncovered, but he never made claims to be either a businessman or a financier. David is a super, passionate, committed journalist with a fierce love of and loyalty to his staff. Here is a man who openly wept when one of his crews went missing during the Gulf war. His bafflement and pain at the saga of ITN's financial troubles is one of my least enjoyable memories.

ITN always chose Monday for their board meetings and on 17 June events took a further convulsive turn. Before the day's routine business was started, Chief Executive Bob Phillis told the assembled Directors that Sir David wished to make a personal statement. Clearly in an emotional state, Sir David read out a brief, dignified resignation speech. He wished to vacate the position of Chairman immediately and allow the new management structure under Bob Phillis to get to grips with the awesome problems that still loomed for the news giant.

When Sir David finished, there was an eerie silence. Tony Brook of TVS cleared his throat and we all looked faintly embarrassed until David, with a smile, gathered his papers and left the room.

Richard Dunn assumed the chair and the day's agenda was re-addressed. For me it was the end of an era and I confess to a feeling of sadness at this dramatic turn of events. Debate was lacklustre and prolonged even though we had deeply serious issues to tackle and resolve.

I had arranged a dinner party that evening at my house in Surrey to which Bob Phillis and his wife Jean had been invited. With the agenda unfinished at 6.30 p.m. I began to reconcile myself to the fact that Bob and Jean would have to cry off and I excused myself from the meeting at 6.45. On the Chiswick flyover I phoned Bob's PA at ITN and told her that I fully understood if he had to take a rain-check on dinner. She laughed.

'Bob will *be* there,' she said. 'He's looking forward to a break in routine.'

And so he was. His chauffeur pulled into my drive at 8.30 p.m. and Bob, still fresh and full of zest, bounced into our conservatory to take a glass of champagne with our other guests, including Peter Marsh, flamboyant ex-Chairman of advertising agency ABM and Brian Luby, boss of publishers BLA and Associates.

The chat over dinner was social, although Bob and Jean joked about the pressure the ITN job now placed on their private lives. It was well past midnight when we said our goodbyes and Bob drew me to one side in the hall.

'Save me a phone call tomorrow,' he said. 'How about Richard Dunn as Chairman now that David's gone?'

I nodded, but entered one caveat. 'It has to be temporary,' I said.

I knew many of my colleagues on the ITN board would agree with this. What ITN needed was a non-Executive Chairman who came preferably from outside the magic circle of independent television. Richard would be fine as Deputy Chairman, but I had a real fear that if he were ever confirmed as Sir David's successor we'd have *two* Chief Executives, not one. That would be a *bad* deal for ITN and an impossible scenario for Bob Phillis.

The month that followed saw further frenetic activity at Gray's Inn Road. A committee of ITV Finance Directors was convened and they crawled all over the accounts. Bob prepared a paper for the board which was bold and imaginative. To start with the board itself was too large and unwieldy and Bob proposed some radical changes. Round the table sat Tony Brook of TVS, myself, Leslie Hill of Central, Clive Leach of Yorkshire, Andrew Quinn of Granada, Greg Dyke of LWT, Richard Dunn of Thames and Ian Ritchie of Tyne Tees who had just succeeded David Reay. Plus of course Bob,

138

Clive Timms, the Finance Director, and Paul Matthews.

Bob felt that there should be no more than three non-executive Directors from ITV and that additional non-executives should be recruited from outside. This was not for *now*, but a scenario for 1993. As a tiny shareholder I could see the logic of this – indeed what clout did I bring to the table with 2.5 per cent?

But more important than the future composition of the board was the state of the company as a whole. After our board meeting on 15 July, Bob tried to reach agreement with the unions for further, urgent staff reductions. The unions weren't prepared to play and management had no alternative but to push ahead with their plan without any union support. The 42 'voluntary' redundancies included star names like veteran foreign correspondent Desmond Hamill and reporter Keith Hatfield. (Sir Alistair Burnett had already agreed to 'phase out' later in 1991 although he might be retained to 'advise' on such things as general elections. To all intents and purposes however, Sir Alistair's day was *done*. Another era biting the dust.)

Sara Cullen, another long-term ITN star with 19 years' service, also faced the axe having returned from maternity leave the previous September. Giles Smith the journalists' leader at ITN protested at what he described as 'carnage'. ITN staff met, after receiving their white redundancy envelopes, in the wine bar opposite the new 'glitter palace' in Gray's Inn Road. Desmond Hamill was sad, but not bitter. He told *Daily Mail* reporter Peter Usher that he had decided to leave ITN because 'they can no longer afford to pay correspondents like me to move around the world.' Hamill had been with ITN for 24 years, a stint that included being kidnapped in Lebanon and then freed after a ransom payment not unadjacent to £20,000 had been negotiated with the terrorist group.

Cameraman-recordist John Phillips, who was also one of those on Bob's redundancy hit list, had also experienced tough times in his career. Apart from brief periods in jail in both Uganda and Angola he had been part of the team who had captured those heart-stopping pictures of the little girl in

Vietnam who was filmed running naked along a war-scarred road, her tiny shoulders splattered with napalm.

Asking people to leave is never a pleasant duty and made doubly difficult when emotions run high. When the pain and anguish subside, as they will, and the balm of time replaces passion with reflection, most people will accept that if ITN was to survive in any shape whatsoever, the decisions made in June and July of 1991 were inevitable.

Since then, ITN has experienced a series of further convulsions and its new shareholder structure will include a major holding by Carlton Television, headed by Michael Green, the new kid on the block who ousted Thames from their lucrative London weekday franchise.

Ironically, Bob Phillis, ITN's Chief Executive, was Green's Managing Director in Carlton's non-broadcaster days, but left to join ITN because Green's hands-on style was a little restrictive to a free spirit like Phillis. Ownership aside, ITN faces a tough, competitive future and it will need every ounce of management skill and journalistic enterprise to emerge as one of the world's leading news organisations.

When I resigned in July 1992, Bob and his team gave Carolyn and me a valedictory dinner at ITN headquarters and Bob thanked me for being 'one of ITN's most enthusiastic and committed' non-executive Directors. It is a compliment I shall forever cherish.

But the upheavals continued. Bob Phillis, perhaps sensing the looming presence of his old boss Michael Green, decided in January 1993 to quit ITN, his work on laying solid foundations done at last. He announced his intention to join the BBC as Deputy Director-General. I reflected sombrely that ITN's loss would be the BBC's gain. He didn't stay long, departing to rejoin the newspaper industry.

CHAPTER 13

Franchise fever again. TSW conned by a master fraudster, red faces all round – especially mine!

The beginning of 1991 saw franchise fever reaching a point of near delirium. The 15 incumbent companies were, not unsurprisingly, determined to defend their own turf. Key staff were offered a range of mouth-watering inducements to stay with their respective teams until the end of 1992 when the current franchises expired. Stock options, extended contracts, winners' cash bonuses and Jaguar motor cars were all on offer.

At TSW we targeted a small group of managers and offered them attractive cash bonuses for staying. Nothing spectacular, but worth in some cases nearly a year's salary in a lump sum. The payment was not to be until after 31 December 1991. Was it enough? With the benefit of hindsight, I wish we'd been a touch more generous, particularly in the light of some of the 'golden handcuffs' offered to key people by LWT and Thames. We did however offer *every* employee, without exception, a cash or shares 'prize' for staying the course and I believe we were the only company to do this.

On the downside, the word redundancy was much bruited abroad. For years, ITV had been the 'fat cat' industry with bloated armies of technical staff and excessive layers of management. It was perhaps inevitable that a commercial monopoly should, over its 30-plus years, start to accumulate fat and become complacent.

1990 and 1991, however, saw Draconian cuts in manpower and ruthless pruning of unprofitable activity. The rush towards leaner, fitter ITV companies was driven by two major influences. The first and most obvious was the looming franchise battle. With 'highest bid' hanging like a sword of Damocles over the contractors' heads, they had no choice but to slash their wage bills. At TSW we had two major redundancy phases, shedding well over 100 staff and saving nearly £3 million a year. It was not pleasant, indeed in terms of human misery it was a deeply distasteful exercise, but it was a matter of survival. The logic was inescapable. A huge staff drove up your costs to a point where a successful bid was impossible. Outside predators sniffing at a franchise would inevitably start with a much lower cost base than any incumbent. The fashionable 'publisher contractor' concept meant minimal wage bills, generally modest overheads and thus a great deal more cash to throw into the bid.

The second influence was that the deepening recession had made tough economic retrenchment a feature of British industry and as far as ITV was concerned it was just as powerful a reason to cut staff numbers as anything else.

Early in 1991 the ITC issued their draft document – or invitation – to apply for an ITV licence. It was a weighty tome, thick as an airport novel and couched in the lifelessly pedantic prose of a civil servant with a bent towards accountancy. Amendments followed, each more verbose than the original draft, until before the first buds of spring had even filled with sap, the document was issued. To an existing contractor it was a formidable piece of work. The guidelines and the preamble were dense with 'caveats' and 'notwithstandings' and 'on the other hands'. The actual questions were long, very detailed, occasionally complex and remarkably comprehensive.

There was little opportunity to 'write up' an application in selling language as each applicant was sternly warned to answer each question in full. Only ten A4 pages were to be permitted in the foreword, or mission statement. The financial section was the most precise and detailed of all. A ten-year cash flow forecast was demanded, plus revenue and cost estimates, staff numbers, depreciation policy, sensitivity tests in the event of a 10 per cent revenue shortfall and a justification of the final cash bid figure. At TSW we knew that preparing

142

answers for this vast questionnaire would occupy senior executives for nearly two months.

If we found it tough, which we did, how on earth, we mused, would an outsider tackle it? We at least had a track record, were in possession of performance records, had an infrastructure and an experienced staff. We also had a cash flow of £3 million a month which enabled us to engage the services of advisers, consultants, merchant bankers, lawyers and public relations experts. To a new bidder, with no existing business, the problem would have been daunting.

Outsiders wishing to wrest a franchise from an existing holder needed, above all else, two vital things: money and information. A speculative bid could cost a punter anything from £1 to £5 million. Unreturnable. This was gambling on a very grand scale indeed. In such a maelstrom of angst, neurosis and overheated ambition it was perhaps inevitable that villainy would also manifest itself.

Now Cassell's dictionary defines a villain thus: a scoundrel, a wretch, a rogue, a rascal – plus a few other equally unflattering names into the bargain. I had the misfortune to come into contact with a man who made these descriptions seem faintly pallid, if not downright mild. The tale I am about to unfold will stretch readers' credulity to the limit and strike them as being more reminiscent of John Le Carré than the real world of commercial television.

It happened like this. In London in early April 1991 I received a phone call from Genoa, Italy. My secretary, Rhonda, said that a man called 'Marcus' wished to speak with me on a matter of vital and urgent importance. It was, the caller insisted, about our coming franchise battle. Just a touch intrigued and not a little apprehensive I took the call. Marcus had a clear Australian accent and immediately told me that my company was in 'grave danger' from industrial sabotage. A rival bidder for our licence in the South-West was already up to a series of 'dirty tricks'. Our studios in Plymouth had been bugged and surveillance equipment of great sophistication had also been installed, clandestinely, in our London offices at Knightsbridge.

Marcus, it transpired, had been hired by the rival bidder on the recommendation of the First National Bank of Boston in Luxembourg, who knowing his reputation as a special enquiry agent, passed his name on to a group of men who claimed they wanted to utilise his ultimate skills in 'information gathering'. On meeting them however Marcus discovered that they were asking him to perform duties 'beyond the law' and furthermore had failed, or refused, to pay his initial expenses during the first few preliminary meetings. He was, therefore both disgruntled and professionally outraged, hence his call to me.

I will own to an initial scepticism. The tale of bugs and electronic listening devices struck me as fantastic and I said so. But Marcus was insistent and, let it be stated plainly, very convincing. He turned on the heat by telling me that in addition to the bugging he suspected we might have three 'moles' inside our company who were assiduously passing sensitive information to the rival bidder. Marcus quoted phone numbers which I at once recognised. They were all on the Plymouth exchange. My anxiety was increased when he added, in darkly sepulchral tones, that a 'convicted felon, a known burglar' had also been engaged to spy on TSW executives during their leisure hours to ascertain whether they were 'up to any nocturnal naughties'.

At this stage his money ran out in the Genoa public call box and I asked him to reverse the charges and continue the conversation. This he did and promised that he would even phone me again the following day with further startling revelations. Now thoroughly alarmed I finished our conversation and contacted our Company Secretary in Plymouth, Ivor Stolliday. Ivor in turn telephoned our solicitors, Foote & Bowden. The partner who looked after TSW's affairs was Tony Jaffa, a talented young lawyer and public notary. His advice was for me to receive the second call from Marcus and make careful note of what he said.

The next day at 4 p.m. Marcus telephoned again, reversing the charges. He had new and sensational information. He knew the name of a Swiss hotel in Geneva where key figures in the rival bidding group had assembled like thieves in the night. From this hotel they had made phone contact with key officers in TSW at their home numbers.

'Do the following initials mean anything to you?' said Marcus. He then proceeded to give me some initials which made the hair on the nape of my neck stand up. The initials were unmistakable. We had traitors in our midst. Marcus had acquired tapes of these vital conversations and would be willing to hand them over to us. Money had been discussed. Bribes negotiated. Treachery was to be handsomely rewarded. Not only that, Marcus would be willing to 'swear an affidavit' and give evidence to the effect that TSW was being illegally bugged and that he had information which would identify the moles in our midst. A meeting between us was therefore most urgent. Marcus couldn't get to England – his work was already in arrears due to his abortive association with the rival bidders. Could I meet him in Genoa? Not possible, I told him and not very wise. I might be recognised at Heathrow and this would set alarm bells ringing.

I therefore decided to send Ivor Stolliday, as the company's senior officer in charge of legal affairs, together with solicitor Tony Jaffa. Under conditions of utmost secrecy they were booked onto a flight to Genoa through our travel agency, Thomas Cook in Plymouth. Marcus had suggested they meet him in the lobby of a hotel in the city centre – where, he added mysteriously, he would identify himself once he was satisfied of Ivor and Tony's credentials. Just how he would verify their bona fide nature before revealing who he was puzzled me a little, but I didn't argue and agreed to the arrangements he had proposed.

On 23 March 1991 Ivor and Tony, equipped with a tape recorder and a $1,000 in cash took an early flight to Genoa, a city described as being about as romantic as Accrington. The hotel Savoia Majestic was of middling quality and it was here in the marbled lobby that my two couriers awaited their rendezvous with Marcus in a state of growing anticipation.

When he arrived and identified himself it was something of an anticlimax. They were confronted not by a dashing spy in velvet cloak and snap-brimmed fedora, but by a middle-aged man of neat, but otherwise unremarkable, appearance. He could, Ivor said later, have been an insurance salesman or government official. He had greying hair, spectacles, a small paunch and an Australian accent. The three men made brief but polite introductions and then settled into a small lounge on the first floor above the lobby to start talking. The tape that was played back to me later in England ran for two and a half hours.

Marcus repeated much of what he had already told me on the telephone and both Tony and Ivor questioned him closely. It seemed that here was a genuinely nice man, a true professional who conducted work of a sensitive and confidential nature for foreign embassies, banks and blue chip organisations. The nature of his business naturally brough him into contact with people of dubious reputation and from time to time clients might ask him to perform duties of a questionable legality which he always refused.

This brought Ivor and Tony to the nub of the matter. The rivals for our television franchise, all rogues to a man, were trying to bribe our own key staff to pass over confidential information and at the same time persuade Mr Marcus to set up an illegal bugging operation at our two offices in London and Plymouth. He had bluntly declined, but warned my two colleagues that the operation was still going ahead through another contact in England – a known and convicted felon who was skilled at burglary and the placing of 'listening devices' in commercial premises. Marcus's refusal to play such dirty games had led our rival bidders to turn nasty with him, or as he quaintly put it, 'They started pissing in my pocket.'

Far worse however than Marcus's Harris Tweed being rotted by uric acid, was the fact that they had refused to pay him his genuine expenses. He had travelled across Europe for their initial meetings – before of course he realised they were up to no good – and he had wasted valuable time on some preliminary research which we presumed was into the background and structure of our company. He confirmed that his

146

motivation in helping us was twofold: old-fashioned revenge and a desire to recoup his expenses. I had already agreed that we would pay these expenses as they seemed both modest and reasonable.

The conversation meandered on, with Marcus doing most of the talking. Our company was in grave danger, that much was clear, but there were still many loose ends to be tied up. Tony politely explained that much of what Marcus had told us was uncorroborated.

'I don't want you to feel that I am suggesting for a moment that you are lying,' said Tony to a slightly miffed Mr Marcus. 'But it would be foolhardy for me to advise the company to proceed on your statement alone. We'd need that corroboration.'

Marcus nodded. 'In other words, you'd like an affidavit from me.'

'Yes,' said Tony. 'And if you swear it in Europe, it could be before a public notary.'

'Fine,' said Mr Marcus. 'I really want to help you guys. I'd even be prepared to come to England.'

Another hour of talking took place and Marcus agreed to try and obtain a copy of the Geneva hotel bill, complete with details of phone calls that would prove that our rival bidders were contacting our key staff at their homes in Plymouth. Heady stuff. There was even the chance that we might get transcripts of what was said. Treachery on tape! A hideous, but nonetheless thrilling, possibility. Our appetites were whetted, our hackles fully risen, our adrenaline churning.

Back then to England came Tony and Ivor, hotfoot from the airport to my house in Surrey. We listened to the two and half hour tape. We talked. We pondered. We fretted. We talked some more. Just a few more details were needed, a few pieces of the jigsaw to be dropped carefully in place and with Marcus's promise of a sworn affidavit we could issue writs against our rivals and summarily dimiss those staff who had been deceiving us by selling secrets to the enemy. Marcus had also given Tony and Ivor copies of a brochure which showed illustrated details of the highly sophisticated equipment that

147

was being used against the company. It made James Bond seem like a character out of *Noddy in Toyland*. He also provided photographs – secretly obtained – of the known felon who had been engaged in England to break into our offices and place these devices in sensitive areas. I decided that as few people as possible should be informed of the Genoa visit and Marcus's revelations.

Early the following week, on the same day as a Plymouth board meeting, Ivor, Tony and I briefed our Chairman, Sir Brian Bailey, at the Grand Hotel overlooking Plymouth Hoe. He listened to the two and a half hour tape with incredulity. Now we had to decide on what precise action we were to take. Legal moves against our rival bidder would have to be delayed until we received the sworn affidavit – and certainly we were not yet in a position to accuse staff of wrongdoing. However, we felt such action could not long be delayed.

We briefed the board with just the outline of recent events, telling them that we were 'investigating a security risk'. They seemed satisfied and agreed that I and my executives should pursue whatever course of action we deemed necessary.

On 27 March Ivor, Tony and I visited the London offices of the ITC where we had arranged a meeting with their two most senior officials, the Director General, David Glencross and the Commission Secretary, Ken Blyth. We told them of our suspicions and showed them the fat 57-page transcript of the Genoa meeting with Marcus. They were shocked, but we said that no action was requested or expected of them until we had more proof – the corroboration that we knew would square this circle and enable us to bring the affair under the scrutiny of the law. We left the Knightsbridge headquarters of the ITC and treated ourselves to an Italian lunch at the Signor Sassi restaurant close to TSW's London office. Over some excellent pasta and a bottle of Frascati various tactics were discussed. Tony spoke of invoking the rare Anton Pilar manoeuvre, not a wrestling tactic, but a curious legal device that enabled the court to grant permission for a solicitor to enter and search the premises of a person 'reasonably suspected of wrongdoing' *without police* being in attendance. Things were getting heavy, we mused. Murky waters were about to be charted, dies were about to be cast.

Tony, while a fully qualified solicitor, felt we should take some further advice from a Queen's Counsel, a barrister-at-law with chambers in Fleet Street. Meantime, he had arranged to go back to Genoa with Ivor for a second meeting. This trip necessitated driving over the border into Italy to see Marcus at the Motel Provenze, Ventimiglia. Here on 4 April the affidavit Tony had prepared was handed to Marcus. Not much else happened at the meeting, but there was more to come.

On Friday 12 April Tony flew to Genoa alone and once again met Marcus at the Motel Provenze. At this meeting Marcus promised to record a conversation with his mysterious contact 'BB', a roguish but shadowy figure who was close to our rival bidders and in possession of some 'hot' information. Later that same day Tony received a phone call on his return to Genoa and was told that the recording had not been obtained. Once again Tony returned to England without sufficient material for us to take any further positive steps.

Recognising how vital a sworn affidavit was to underpin our case Tony flew out again, this time to Milan on 18 April to see Marcus at the Milan Hilton. Marcus handed over the signed document which had been sworn before a local notary and Tony returned home the next day. We felt we had made progress, but still not enough to thwart our dastardly rivals.

On the following Monday Tony, Ivor, myself and Sir Brian agreed to meet at the London offices of our Queen's Counsel at Fountain Court Chambers in the Temple. I met them at Paddington and when they arrived on the early train from Plymouth we all crammed into my Jaguar and whisked across London to Fleet Street. Tony looked pale and strained. His office had received a phone call from Marcus that morning just after he had left for the station. The news was a bomb-shell – Marcus had told Tony's assistant that we should not proceed with the investigation as the 'whole thing was a hoax and we'd end up looking foolish if we went to court'.

Frankly, none of us knew how to take this news. A hoax? What the hell was Marcus playing at? Then the penny dropped. He was running scared. Coming to London and swearing on oath in court might mean him 'shopping' some of his contacts. Honour among private detectives, we reasoned, was as likely as honour among thieves.

Furthermore he had told Tony that he was going to a final meeting with our rival bidders – a dangerous move to be sure – but armed with a miniature recording device he was to tape the words which would seal our rival's fate. So what had gone wrong? Of course! What fools we had been. At this last meeting with our rivals they had bought him off! Danegeld, perhaps, but it was a risk they were prepared to take in order to secure his future silence. The bastards. The villains. The unmitigated swine!

Somewhat downhearted we filed into the book-lined chambers of our Queen's Counsel Thomas Morrison. He read the affidavit Marcus had sworn under his real name of Harold Gray, but he frowned and shook his head.

'It won't stand up in court,' he said. 'Too circumstantial. And furthermore the man has only given a post restante address.'

Plunged into gloom we sat hunched around the big desk and tried to gather our thoughts. Tony contacted his office again and there was a further message from the ubiquitous Mr Marcus. Tony was to phone a Paul Charmain at a London number, mention Harold Gray (alias Marcus) and ask him if he knew anything about a man called Joe Flynn. This instruction made absolutely no sense to any of us, but Tony made his call.

It was at this precise moment that I felt the bottom dropping out of our world. Charmain was a freelance journalist who, some years earlier had written a long feature in the magazine *Time Out* about one of the world's most accomplished confidence tricksters – one Joe Flynn, otherwise known as Harold Gray, or Marcus, or more colourfully, the King of the Sting!

Had we been stung? We had been stung, screwed, fucked, turned inside out and hung out to dry. Marcus had coolly separated us from nearly £4,000 in cash by spinning a tale which was no more than a cleverly constructed tissue of lies, half truths and brilliantly hinted innuendoes. If a revolver had been handy at that moment I would have shot Ivor and Tony and saved the last four bullets for myself!

When Paul Charmain had stopped laughing and made arrangements to dry his trousers out, he faxed us a copy of the article he had written 'exposing' Marcus and we all read it with a sense of frustration and anguish.

Worse, however, was yet to follow. Only a year previously Charmain had fronted a Channel Four programme in the *Hard News* series in which Marcus had actually appeared. When the tape arrived a few days later I played it in my office to Ivor and Sir Brian (Tony was to view it at home later). As Marcus popped up on the screen, for all the world as mild and ordinary as a friendly bank manager, I thought Ivor was going to implode.

'That's *him*,' he yelled. 'That's the man!'

Some strange compulsion inside him had made Marcus anxious to 'confess' on film. He was particularly keen for the world to know just how devious and clever he was. Indeed the tale that unfolded remains one of the most extraordinary I have ever witnessed, made doubly poignant by the fact that we had experienced the alchemy that Marcus worked at first hand.

Australian by birth and itinerant by nature he had made a living by preying on the gullibility of people who should have known better (and I include myself). By way of mild compensation we were in good, even illustrious company. Marcus had conned Rupert Murdoch of News International out of over $50,000 by pretending he knew the identity of the assassins who had 'iced' Jimmy Hoffa the American Teamster's union leader. His *modus operandi* was now familiar to us. The initial phone call to Murdoch in New York was plausible, and seductively persuasive. He was offering Murdoch's New York tabloid *The Daily News* an exclusive scoop. Evidence would be produced – in Europe of course – of Hoffa's murder and the world would stand in awe as the Murdoch press ran a truly sensational story.

So impressed was Murdoch with the validity of Marcus's

evidence – one down-to-earth Aussie to another – that he decided to take control of this story himself. He flew to Europe and handed over the cash. Absolutely all he got by way of evidence was a pair of second-hand shoes, claimed by Marcus to be Jimmy Hoffa's own. Later when the scam was realised, Hoffa's son remarked succinctly that 'they weren't my father's size'.

More daring con tricks were performed – twice more on the Murdoch press. *The Sunday Times* ran a story based on a Marcus 'invention' about Middle East terrorists and subsequently had to publish a retraction. The *Independent* newspaper, the FBI, the CIA, the BBC, Central Television and even a henchman of Colonel Gaddafi fell for the Marcus black magic. In each case Marcus sold them utterly spurious stories which were without a shred of truth. In the case of the BBC and Central they 'bought' the Marcus line, but didn't in the end transmit the material.

The Gaddafi scam was breathtaking in its audacity. Two of the Libyan leader's aides were in Geneva on a diplomatic mission and Marcus learnt of the hotel they were staying in. At the time there were anti-Gaddafi groups active in London who had received a certain amount of press coverage. Using this brief, second-hand knowledge, Marcus approached the Libyan aides and posing as a professional assassin offered to eliminate these 'dissidents' in London for a fat fee. It's hard to credit that two hardened Arab tough guys would actually fall for such a preposterous line, but they did – hook, line and sinker.

'How will you do it?' asked one of the Arabs. 'Will you shoot them?'

Marcus, bland and suburban, smiling like a Cheshire cat, shook his greying head slowly. 'No,' he said. 'Too noisy. I'll probably poison them.'

The two Arabs practically fell over each other in their scramble to get bundles of cash out of the safe in their suite and press the notes into Marcus's eager hands. As Marcus himself commented, somewhat wryly, 'They couldn't wait to pay me – it was like stealing sweets from a six-year-old child.'

After the payout, needless to say, they never saw Marcus again and the London 'dissidents' remained unscathed.

At the time of writing this we do know that Marcus, not unlike the Scarlet Pimpernel, is being sought all over Europe by various people he has ripped off, including Interpol. He has served one short prison sentence for fraud, but although he pops up in Genoa, Paris, Geneva and Venice on a regular basis nobody knows just where he really lives. His ability to seduce and bamboozle remains undimmed and I have little doubt that we have only heard a fraction of the cases in which he has been involved. His skill is in only taking modest sums of money from his victims. This makes the cost of legal pursuit hardly worth the trouble. With the possible exception of the $50,000 Murdoch scam, his 'fees' are always within the bounds of acceptability or 'petty cash'.

I would like to meet him face to face one day – although just what I shall say to him in the event of such an unlikely confrontation remains a matter of idle speculation. Would I grab him by the throat and demand my money back? Would I frogmarch him to the nearest police station? If the latter, just what, precisely, would I accuse him of? The police may well shrug and say 'this kind of deception, while deplorable is hardly *actionable*!' I just don't know the answer. And probably never will. A small, very secret part of me rather hopes that such a meeting doesn't ever take place. Not because I fear that I might throttle the little shit, but rather because he might sell me the Eiffel Tower for £15 in six easy instalments. Of the mixed emotions Marcus arouses in his victims almost all of them would admit, in the long reaches of the night, that grudging admiration is one.

There is something of the Robin Hood in his style. His 'marks' are always corporations or very powerful individuals who can afford to part with the money he so artfully extracts from them. And his eleventh-hour phone call to us prevented me from taking the ultimate, horrible step of accusing innocent colleagues of wrongdoing when they were as pure as driven snow.

Has the experience made me more cynical about my fellow

man? Will I ever trust anybody completely again? The answers are 'no' to the first question and 'yes' to the second. Marcus is just another dazzling thread in the rich tapestry of life. We are wiser and a touch sadder as a result of getting taken in by him, but I cannot bring myself to hate the man too much. Certainly I'd like him brought to justice, and I'd like my money back, but in real life stories don't always have happy endings.

CHAPTER 14

The new franchise battle. We contemplate a big bid, but there are many hurdles to overcome.

It is early spring, we have emerged from the Marcus fiasco with invisible bruises, but are otherwise unharmed.

Work of a complex and highly intensive nature has been done on our application document. It is now a weighty tome replete with ringing assertions of our broadcasting integrity, our financial rectitude, our social awareness, our marketing expertise. John Roberts, Finance Director and Ivor Stolliday, Company Secretary have constructed the financial parts of the document brick by brick, with Sir Brian providing the flow of elegant words which will act as mortar to hang all these bricks together. Paul Stewart-Laing, Director of Programmes, being creative, is always on a short fuse and complains to me that he is 'being left out of the discussions' and that Ivor and Sir Brian are 'playing it far too close to the chest'. Martin Bowley, Sales Director, shares Paul's apprehension – after all what is TSW all about if not programmes and revenue?

I intervene, warning Sir Brian that we must include these two key executives in our deliberations. Sir Brian, who loves writing, is loathe to surrender any part of what he is doing, but I insist that he can write down no commitments to future programme plans until and unless they have been approved by the Director of Programmes. Likewise sales forecasts. Tension fills the air like electricity, but is soon dispersed when we realise we are all in the same boat and striving to achieve the same objectives.

The half-completed document is awesome. National Economic Research Associates (NERA) have helped construct

155

the economic model on which our business plan, revenue forecasts and future balance sheets are based. Their contribution has been prodigious.

As the deadline of 15 May hurtles towards us we begin to worry if we are going to get finished in time. Midnight oil is burned. Candles glow from both ends. Ivor and John lose weight. Ivor's hair turns a lighter shade of 'John Major' grey. Paul Stewart Laing's shirt strains across his waistline like a small balloon and I too gain a few pounds from 'stress eating'. This is a new, fashionable condition. The posh newspapers are full of it. Paul and I share the same medical problem – greed. Tempers flare and subside. Executives wake up at three in the morning covered in sweat and screaming silently. This truly is a visitation of the curse of Thatcher!

The weekend prior to 15 May Ivor Stolliday pitches camp at the Tower Hotel in London, close to our specialist printers and Martin Bowley and I, with our wives, join him and Elaine Dowling, from Personnel, to help with the painstaking business of proofreading. In the event Ivor doesn't go to sleep that night at all, but works till the wee hours. We are now getting down to the wire and everyone is becoming jagged and hypersensitive.

A board meeting has been arranged for Tuesday 14 May in London and I have asked directors to spread themselves around the town rather than all bunch into the Hyde Park Hotel. The plan is very straightforward. At 4 p.m. we assemble in my office in Bowater House. After a liberal dispensation of tea and biscuits a brace of limos whisk board members to the Stratton Street HQ of NERA where they will receive a comprehensive presentation. It will comprise the details of NERA's economic model and the step-by-step process by which we half-reached our cost and revenue projections.

Robin Foster of NERA, unassuming but brilliant, as always, takes us through a maze of figures, charts and graphs until I see some colleagues' eyes glazing over. Crunch time comes late in the evening when we focus on the various cash bid options we have to consider. Whatever the final bid, we all agree that it should reflect the following fundamental principles:

156

1 The maintenance of dividends to shareholders.
2 If trading losses occur they should not continue beyond year one.
3 From year two, break even at least, and thence into profit.
4 Cash accumulation on a progressive scale through till 2003.

The process we employ to arrive at our bid can best be described as a mixture of financial logic and Byzantine alchemy. After lengthy debate, punctuated by occasional flashes of emotion, the board agree that the maximum bid figure should be £14 million. It is a fine round sum. It sits up there on the computer screen, its string of noughts quivering like a row of virgin brides. We all stare at it in absolute silence. Fourteen million quid. Bloody hell!

But the strict financial logic behind this figure has been scrutinised not just by NERA, but also by our accountants Ernst & Young *and* our merchant bank, J. R. Rothschild, both companies with impeccable business credentials.

Sir Brian, who has sat motionless and Buddha-like for the past five minutes suddenly stirs. 'It's too *round*,' he says enigmatically.

We all snap out of our stunned reverie. Too *round*? What can Sir Brian mean?

'Let's add in the date,' says Sir Brian, 'just for luck.'

John Roberts grabs a pencil and scribbles furiously. 'That makes it £14,591,000,' he says.

We all laugh, somebody claps. We nod sagely. That's it. £14,591,000.

NERA have laid on supper in a room upstairs and with visible relief the board start to gather their papers and file out. John Ivor and I hang around to thank Robin Foster and his team. John and Ivor exchange glances. Something wrong? I enquire. Nothing is wrong exactly. But it is a whisker short of being absolutely right. The figure of £14,591,000 is in 1991 prices and the ITC application document specifies 1993 prices for the cash bid. John's fingers are a blur as he adds in two

157

years' standard inflation. Voila! £16,117,000. Blimey! But that really is it. No question. It fits the bill exactly, and we can stick to our agreed policy. No break in dividends. No losses beyond year one. But to achieve this goal we all know there will be further economies to be made, more staff to be made redundant. But the new, post-1993 streamlined TSW will be on a steady, profitable journey towards 2003 with the prospect of very healthy cash generation on the way. We break for dinner and I am surprised to find that the back of my neck is damp with perspiration.

I have written the magic figure down on the small slip of paper provided by the ITC – it appears on no other document. I lick the envelope, stick it down and give it to Ivor as Company Secretary for safe keeping. We are to meet at 8.00 a.m. the next morning for a final breakfast meeting at Bowater House before I take the sealed envelope to the ITC's headquarters in Knightsbridge.

The press meantime have been running speculative pieces about just how the various bids will be delivered. Noon on the 15th is the closing deadline. High noon. I ponder on whether to deliver TSW's bid on horseback as the Hyde Park riding circuit runs within a few hundred yards of the ITC building. And why not? We're in showbusiness are we not? But what if Joe, my horse, does a quick 'Ratner' on the ITC's doorstep. Bad vibes all round. Forget the horse. Helicopter? Parachute into Hyde Park? No. Too risky. Might land in the Serpentine. I must think of *something* special though, as 15 May, although a critical day in the life of ITV, promises to go off like a damp squib. Most ITV Managing Directors will just turn up, discreetly, deliver their bids and vanish. The press are looking for a bit more than this – but there's no story in a bunch of middle-aged men climbing out of nice cars with envelopes in their hands. I decide at breakfast to take Gus Honeybun and this simple decision ensures we have more press coverage than any of the other bidders, whether existing ITV companies or new hopefuls. Gus and I appear in photographs in *The Times*, the *Guardian*, the *Independent*, the *Telegraph* and the *Daily Mail*.

At lunchtime I leap aboard the Plymouth train so that I can meet the local newspapers for a brief press conference. It goes well, even though I insist on playing the tape of TSW's 'battle hymn of the franchise', a rousing, emotional piece written specially by our music consultant, Ed Welch.

Friday morning and I am back in London to give another press conference to the trades' and the national papers. Peter Fiddick, ex-Editor of the *Listener* and Martin Jackson, publisher of *Broadcast* are both rude about my singing, but what the hell. My sister Mary was a professional opera singer in the 1950s; maybe these skills don't transfer from sister to brother.

'That's the last time I sing in public,' I tell Gilly, my PA. The look of relief on her face is remarkable. I resolve to take up the nose flute and anklespoons instead.

It is the ITC's intention to set a measured timetable for the licence award process. They have close to 40 applications to consider and they wish to be diligent in the way they appraise the 'quality threshold'.

After various specialists within the ITC have pored over the fine print, Hill Samuel, their financial advisers, will eyeball the business plans. We know that the Chairman of the ITC, George Russell, has had a quick peek at the actual cash bids in order to satisfy himself that nobody has inadvertently stuffed their grocery list in the envelope, but the full membership of the ITC won't make a final decision until the procedure of reading several *thousand* pages of special pleading has been completed. Three contractors appear to have been born lucky. Central, Scottish and little Border are all unopposed.

It is only a few weeks after 15 May that speculation in the press begins to mount. Ray Snoddy of the *Financial Times* takes the view that the whole process of the blind auction is a farce and that the ITC will be unable to prevent leaks long before the October decision date.

As the ITC propose no public meetings for this franchise round, the *Guardian* newspaper and the British Film Institute decide to step into the vacuum and run their own at various venues across the country. At first the ITVA Council reject this as unacceptable. The incumbent contractors, it is felt, will be sitting targets for ambitious new bidders who have little or no track record and the debates might be counter-productive. I share this view, but am persuaded by Georgina Henry of the *Guardian* that *not* to be represented at the meetings will smack of arrogance. We occupy the high ground, so why not use the occasion to make a bold, confident statement about the company? My own Arts Advisory Board at TSW take this line also. So we go.

Our public meeting is to be held on 18 June at the tiny Barbican Theatre in Plymouth. Paul Stewart-Laing and I will take the platform and state TSW's case in the ten minutes allotted to each bidder for the South-West franchise. In the event we trounce the opposition.

Telewest is represented by Mallory Maltby, a pleasant man with an easy, unassuming manner. He has been a producer of some distinction, working largely as a freelance for Anglia. He apologises for being the only representative of his group.

'The others,' he explains rather sheepishly, 'are all in confidential brown envelopes.'

We are offered instead a video tape of Angela Rippon, one of Telewest's 'stars'. She talks sincerely to camera in her own inimitable if faintly schoolmarmish style. Telewest are a 'super' group. Full of smashing ideas. Fresh. Packed with innovation. And so on. It is not a wholly convincing performance. Angela is an ex-colleague from Westward days and my guess is she was recruited very late in the life of Telewest. She and I lunched at Waltons in Chelsea only a few months previously and she was full of how much she now enjoyed living in London, 'where the work is.'

Maltby tries to summarise as Angela fades from the monitor screen, but is counted out by Chairwoman Sara Davies as they have exceeded the ten minutes allotted them.

Next comes West Country Television, formidable enough on paper and backed by South-West Water, Brittany Ferries and Associated Newspapers. Those of us at TSW who have read their application reckon it is superficially attractive, but flawed. Paul Stewart-Laing describes it as a 'mirage' application.

Tonight they field television veteran Frank Copplestone, ex-IBA mandarin and one time Managing Director of Southern Television. Frank kicks off with a perfectly respectable opening statement using words like 'commitment' and 'professionalism'. He voices concern over WCTV's press treatment at the hands of both national and local newspapers.

'The fact that South-West Water is a twenty per cent shareholder will not influence the editorial freedom of our journalists in pursuing stories,' Frank tells us.

But this is an issue that simply won't go away. Comparatively recently, TSW exposed to a startled world the scandal of the Camelford water incident where aluminium waste was dumped into the domestic water supply. South-West Water have never quite recovered from the lambasting they received over this affair and are today still hypersensitive about it.

The press, unprompted by anybody at TSW are asking if it is right and proper for a water authority to invest their money in a speculative bid for a television franchise. Shouldn't they stick to investing in an improved water supply? It is good rousing stuff and I am enjoying every minute of it. Frank concludes and then introduces his Chairman designate, John Banham, Director General of the CBI. But on video. A tactical error my view, but I suppress my elation. Banham comes across with all the personality of a game show host. He is after all, just a local lad, oozing sincerity from every pore. He arches his eyebrows in a man to man, straight from the shoulder pitch and I feel my lower intestine contract sharply. His knowledge of television can clearly be drowned in a thimble and I am deeply underwhelmed.

My Chairman, Sir Brian Bailey, has already written to the CBI Chairman protesting at Banham's involvement. We are members of the organisation and we find it odd to say the least that a man whose salary we pay in part should mount a hostile bid against us. Shome mishtake surely, As *Private Eye* would say.

After Banham's tape, which I vote the worst piece of video

161

I've seen all week, Frank Copplestone hands over to his head of news designate, Richard Myers. Richard is an ex-TSW Head of News. A nice man, but an ex-Head of News nevertheless. He trundles out the usual patter about 'more comprehensive coverage of the region' and finishes with a weak jibe at me, promising that WCTV will have 'no gimmicks and no *cigars*!' The audience do not break into spontaneous applause. Before Richard can hand over to the third member of their team, a lady called Jane Clarke, they too are 'gonged' by the chairwoman for overshooting their ten minutes. The lady looks decidedly pissed off, as well she might. A thought occurs to me. These guys are hoping to win a television franchise. Television is about split-second timing. Handovers. Links. Preparation. So far both our rivals have screwed up on all four. If you can't plan a ten-minute pitch at the Barbican Theatre without overrunning then how the hell are you going to run a television station?

Now it is our turn and we do *exactly* ten minutes, without frills.

'This is *us*,' I say. 'If you *really* want to know what TSW is all about you shouldn't be here in this stuffy old theatre, you should be at home with your feet up, watching telly!'

Paul weighs in with a comprehensive run-down of our programmes past, present and future. It is no contest. We have widdled on them from a great height. But *politely*.

Questions follow. Most of them are directed at WCTV over their choice of shareholders. South-West Water aside, doesn't the involvement of Associated Newspapers pose questions of public interest too? Associated already own the *Western Morning News* and the *Exeter Express* and *Echo*. Isn't it unhealthy for one media owner to dominate the communications business of a small region like the South-West? A number of people in the audience obviously think so.

I field a couple of wobblies about TSW's attitude to women, equal opportunities and other 'green' issues. No meeting is compete without somebody flashing their social conscience. But we have no apologies to make on these items. Our record

162

is fine and it is, after all, a *Guardian* BFI evening. All that is missing are sandals and muesli.

The meeting winds up with a good-natured natter over glasses of outstandingly awful red wine and all the contestants shake hands in a sporting, British fashion. Georgina and I then walk the mile or so to Plymouth's only Michelin starred restaurant, Chez Nous where Georgina buys me a quite delicious dinner.

The evening, I admit, has been most worthwhile and Georgina, to do her credit, doesn't even *look* as if she's going to say 'I told you so'. I hit the sack at my flat on Grand Parade at about 1.30 a.m. and fall at once into a dream-filled sleep. John Banham of the CBI is tunnelling into the offices of the ITC wearing a miner's helmet, while a bugle is playing snatches from 'Colonel Bogey'. On waking I check these dreams in my recently purchased *What Your Dreams Mean* book. They mean very little that I can discern so I resolve to pamper myself with an enormous British Rail breakfast on the train back to London and to hell with cholesterol!

CHAPTER 15

Talking to the politicians. An exercise in masochistic futility. I get handbagged by Mrs Thatcher.

Much has been written about the Tory government's White Paper and subsequent Broadcasting Bill, *so* much in fact that many students of the television media are heartily sick of the whole subject. With the passage of time and the luxury of hindsight, I join many others who still believe it was ill-considered, doctrinaire and unnecessary.

It is true nevertheless that one politician emerged from the long and sometimes tedious debate with honour: David Mellor, Minister for Broadcasting and subsequently Minister for the Arts. He, virtually alone, was willing to listen, to modify, to make fair compromise and to ultimately ensure that the final bill was less Draconian, less silly, and more attuned to the reality of broadcasting than the raw and ghastly first draft. Mellor was also the only Minister who took the trouble to try and understand the broadcasting medium.

The first draft of the White Paper was prepared during Douglas Hurd's time in office as Home Secretary. His patrician style and obvious dislike of commercial television made him a difficult man to deal with. He thought we were all fat cats, and took every opportunity to tell us so. Indeed, the fat cats of ITV, it was made abundantly clear, were to receive a short, sharp shock.

We were to be exposed to the cold blast of competition: The feather-bedding days were gone. It was irritating in the extreme to be lectured by politicians, most of whom had never done a hand's turn of work in their lives. Of course they all took their cue from the Prime Minister who had an obsession about television and the need to cut it down to size.

After Hurd, we had brief periods of Waddington and Baker at the Home Office and it has always intrigued me that Ministers can be moved from discipline to discipline without any formal training. We are expected to believe that when a new Home Secretary takes office, he is possessed of a broad knowledge of the complex broadcasting industry. It's nonsense of course, as Baker demonstrated on more than one occasion.

But the ITV companies had to accept the hand they were dealt and they had one objective: to get the Broadcasting Bill modified.

When the companies decided to lobby for changes in government's proposed Bill, a general agreement was reached that we would cast the net as widely as possible. For my own part, I wanted to make the case to key decision-makers in the Tory leadership and to those opinion-formers in industry who might themselves influence government thinking. I was delighted therefore when my political adviser Michael Stephen told me he had arranged for me to meet the Prime Minister, Mrs Thatcher, at the Carlton Club in London's St James.

The meeting was to be at 11.30 p.m. after a cabinet dinner. Michael and I had a drink at the bar and smack on time, Mrs Thatcher came sweeping into the club followed in single file by her cabinet.

The men looked distinctly exhausted, faces gleaming with perspiration, dinner jackets faintly rumpled. The Prime Minister, however, looked magnificent. Not a hair out of place, exuding energy and good health like a beacon.

I was introduced to her in an upstairs ante-room. It was formal, not unlike meeting Queen Victoria, and we shook hands. I told her of my reservations about the proposed broadcasting legislation and my concern over the possible emasculation of regionalism. She stood inches away from me and fixed me with a basilisk stare.

'Not afraid of competition are you Mr Turner?' she said, and before I could utter another syllable, she proceeded to handbag me about the evils of monopoly, the joys of competition, the sluggish complacency of ITV management and much more besides. She was remarkably well-briefed and seemed obsessed with the need to give ITV a 'kick in the pants', although she didn't use those exact words. It was a *tour de force* and, to coin a phrase, I was gobsmacked.

Finally, softly-spoken tirade over, she treated me to a glacial smile. 'If you have any questions, Mr Turner,' she said, 'speak to Lord Young.' And then she was gone, striding away on high heels like a latter day Boadicea after a brisk chariot race.

Later I lobbied Masden Pirie, another free-market guru and one-time member of a Number 10 think-tank; Lord Chalfont, recently appointed Deputy Chairman of the IBA; and even Lord Whitelaw, who, one deduced, was not entirely comfortable with the proposed legislation, but whose influence was less than it had once been with the Iron Lady. I saw civil servants who were involved in drafting the Bill, like Chris Scoble, a brilliant young mandarin destined for greater glory than cobbling together the patchwork White Paper.

I was helped in these seemingly interminable visits by Michael Stephen and Nerj Diva who ran a public relations pressure group specialising in discreet political lobbying. Both men became Tory MPs eventually, Nerj being the first Asian candidate to win a seat for the Conservative Party. We plotted and planned and lunched at Whitehall clubs and dined journalists and editors and rammed the message home: the Broadcasting Bill was substandard and needed to be radically amended.

Perhaps the most effective lobby group however was the Campaign for Quality Television led by Simon Albury, now one of the Directors of the triumphant Meridian TV who ousted TVS from their lucrative southern franchise. Simon, who was a former *What the Papers Say* producer, is a voluble and energetic man with a fuzz of grey hair. He knew that to have credibility, his lobby group should be separate from the fat cat ITV companies who after all were just defending their own lush patch of monopoly. Among Simon's colleagues were Stuart Prebble, a Granada *World in Action* producer who initiated the original concept of a 'quality television' cam-

166

paign, and celebrities like rubber-faced comedian Rowan Atkinson and *Monty Python* star Terry Jones.

They were well-received by David Mellor during his time as Minister of State for Broadcasting and they sowed the seeds for the final, revised version of the dreaded Broadcasting Bill.

CHAPTER 16

A visit to New York and Hollywood, while in London the press universally condemn the government's proposed Broadcasting Bill as flawed.

It is the declared intention of the ITC to stick to the timetable they have set for the licence award process. From 15 May until mid-October their officials and advisers will deliberate, cogitate, investigate and for all I know probably masticate over the 38-plus applications they have piled up before them.

TSW's advisers have warned us that as we are in possession of 'inside' knowledge in relation to our own bid no Director or member of a Director's family may trade in our shares. Colleagues are given an awful caution that to break this embargo could cause a nasty touch of the 'Pentonvilles', so we all sit on our hands and refuse to be seen eating lunch with our stockbrokers unless chaperoned by a state registered nurse.

During these strange, lifeless days of early spring, TSW, at my behest, takes a shareholding in a consortium who are bidding for our neighbouring region, Wales and the West. The group, chaired by voluble Labour Peer Lord Morris and a team of impressive television professionals including Tim Emmanuel, John Edwards and Willie Wilks have convinced me that they stand a very good chance indeed of ousting the present franchise holder HTV and picking up this very lucrative contract. We take 19.2 per cent of the equity in their company, C3WW, and I join their board as a non-executive Director. This is, at first blush, in contradiction to TSW's declared policy of only bidding for its own South-West area licence, but we justify it on the grounds that it is no more than an investment opportunity. We are 'punting' £150,000 up front. This is not too painful an exposure for the company and any guilt we might have felt at pitching against our neighbour HTV is assuaged by the knowledge that they too have actively considered joining a group to take a run at us. All's fair in love, sex and television franchises.

My non-executive directorship with C3WW is not as tranquil as I first anticipated. As a major shareholder we offer to help raise the rest of the investment capital. I am also conscious of the fact that if they win we will have to stump up another £5 million. The fundraising is led by Barclay's de Zoete Wedd and before long I am exposed to the unreal world of corporate finance and venture capital. 'Mezzanine venture capitalist' is a gross misnomer. Most of those I meet are more cautious than a bunch of actuaries and about as voluble as Trappist monks. I look in vain for a sense of dash or daring. There is none. The City is a grey, unexciting place where in corporate boardrooms panelled with old ship's timbers nursery food is served in an atmosphere reminiscent of ancient British public schools.

At C3WW Lord Morris, a Welsh academic, conducts board meetings like Mussolini, speaking in clipped, no nonsense tones and not allowing any extraneous waffle. He is also obsessed that no meeting, not even the Security Council of the United Nations, should last more than two hours. This is in stark contrast to TSW's board meetings where Sir Brian encourages all directors to say their piece even if the meeting runs to five hours or more.

As a damp spring turns into a wet summer, press speculation over the ITV licence bids starts to boil over. July and August are not good 'news' months for the newspapers and editors are anxious to fan any story, however slight, into a blazing 'issue of the day'. One reporter, however, trumps all his colleagues in the pursuit of the ITV licence 'hare'. He is Ray Snoddy of the *Financial Times*. Ray is a softly spoken Irishman cast in the traditional investigative journalist role.

Slightly built, faintly academic in appearance and bespectacled, Ray doesn't *look* like a reporter even though for a season he fronts Channel Four's *Hard News* programme.

In July Ray runs a piece on the front page of the company news section in the *Financial Times*. It states in bald terms: 'TVS bid £55 million a year to retain television franchise'. In the accompanying text there is no qualifying 'it is believed' or 'sources close to the top have indicated'. None of that pussy-footing shit. What Ray writes is, effectively, 'TVS *has* bid £55 million a year to retain its *commercial* television franchise.'

The effect of Ray's piece is explosive. Is it true? How did he get hold of the information? Who is leaking? TVS's executives' lips are sealed. But rivals for the TVS franchise howl in dismay: 'Such a bid is not sustainable.' The furore has scarcely died down when Ray runs another piece, this time about the North-West franchise. Once again the headline is unequivocal: 'Television rival outbids Granada'. Ray's following piece claims that North-West Television, a consortium including Mr Phil Redmond's Mersey Television *and* Yorkshire Television, has bid £35 million a year for the licence to broadcast in North-West England. They have outbid Granada, one of Britain's oldest commercial television companies, by more than £15 million.

Phil Redmond is an independent producer who makes the *Brookside* serial for Channel Four. If North-West get through to the final stage, Granada's only chance of survival will be if the ITC decides there are 'exceptional circumstances' that would justify setting aside the highest cash bid.

Shock, horror, palpitations and damp trousers in Manchester and Brompton Road. Just what is Ray Snoddy playing at? It certainly isn't cricket. Mind you, grumble some around the ITVA Council table, all Ray is trying to do is trash the whole licence award system and force the ITC to show their hand early, rather than wait until October. But Brompton Road is not to be cajoled or panicked in this way. Stiff upper lips are the order of the day. Indeed the existing ITV companies are all in *purdah* and cannot socialise with ITC

170

officials in case rivals smell 'favouritism' towards the incumbents.

Back in June at the screen advertising festival held in the South of France, Frank Willis, ITC's Head of Advertising Control, refuses TSW's invitation to lunch at the Colombe d'Or in St Paul de Vence because, as he wittily puts it in a faxed reply to Martin Bowley, my Sales Director: 'I know that if I did accept, the Editor of *Broadcast*, the Director General's aunt and the Head of ITC Personnel would be bound to be sitting at the next table'.

More Snoddy revelations follow in quick succession. It is now obvious that Ray has got an inside track on really hot information and intends to break a new 'franchise' story every week. 'HTV outbids rivals with £20 million plus' scream the headlines. At C3WW we are not too downcast because we have bid close to this at £18 million and believe our *quality* will see us through to victory. 'Central Television bid only £1 million to retain franchise. There are no other bidders.' Scottish and Border are likewise unopposed, and as the *Financial Times* put it: 'Row looms over television share prices'.

It is clear that the Stock Exchange is getting some stick from analysts, merchant bankers and television companies who are all concerned over the way television company shares have reacted to the reports in the *Financial Times* giving details of the various franchise bids.

The Exchange has been in touch with ITV Chief Executives seeking assurances that the companies themselves have not leaked details of the bids and thus broken Stock Exchange rules. They receive such assurances and decide there is no basis for declaring a false market in television company shares. This *in spite* of Central Television's price rise of 26 per cent (up to 790 pence) and Scottish Television's hike of 45 per cent (up to 500 pence). It is clear however that without formal confirmation of the size of the various bids the market in television shares has become something of a lottery.

One merchant banker advising a television company describes what is happening as 'farcical, but predictable'. He

171

argues that it is inevitable that leaks would occur and share prices react. The television industry is notorious for gossip and soul-searching and nothing that has occurred is really so outrageous.

A few days later Ray Snoddy phones me in Plymouth and tries to draw me on the size of TSW's bid. Here I observe a master at work. Ray has a beguiling, soft Irish brogue and can deduce more from a silence or a 'no comment' than most other journalists can from reading a printed document. We fence verbally for a while and it is clear to me that Ray is very close indeed to guessing what our bid is. He also contacts our rivals and teases out a few more snippets of information about their bids. Nothing specific. But enough for Detective Inspector Snoddy to fit together the jigsaw pieces and run an article in the *Financial Times* that says: 'TSW follows ITV trend with £16 million franchise bid'.

We decide at TSW that our best tactic is to neither confirm nor deny Ray's story. Indeed we have been advised by our stockbrokers, Rowe Dartington, that this is our *only* course of action. Our share price moves up a penny to 86 pence.

Ray runs a 'round-up' piece in the Saturday edition of the *Financial Times* on 20 July which is headlined: 'The Great Television Lottery'. In it Ray comments on the weakness of the government's tendering system. It is 'capricious' says Ray and nobody would disagree with him. He concludes the piece by declaring:

George Russell, Chairman of the ITC has been given the power to turn a misconceived Government policy that few now support into a system that might prove workable.

Many in the Industry now believe that it is time to remove some of the uncertainty by bringing all the bids into the public domain so that there can be sensible debate about whether the sums of money involved can be reconciled with the production of quality programmes. It might not add up to the better way Lord Thomson sought. It might however, make the awarding of franchises a

172

little less secretive – though no less subjective – than last time.

On 21 July, the day after Ray Snoddy's round-up piece, *The Sunday Times* jumps onto the bandwagon with a full-page business focus article written by Margaret Park. A league table of estimated bids is published showing who is tipped to win and which incumbents are in danger of being unseated. The latter present a surprising list: Grampian (rumoured to be out-bid by North of Scotland Television by a mere £600,000); Bruce Gyngell's TVAM are said to have bid a lowish £30 million against both Daybreak at £34 million and Sunrise at £35 million. Bruce remains defiant and when I phone him he says,

'Fuck them. If I lose I'm closing the station.'

Perhaps the biggest shock is to see that Thames, the biggest ITV company in Britain, is likely to have been outbid by Carlton Television at £53 million. The Thames bid is rumoured to be £50–£52 million. The third bidder, CPV-TV, are not rated as serious even though they have put £58 million on the table. All the other incumbents including TSW are now hot favourites to win.

Margaret Park's long article finishes with the following: 'Excluding advertising revenue, in 1993 the Government is limbering up to collect at least £300 million – a sum which could justify the whole controversial auction process very nicely'. I think, 'Shit! Who is this woman kidding?' £300 million to those faceless bureaucrats in the treasury means £300 million less to spend on programmes. It confirms my long-held belief that all taxation is theft and that governments are great, lumbering, insensitive monoliths who understand little and care even less.

Back in Plymouth my staff are getting understandably edgy and rumours are beginning to bubble up from canteen and studio floor. Have we bid too much? Is there any truth in the story that we've got company money in BCCI? I decide to send all staff in London, Plymouth and Bristol a note which I reproduce here.

173

You will have seen speculation in the Press about the various bids claimed to have been made for Channel Three licences.

I have to tell you that the bids must remain confidential and it is worth remembering that the final decision will be in the hands of the ITC and not the press!

As a public company, with a legal responsibility to our shareholders, we are not permitted to comment on TSW's bid before our shareholders are officially informed, but I can tell you that our bid was arrived at after a most comprehensive and extensive analysis by our Financial Advisers including N. W. Rothschild, Ernst & Young and National Economic Research Associates.

You may wish to note a further few points of interest:

1 All the bids are expressed in 1993 prices and are tax allowable. TSW's bid was based on sound business principles.
2 TSW will not be paying levy at the rate of £2 million annually in 1993.
3 TSW will not be subscribing nearly £5 million annually to Channel Four in 1993.
4 TSW, along with the other smaller companies, will enjoy substantial discounts on Network Programme Supply in 1993 (£2 million annually less than we pay now).
5 TSW has already reduced its operational cost base by well over £1 million annually.

Finally let me assure you that the bid we have made was designed to fulfil our long-term objectives of providing a proper return to our shareholders and maintaining a quality television service to the viewers of the South-West. Although speculation may continue in the press we must all be patient until the ITC make their final announcement.

I also enclose a chart which shows the current 'bid' situation based on press 'estimates' and information published in the ITC Application Document and also by the ITVA. 'PQR' stands for Percentage of Qualifying Revenue – the 'fixed' element of the bid.

At the end of July I fly on holiday to my villa in Spain. As I leave Gatwick it is grey, cold and raining and Carolyn and I are looking forward to a week of uninterrupted sunshine by our poolside. My sister and brother-in-law are house guests and we plan to eat, sleep, sunbathe, read and swim.

On the fifth day however my PA, Gilly, phones to tell me that *Broadcast* magazine and the *Observer* newspaper have both run stories about the TSW licence bid. They suggest that if we have bid £16 million plus we are unlikely to make a profit for the first few years of the new franchise period.

I am relaxed. This is exactly what I have warned colleagues will happen. People will try to trash our bid and unsettle our institutional shareholders. There are assholes in every walk of life and they are thick on the ground when lucrative television franchises are up for grabs.

I speak to Ivor Stolliday, my Company Secretary, but he is far from relaxed. But this too is not unusual. Ivor, a most talented executive, is permanently wound up like a coiled spring. He has spoken to our lawyers who advise him that the two articles may be damaging. 'Malicious misinformation' are the words used by the solicitor Ivor consults with. Ivor suggests we snap off a quick letter to both *Broadcast* and the *Observer* to act as a warning shot. I agree, but without enthusiasm. Nobody knows the *basis* on which we have made our bid except *us* and the ITC. Everybody else, Ray Snoddy and the Pope included, are basing their conclusions on incomplete data.

I go back to my pool and plunge in. London and Plymouth seem a long way off and I am not surprised to hear from Ivor that it is pissing with rain in Plymouth. Why does this information please me so?

Sitting by the side of my pool at 7.30 p.m. with a gin and tonic in my hand, the sun is still strong and high with temperatures in the early eighties. To my right is a mountain range running like huge, jagged teeth along the skyline. To the left at the bottom of the hill I can see the azure sheen of the Mediterranean. Do I relish getting back to the cut and thrust of commercial television in Plymouth and London? Take a wild guess. It's not just that the business is going through a major advertising recession with our revenues well down, but I have come to the considered conclusion that I have enjoyed the best of the golden years.

A lot of sheer fun has gone out of the business. This is the age, not of the creative man or even the huckster. This is the age of the grey people. Accountants. Lawyers. Analysts. John Major. None of whom are likely to inspire me to bust a gut for abstract principles.

Certainly I want to see TSW win its new licence. I intend to see it through until victory is confirmed. And then? Who knows? Spanish sunshine and good wine tend to unglue the mind a little. I am 56. Do I want to flog on as Managing Director until I'm 60? If I quit early I still have a pension and I've managed to save a few thousand. I'm not rich. I'm very comfortable. But am I going soft? Sliding into the abyss reserved exclusively for old farts in check slippers and beige cardigans?

I pour a second gin and tonic and decide to put such profound thoughts on the back burner. The sun is dipping now and a flock of tiny martins are swooping low over my swimming pool. They skim the water's surface and allow their wings to gather a few cooling drops before soaring up above the trees and vanishing. What do these elegant little creatures know of the burdens we humans create for ourselves? And if they did know would they give a shit? I think not.

Tonight, I decide, we shall dine out at Tiberio along the coast near Marbella and I shall not utter another word about franchises, television or lawyers. Not until I get back to England, a thousand years from now, in three days time!

In spite of being the silly season as far as newspapers are concerned, stories about the size of Channel 3 bids continue to bubble to the surface. It is as if the editors of the national press have formed a coven and sent out a joint directive to all journalists: 'For God's sake keep the franchise story alive'.

176

Considering the yawning spaces that must confront them each day, the editors cannot be blamed too much.

It is only the historic events in Moscow over those 48 amazing hours in August when Gorbachov is ousted and then reinstated that drives the franchise stories from the news pages. Up until then speculation, rumour and hysterical half-truths bounce off the walls of Fleet Street with machine-gun rapidity.

Phil Redmond threatens legal action against the ITC should it invoke the 'exceptional circumstances' clause and award the Granada licence to a lower bidder.

Tory MPs, stirred from their summer lethargy are reputed to be alarmed at the size of the bids being submitted for Channel 3 licences and plan to lobby the Treasury to reduce the levy on the companies. Fat chance, I think. The horse has long bolted and the stable door gapes. David Mellor, Chief Secretary to the Treasury is mentioned as a potentially sympathetic ally. Excitement mounts. Then collapses. Stuart Prebble, Head of Regional Programmes at Granada says, 'I can't think of a worse way to allocate franchises'.

I can. How about a blindfold and a rusty pin?

Bruce Gyngell, my chum at TVAM, appears to be reconsidering his threat to close the station if he loses. Now, it is said, he will pitch for a Channel 5 licence instead. Philip Carse, one of NERA Communications' consultants fires off a letter to the *Financial Times* on 19 August 1991 which suggests that the Fleet Street commentators have got it all wrong. The bids that are being criticised are not so outrageous after all. 'Over the ten-year period 1990 to 2000,' he writes, 'we expect real advertising revenue growth to average 5.1 per cent a year. This compares with an average of 6.2 per cent a year for 1980 to 1990 and 9.4 per cent a year for the "boom" period of 1982 to 1988.'

Leslie Hill, Central's ex-accountant Chief Executive is described as either the luckiest or bravest man in the country. His unopposed bid is now reported to be £2,000 a year! I send him a short note: 'Only a fiver a day, Leslie. You lucky sod!' I enclose a Gus Honeybun puppet which he says he will keep on his drinks cabinet at home.

177

Stockbroker James Capel issues a sombre statement suggesting that advertising growth will be very low in the 1990s. What, I ask myself, the hell do they know about it? I lunch at Orso's in Covent Garden with the delectable Jane Thynne, Media Correspondent on the *Daily Telegraph*, but even her skill and glamorous charm fail to prise any information from me about the size of TSW's bid. My lips are sealed save for the ingestion of pasta and champagne.

Other executives inside ITV say that analysts have failed to grasp the likely impact of economic recovery by using forecasts gleaned from 'dubious' or 'bucketshop' operators as their flawed basis for making revenue projections. I share this view and say so. Frequently. A number of ITV companies, including my own, announce pay freezes to a muted, but nonetheless unhappy reaction from the unions. Bruce Gyngell allows himself to be interviewed by the chief female Rottweiler, Lyn Barber, in the *Sunday Independent*. While not exactly a hatchet job it is an acerbic piece which majors on Bruce's eccentricities: Buddhism, macrobiotics, Shiatsu massage, the Japanese technique of visual diagnosis called Bo Shin. The *Daily Express* picks up the theme and runs a piece which is headlined: 'Three In A Tub Plunge Changed Television Boss's Life'.

I think, ye gods and little fishes, what will the press make of it if they learn that I once smoked pot in California? The fact that the experience was about as uplifting as having your sinuses drained will be neither here nor there.

As these and other stories pop and fizzle in the national press I prepare for a short visit to America. I am due in New York, Los Angeles and Florida at the end of August where my American friends will no doubt ask me to explain just what is going on in the British television industry. I know this will be difficult, if not impossible. To observers on the other side of the Atlantic we must appear to have gone barking mad.

Just as we are resigning ourselves to another wet, windy and disappointing English summer the sun bursts out and a mini-heatwave engulfs London. With less than a week left in August we are still grateful for this meteorological bonus.

White-limbed office workers throng Hyde Park, while Australian visitors in repulsive shorts and silly hats waddle oafishly in Knightsbridge. Cars overheat and stall. Arabs invade Harrods and snaffle the late summer bargains – a 60-piece set of china goes for a mere five grand. An exquisite silliness hangs over the City and four days before I fly to New York I lunch with one of my favourite clients, Barry O'Connell, boss of KP Foods. We eat at Barry's club, Mosimanns in Belgravia, and the conversation moves inexorably from sex and fast cars to what is happening to the British commercial television industry. I remind Barry that one of the prime factors in persuading Mrs Thatcher and her Tory cabinet to impose the 'blind auction' system of awarding television licences was the advertisers' lobby. It was they, through their Trade Association, The Incorporated Society of British Advertisers (ISBA), who demanded the break-up of the old ITV monopoly, more choice for advertisers, competition red in tooth and claw and all the rest of it. What they are likely to get is not necessarily going to be entirely to their liking: a weakened network, fragmentation of audiences and over £300 million a year that could be spent on programmes being siphoned off to the Treasury.

During the drive home that evening I find my mind reflecting on the changes and convulsions that ITV has endured in recent years. What was once a settled and successful part of the British broadcasting landscape is now a destabilised plaything of itinerant politicians who, having successfully kicked the industry in the groin now leave it to a hard-pressed ITC to act as nursemaid. George Russell, it is clear, has been told to make a silk purse not out of a sow's ear, but a horse's ass.

George is a clever bloke, but getting the blind auction deal to work to the satisfaction of all parties would tax the intellect of Socrates. To an intelligent visitor from Mars, the running of a successful television operation in a market economy would seem straightforward enough. Programmes would rise or fall on their acceptability or otherwise to their audiences. Allowing for a balance to be struck between the 'public service broadcasting' ethic and raw commercialism it would be

179

relatively easy to assume that the industry would be demand-led and service orientated. What has happened over the past few decades of course, is that a patina of unreality, protectionism and government meddling have turned the industry into a hydra-headed mutant. It is neither fish, fowl or unicorn.

Back in the golden 1950s, when Lew Grade still had hair and Michael Grade wouldn't have known the difference between a schedule and a back number of the *Beano*, things were all rather British and secretive. The government quango, the ITA, was composed almost entirely of light-viewing, middle-class academics, civil servants and token trade unionists. The latter being chosen specifically for their intellectual dullness and supposed 'common' touch. Forelock tugging to the mandarins in Whitehall was the order of the day, but after a dodgy start the lucky contractors appointed by the ITA began to demonstrate that, given a regional monopoly to sell advertising airtime, you could make a lot of money.

Roy Thomson, the pear-shaped Canadian with a stunningly low taste in popular television programmes even coined a famous phrase that was to hang around the neck of the industry like an albatross for years to come. 'A licence to print money'. How quaint it sounds in 1991.

By 1967 the mood had changed. But the ITA's deliberations remained clandestine. They discussed in secret and they disposed their largesse like a medieval Pope issuing decrees from the Vatican. The odd Labour politico suggested that the procedure for dishing out lucrative television franchises might be a bit more open, a bit more democratic, but this view was not popular with one of the most disastrous Postmaster-Generals in the history of the known universe, one Edward Short – a man so grey and boring as to make our own John Major seem like Liberace on speed by comparison. Then there was the famous LWT fiasco when the ailing station had to be rescued by Rupert Murdoch, already a man regarded by Labour MPs as having a tail and a pair of horns.

Various nostrums were wheeled out by politicians who watched aghast as the genie of commercialism, now out of the bottle, refused to be stuffed back in again. A television levy of 11 per cent was whacked on. And then taken off. There was the Pilkington Report, a fairly useless document that proposed little that was practical. Indeed my then Chairman, Peter Cadbury, burnt an effigy of the wretched Pilkington on a bonfire in his garden. But we still got BBC2 on Pilkington's recommendations.

There was also the Crawford Report, but like the Schleswig-Holstein question only three people understood it and they are either all dead or mad. Advertisers began to rumble about the abuse of monopoly until the famed Annan Report declared that the 'bushy tailed' sales teams within the companies were preferable to some centralised, bureaucratic selling organisation.

And of course we had Peacock. Sir Alan's committee once again plucked the squawking ITV chicken out of its hen-house and examined its entrails. By now, those of us in the industry were hardened to these regular examinations. But in spite of it all, in spite of the overmanning and the Spanish customs and the tendency to become complacent, the commercial companies served their audiences *and* their advertisers pretty well. There are household brand names on shelves throughout the country that have made fortunes for their manufacturers *only* because they advertised on television. The medium has been an indispensable tool to very many blue chip companies in this country and they display hypocrisy of a high order when they whinge and criticise it.

Throughout the tumult of the 1970s and the 1980s the ITV companies grew more sophisticated, virtually all of them becoming plcs with quotations on the Stock Exchange. This itself has changed the culture of the industry. Some would say for the worse – but only history can be the judge of that. Regionalism has survived and I take some share of the credit for this, as during the great 'White Paper' debate of the middle-1980s there were many who saw federalism and the 15 companies as a wasteful duplication of resources and something that mitigated against an ITV network acting in unison against the BBC. I spoke on public platforms and argued that freedom of choice would best be served by pluralism and that

181

a move towards say, six large mega-regions would not be in the public interest. It would also, I maintained, present the advertisers with another quasi-monopoly in disguise. It was in the commercial interest of the big manufacturing companies represented by the ISBA to have 15 regions. The ISBA agreed, much to my surprise and relief, but the advertising agencies through their Trade Association weren't so sure.

These thoughts bounce about in my head as I pack my suitcase for the Sunday flight to New York. My defence of regionalism is not universally popular, particularly with the exponents of the 'economic inevitability of bigger units' school of thought. History, they tell me, is on their side.

The acerbic William Phillips writing in the erudite and obscure *ADMAP* magazine in August not only doesn't like regionalism, he positively abhors it: 'The curse of regionalism has cast a long shadow', he writes, 'loading superfluous costs on an unnecessary number of companies and forcing them to fight their own corners to the detriment of Network co-ordination'. Well, William, it's a point of view. By 1994 we shall see just how robust the regional concept is when the moratorium on take-overs is lifted. What do I think? Very sadly, and reluctantly, I think that wholly *independent* regional television will indeed disappear. Avaricious conglomerates, benign European media moguls and the sheer pressure of extraterrestrial competition will all hasten its demise. If demise is too harsh a word, then let me put it another way.

The very smallest regional companies, if they are to survive at all, will need to be part of much larger groups who themselves have access to resources and markets on a grand economic scale. My romantic dream of diversity and choice shattered? No, not entirely. A form of regionalism can emerge from this future scenario, but in a different form. It depends of course whether the big company umbrella beneath which it shelters is held by a cynic or a believer. Will my company, TSW, for example, still be recognisable *as* TSW in the year 2002? Don't hold your breath.

As we arrive in New York the temperatures hit the middle

182

eighties. The traffic is horrendous and the state of the roads in central Manhattan is worse than in a banana republic.

During my brief forays along Madison Avenue to visit old friends in the J. Walter Thompson advertising agency, I am struck by how up to date they all are on the latest news about British television. The consensus seems to be that we are a mirror of what has already happened to the networks in America. I protest that it is unreasonable to draw so close a parallel, but the evidence is chilling. The changes wrought by the Broadcasting Act, plus the blind auction, increased competition and all the rest, are going to hit British television a sharp blow in the solar plexus. My friends sketch a devastating scenario, reminding me of the way in which ABC, CBS and NBC have been affected by competition and more alarmingly, by their long-standing complacency and belief that they were unassailable. The big three have seen a rollercoaster nosedive in their audience share and their revenues. About 12 years ago they could claim 90 per cent of the nightly viewing. In 1991 they have lost a third of this audience and their collective profits have slumped from $800 million in 1984 to $400 million in 1988, with latest forecasts suggesting only a break even position in 1991/92.

The average American home now has over 30 channels to choose from and VCRs are in about 68 per cent of all homes. Murdoch's Fox Network, once laughed off as an upstart adventurer, now programmes five nights a week. There are video stores in every neighbourhood and the exercise of consumer choice is devastating the network's ratings. In the last week of August 1991 the *highest* network rating was a nine (per cent). It's only a few years ago that a network commercial screened in prime time would cost $450,000 for just one transmission. Now the salesmen have their backs to the wall and are forced to deal. The buyers in the big advertising agencies and the specialist media shops are scenting blood and going for the network's jugulars.

These facts are startling enough, but another piece of evidence alarms me even more. After decades of stability, all three network companies have new owners. CBS, NBC and

ABC are now all part of huge conglomerates who do not share the old 'pursuit of programming excellence' philosophy. They are run by hard-nosed, granite-faced money men who have already ruthlessly pruned staff and slashed costs to the bone. Television is just another product. A washing machine with pictures. The talk in the boardrooms of the big three is now more about the bottom line and how to increase the value of shareholders' investments rather than the quality of the programmes to be transmitted.

That will be the pattern in Britain by the mid-1990s, my American friends tell me. But a lot of our troubles are self-inflicted, or at least government inflicted. They voice a further warning: once British television is snatched from the hands of television professionals and becomes the property of accountants and financiers its quality will slide inexorably downmarket. This doom-laden prognosis lowers my spirits somewhat and even a dinner of salmon caviar and blinis at the Russian Tea Rooms doesn't evaporate my forebodings.

Three days later we fly to Los Angeles where I plan to talk with friends in advertising and broadcasting to see whether the Californian climate inclines them to take a more sanguine view of the future. Arriving at the fabulous Bel Air hotel, nestling among palm trees and tropical gardens, I feel my spirits rise again. California is synonymous with optimism and hope. Everybody here seems to believe that whatever it is you want in life, you should just get up and 'go for it!' The sun shines brightly, the pool shimmers and the Napa Valley Chardonnay is chilled to perfection. As I settle onto my lounger to plan the week ahead, poolside telephone at the ready, I spot the American actress, Elaine Stritch, on the small terrace of her room alongside the pool. She is reading aloud from a fat script and even though she reads more or less to herself those gravel tones are unmistakable. This is Hollywood. I am probably the only person around the pool who I don't recognise. All the others are clearly bit part players from various television mini-series. Surely that man with the hairy shoulder blades and the solid-gold Rolex was a policeman in the last *Kojak* series? What the hell. I telephone my friend,

Judy Kauffman, who was, until recently, a drama producer for the Grundy Organisation and we agree to meet for dinner tomorrow at L'Orangerie, one of LA's most fashionable restaurants where to be seen is everything. The food's not bad either, although most Los Angelenos are on a diet and think nothing of paying $50 for a plate of salad and a glass of Perrier.

I also contact Brian Fernee who runs the media independent, RNF. Brian is an Englishman who has lived in Los Angeles for 27 years although there is no trace of Americanism in either his accent or his appearance. He is also an ex-colleague of mine from schooldays when we were both at Sloane Grammar in Chelsea. Brian shares his New York colleagues' apprehension about the future of British television – news of the impending bids and the speculation surrounding them is actually discussed at smart dinner parties in west Los Angeles and Malibu.

Only that morning, Brian Fernee tells me, he sat in on a sales presentation by CBS, and talk of 'deals', 'extra spots' and 'sweeteners' is now standard practice. Brian has a media-man's theory. It goes like this, when the broadcast business becomes a buyer's market (as opposed to a *seller's*), what follows is a downgrading of programme quality. The link is a touch tenuous, but if you think about it, not too outrageous. A buyer's market means downward pressure on prices and this leads to falling revenues for the networks and thus less money to spend on programmes. The problem is the time-lag – investment in next year's schedule should begin *now* – but if money is tight and the bottom line under threat the seedcorn cash for the future is raided as a short-term expedient. As a Chief Executive I am familiar with such pressures.

Brian suggests lunch and we go to 'Eureka', Wolfgang Puck's new west Los Angeles bistro which is a converted brewery. The alterations and decor are reputed to have cost $3 million, but the place looks like a rivet factory. Big metal studs are dotted along strips of chrome and what I take to be ruthlessly modern paintings hang on the high walls. One of these pictures depicts a leaking bucket and stands about ten feet tall.

The paint appears to have been hurled at the canvas by a blind-folded chimpanzee with a dubious sense of direction. Great globules of colour hang like dew from the frame, some of them spilling onto the wall beneath. I say nothing. As a visiting Englishman, the smallest hint of criticism will see me torn limb from limb by excruciatingly fashionable young waiters with razored haircuts and triple earrings. The food is okay. What can go wrong with a vegetable pizza?

After lunch Brian suggests, somewhat unenthusiastically, that I might wish to see those parts of Los Angeles that have been 'captured' by the 'crack' kings and roaming Hispanic gangs. I decline. I have a better chance of staying alive if I go back into the restaurant and criticise the paintings. In the event we do neither, but agree to meet at a Hollywood party on Saturday where, it is promised, media moguls and other trend-setters will congregate.

Later that evening I talk with Judy Kauffman at L'Orangerie, another restaurant that has been decorated regardless of expense. This one however does not look like a rivet factory, more like a French nobleman's seventeenth-century town house. Our waiter, who is about 20, rattles through the menu, pouting. His hair has so much gel applied to it that it looks like patent leather. I try to order, but the pout increases. A ritual has to be observed before dinner is actually discussed. The waiter is going to tell us about his budding career as an actor. There is no escaping this ritual anywhere in Los Angeles. Here's why:

1 All waiters are either 'resting' actors or about to be actors.
2 All waiters have the advanced hearing commonly found in bats and can detect your whispered aside that you work in television.
3 If you work in television and eat in a Hollywood restaurant all the waiters will come and audition at your table.
4 If you ignore them they will tell you whatever you've ordered on the menu is 'off at this time' and pout.

5   After you have listened and made suitably amazed
    noises at being presented with the information that
    your waiter had a non-speaking part in *Popeye* – the
    self-same movie as Robin Williams – then and only
    then can dinner be ordered.

The food in L'Orangerie, when it comes, is outstanding. We
sip a ferociously expensive Chardonnay and talk about the
similarities between British and American television. Judy
Kauffman's views mirror those of all the other Americans I
have spoken with. She, like many Anglophiles, believes we
are heading for a diminution in quality and are in serious
danger of losing our commitment to the public service broadcasting ethic.

I am reminded of the little note I saw pinned up in the media
department of J. Walter Thompson in New York last week. It's
a direct quote by NBC's top executive, communications chief
Bud Rukeyser. It is a remarkably accurate, condensed summary
of what television is, or ought to be about. Its truth applies not
just to the United States, but to Britain as well:

'We do not have a tangible product, yet it is 'used' in
nearly every home in America every day; we buy programmes and sell audiences; we have regulatory con-
straints that many of our competitors do not; our
distribution system is dependent on affiliates who often
have a different business agenda from our own; we are
required by statute to serve the public interest yet every
home we serve has a different idea of what that interest
is; our main business is entertainment, yet we are the
primary source of news for most Americans and we are
the most widely covered by the press.

Later that night, after dinner, we have a nightcap in the
famous Polo Lounge at the Beverly Hills Hotel. It is filled
with women with skin the colour and texture of khaki vinyl
and lots of middle-aged men with their hair tied at the back
in little pigtails. A great deal of boasting is going on.

187

Telephones are being used like weapons, but the noise level in the bar is so high that the conversations must be meaningless. Our waiter, thank God, is old and sounds Polish. He serves our drinks without auditioning and I am so relieved I over-tip hugely. When we get back to our own hotel in Bel-Air, Brian Fernee phones to give us details of the Saturday night party and reveals, with an insouciant tremor in his voice, that somebody has nicked his Porsche from outside his house. This is such an everyday occurrence in Los Angeles that when I commiserate, Brian sounds surprised.

'It's either in Mexico now,' he explains, 'or in pieces for resale in East Los Angeles.' Such is life in LA-LA land.

People are still heavy television viewers in this town, but because they have so many channels to choose from their attention span is short and they tend to 'graze', rather than stay with one channel for any length of time. I notice that many shows are sectionalised into bite-size pieces so that the flickering loyalty of the viewer is not unduly pressurised.

Even the network news, which is usually excellent, goes for short items handled with briskness and urgency. The fashion of two anchors, one a middle-aged, white-haired male and the other a glossy female, often from an ethnic minority, is widespread. The result is a touch artificial. The man will have gravitas; a solid, all American, apple-pie quality about him. And a very deep voice. The female will be glamorous. Not necessarily pretty or even attractive. But she will have lots of hair and teeth. If she is Chinese or Vietnamese she will wear an embroidered silk kimono-type blouse. If she is black she will wear an expensive 'power' suit in either pinstripe or yellow linen. If she is white she will look as if she is just off to a hunt ball, with several kilograms of jangly jewellery. Whatever she is she will be groomed to within an inch of her life. Every skin surface will have been air-brushed, powdered, polished, tinted. Her lips will gleam with an unearthly light as if illuminated from within. Her hair will be the eighth wonder of the world. How do American women *grow* so much of the stuff? Do they use fertilisers? Or wigs? Perish the thought.

Perish the thought that may enter any fantasising middle-

188

aged man's mind that this is hair through which he might
lovingly run his fingers. Try that for real and you'll slice your
hand off at the wrist. This hair has been sprayed with a sort
of perfumed, aerosol concrete and is *sharp*. I mean *razor*
sharp. But these women are good at their work. They're quick,
they handle links between the anchor desk and an in the
field reporter with great skill. The men, although themselves
occasionally drawn to unnecessary blow-dried, bouffant hair-
styles are also good. They exude authority and are usually
very experienced journalists.

The weathermen however, are something else. Can you
imagine the BBC's Michael Fish rolling about on the studio
floor, clutching his throat, miming a drought? Or appearing in
sou'wester and oilskins and pouring a bucket of water over
himself? But of course there is one heck of a lot of weather
in the USA.

Our weather forecasts in Britain tend to be narrow, whingeing affairs with men who speak in the nasal tones of suburban insurance clerks. I have rather tended to support the view
that weather forecasts in Britain are largely a waste of time.
We all know it's going to be lousy. On those rare occasions
when the sun does shine we brace ourselves for the thundery
showers that inevitably follow, as a kind of Anglo-Saxon pun-
ishment for daring to have it so good.

Just before leaving Los Angeles to commence a brief vaca-
tion in Florida, I catch a late-night equivalent of the British
telethon on network television. The worthy cause is muscular
dystrophy and the main host is Jerry Lewis, the comedian. The
local supporting hosts however are grisly beyond imagination.
Clearly the producer has told them to play down the grinning,
upbeat style that is the norm for most game show comperes.
This show is serious. It's about sick people. And how to help
them. The male host therefore adopts a graveyard manner. His
voice trembles with emotion as he reads out the names of
viewers who have pledged money. What names! Miss Wendy
Bubash Campagnano has pledged $50! Mrs Randi Buffington
Mlotek has pledged $10! And Mrs Washington Snuck has
donated $30!

189

The female host, the weight of whose jewellery is threatening to bring her toppling in a heap on the studio floor has the shiny, fixed-tight expression that results from excessive face-lifts. She speaks in the unctuous tones once used by Mrs Thatcher before she had her voice fixed. Every word drips with pathos. It's a miracle she can complete a sentence without bursting into tears. When a small boy in a wheelchair comes onto the set to give her a cheque for $1,000 – collected from school chums – she goes into a spasm and for a moment I think she's going to snuff it in front of millions of viewers. But we are spared the harrowing spectacle. There is a brief moment of danger when one of her earrings, which are the size of tennis balls, swings perilously near the lad's head, but all is well. Just as I think the moment has passed she lunges forward, grabs the boy by the back of his neck and plants a mighty kiss on his lips. The boy looks as if he has been hit in the face with one of those rubber plungers used to unblock kitchen sinks. The hostess turns to the camera, eyes brimming and says, 'We'll be right back after these announcements.'

A Californian vignette.

It is Saturday night in Los Angeles and the temperature is still knocking 90 degrees. We are balancing plates of food on our laps at the spacious, Spanish-style apartment of Derek Rowlett, an Englishman who runs the pension fund for the Television and Movie Directors Trade Association. The fund is huge. Around $500 million. Rowlett, who is 60, is a London boy made good and plans eventually to retire to his home at Richmond, overlooking the Thames. He is a treasury of anecdotes about the movie business and how some directors resent having their fees docked by 7 per cent as a contribution to the pension fund.

'We are talking about guys who can earn *millions* of dollars a year,' he says.

A hot director in his thirties or forties, living in Beverly Hills and driving a Rolls Corniche hardly ever thinks about old age, or how he should provide for it. The conversation swings, as it always does at Hollywood parties, to wealth and conspicuous consumption.

190

'Have you seen Aaron Spelling's new house?' somebody asks me.

Spelling is the mega-rich television executive who brought *Dallas* to our screens. As it happens I had seen his house, a couple of years previously. It has become something of a *cause célèbre* and a talking point. Some regard it with awe. Others with disgust. Standing on a five-acre plot, the Spelling house occupies the site of Bing Crosby's old home – now torn down to make room for what I can only describe as a vulgar monstrosity of idiotic proportions. Nearly 58,000 square feet. Just to accommodate a family of four. From the outside, still heavily guarded by men and dogs while construction continues, it looks at first glance like a medium-sized hospital. As a private home it is entirely devoid of charm. But as older Angelenos point out, this over the top display of huge wealth is the last act in a decade of greed. Already there are rumblings at City Hall that such buildings should be subject to much tighter planning control. I mean to say, a single house that is *bigger* than a football field is a sign that whomsoever the gods wish to destroy, they first drive mad.

Apparently, early in 1991, a Japanese businessman offered $55 million for the house, uncompleted. Rumour has it that it will never be lived in, but just bought and sold as a curiosity. Spelling insists it's just a family home and he will live a simple life there. Just an ordinary Joe. If you believe that you will be the sort of person who thinks Dolly Parton is pigeon-chested.

A 25-minute drive from the Spelling house in Holmby Hills is downtown Los Angeles. Here in crumbling streets of unrelieved awfulness unemployed Hispanics and black families live in cardboard boxes on the sidewalk. Not just a few, but hundreds of them. Shops are gutted, burnt out or boarded up. A parked car will have its wheels removed and its upholstery stripped out within ten minutes of being left there by its owner. An hour away at Malibu, film stars employ lawyers to argue that $5 million for a single movie is no longer acceptable. The contrasts in this town are so vast, so indefensible as to stun the imagination. Television only scratches the surface

191

because most middle-class Angelenos prefer to ignore the festering Third World tide that may one day soon engulf them.

We talk television. The Public Service Broadcasting System (PBS) in America runs a lot of British shows. We are still synonymous with 'quality' and flattering though this is there is no denying the sheer commercial energy of many American products. More than occasionally however your toes curl with embarrassment at what comes tumbling out of the screen at you. I tell my American friends at the Rowlett party that I could scarcely believe the latest 'entertainment' show being trailed by veteran broadcaster, Donaghue. It's called *Grudge Match* and in it people who have a genuine dislike of each other, or some piffling domestic dispute, slug it out in a boxing ring with outsize gloves or wrestle in overripe melons in a plastic bin, or wear huge rubber tyres around their waists and bump each other until one of them collapses. There is a fat referee with a falsetto voice, two judges in tuxedos and an audience of screaming, unbelievably ugly people who stamp and whistle and emote throughout the whole diabolical proceedings.

'It's only a step removed from *It's A Knockout*,' says one Angeleno, defensively.

Well it's another point of view. I try to imagine it transferring to regional television in Britain. 'And tonight folks we have Mrs Enid Trembling of Plymouth who is being driven crazy by her neighbour Mrs Beryl Brusque who plays her Des O'Connor tapes way into the small hours. Tonight in the Plymouth Pavilions the two ladies will face each other in a vat of warm marmalade, blindfolded, and engage combat with rubber brooms, rotten apples and mud pies. Your celebrity judges for tonight will be Bruce Forsyth and Barbara Windsor!' Is *this* the shape of things to come? Who knows. Nobody went broke yet by underestimating the awfulness of mass public taste.

If Los Angeles is a city of contrasts between rich and poor then the State of Florida demonstrates this phenomenon in spades. Our first port of call is Palm Beach. I had been told it was a playground of the rich. The Kennedys keep a place

192

here, as do the reputed princes of the Mafia. We arrive at August end, out of season it transpires, and the weather is oppressively humid. The streets are exquisitely manicured. But empty. Our cab driver, a Hispanic with not a word of English, deposits us at the Colony Hotel. It is as silent as the grave. At first we assume we are the only guests, but no, there are at least four other people staying there. We take a walk down the famed Worth Avenue which is lined with Hermes, Gucci, Laura Ashley, Gap, Cartier, Ralph Lauren. We are the only people on the street. Later we take a cab to the equally famed Breakers Hotel. It is enormous. Utterly vast. Bigger than three Ritz's put together. About seven guests throng the one-acre lobby. Tiny lizards scamper over the outside lawns and we take coffee in the main restaurant. It is like sitting in the middle of a covered Wembley Stadium.

Afterwards we walk back to our hotel past huge, shuttered, silent mansions. On our left the Atlantic breakers crash and foam on a deserted beach. A Ferrari cruises past. Then a Bentley. We count eighteen lizards on the sidewalk during our walk back. This place, all of it, is clearly *closed*. But it is out of season we remind ourselves.

That night we eat in what appears to be the only restaurant open in town, Renato's. It is full of glossy people in expensive clothes and the food is excellent. A pianist plays Lloyd Webber discreetly in the background. Conscious of the American paranoia about smoking I deny myself my usual Havana in spite of ashtrays and matches being prominently displayed on the table.

Three days later we fly to Naples on the Gulf coast. Here we are to enjoy the supreme pleasures of the Ritz Carlton Hotel, a beautiful building which faces a huge beach and a tropical garden with waterfalls and the occasional pelican. We make contact with Mike and Noreen Chamberlain, old friends from England who now live in a huge, luxurious house in one of Naples' most exclusive districts. Mike is an ex-publisher of *Marketing Week* magazine and the man who organised some of the most successful television conferences held in Monte Carlo. Now rich and semi-retired at 43, Mike still does a certain amount of freelance work for ITN (he covered hurricane Hugo for them) and ILR. He admits over dinner that 43 is a bit young to be even semi-retired. We talk television and like most expatriate media men Mike is fascinated by the unfolding drama of British broadcasting. I ask him what he most misses about England during his self-imposed four-year tax exile. He ruminates for a moment and then replies,

'The changing seasons.'

We agree that when he does return to England the British television scene will have undergone its most dramatic upheaval since ITV first exploded onto our screens in the 1950s.

CHAPTER 17

*The IBA goes into a huddle to decide our fate.
Nasty omens on French TV and a phone call from
the clairvoyant Ray Snoddy of the* Financial
Times. *I unveil my own bollard in Hyde Park.*

Arriving back in London and picking up my first English
newspaper for two weeks, it is clear that the television franchise story is still rumbling on.

At the Edinburgh International Festival, David Elstein (now
Chief Executive Officer of Channel 5), then Thames Television's urbane Director of Programmes, has predicted network
chaos if one or more of the big five incumbents were to lose. He
adds darkly that this would also open the door to the BBC who
would 'swiftly establish an output deal which would secure it
such plums as *Blind Date*, *Coronation Street* and the *Darling
Buds of May*'. This doom-laden forecast is made more piquant
by the additional news that LWT may have been outbid by rivals
London Independent Broadcasting to the tune of £8 million. The
rumours are that they have stumped up £33 million to LWT's
reputed £25 million. Oh woe! Oh calamity! London is, or could
well be, burning – at least on Saturdays and Sundays.

TVS Chairman Rudolph Agnew, much criticised for his bid,
is threatening to close his station if he loses his franchise.
Shades of Bruce Gyngell at TVAM, I muse disconsolately.
Agnew also confirms that his £54 million bid was arrived at
not by the executives, but by the non-executive Directors
alone. Curiouser and curiouser.

TSW has not escaped unscathed or un-commented upon.
Various stories appear to have been 'planted' among journal-

ists attempting to cast aspersions on our bid. Every time my name is mentioned it is prefixed by the words 'ebullient', or 'flamboyant' or even 'cigar smoking'. Better I suppose than being referred to as 'ousted' like poor James Gatward or 'disgraced' like John Profumo.

How long do these labels stick? Forever it seems. What happens if I give up smoking or have a frontal lobotomy to remove my 'ebullience' section? The *Sunday Times* strikes the right note of irrelevance by featuring the fact that as a regular horse rider in Hyde Park I have had a bollard named after me in Rotten Row. The *Sun* newspaper, never one to ignore a bandwagon, particularly when it's rolling, manages to find space between breasts and buttocks to faintly ridicule the members of the ITC. The *Sun* however, does cause one to pause reflectively on this issue.

Ten worthy people, the board of the ITC, will decide the future of Channel 3, or ITV as we prefer to call it. Led by Chairman George Russell, ex-ITN Chairman and Geordie businessman, they are:

Jocelyn Stevens, Rector of the Royal College of Art
Pauline Mathias, ex-headmistress of a Catholic girls' school
Professor Sean Fulton, Vice-Chancellor of Queens University, Belfast
Lady Popplewell, Probation Service Chairman
The Earl of Dalkeith, landowner
Pranial Sheth, Asian lawyer
Eleri Wynne Jones, psychotherapist and professional Welshman
Professor James Ring, astronomer
Roy Goddard, business consultant

You can see the common touch shining through. The gritty credentials and down-to-earthness of all of them. Can you not? I acknowledge that these clever and successful people do have a huge responsibility on their hands. Awesome would not be too extreme a word to describe it.

I discuss this with Paul Stewart-Laing, my Director of Programmes, and we wonder mischievously if any of the distinguished members of the ITC inner sanctum actually *don't have* television sets! Wouldn't the *Sun* newspaper have a field day over that? More realistically, we ask ourselves just how much normal, domestic viewing at home takes place among ITC members. I hesitate to cast stones as it is a fact that most television executives within the industry are too busy chattering about television to actually switch on a set and watch the stuff.

Personally, I loathe *Coronation Street, EastEnders* and *Brookside*, not because they are unpopular television – they most certainly are not – but because the people they depict and the themes they explore bore me witless. American soaps on the other hand, while thin on plots and superficial on characterisation are at least aspirational. I never cease to be amazed that British viewers prefer to see mirror images of their own humdrum lives rather than anything else. Yes, we had *Through the Keyhole*, the voyeurs' guide to tasteless furniture, but that's about it, and *Keyhole* was not a soap. Or was it?

It is late September and England is embracing a balmy, Indian summer. After a fine day's racing at Haldon near Exeter sponsored by TSW, I drive to Cambridge for the Royal Television Society Convention. Everybody who is somebody in television is gathering in this magnificent city with its ancient, mellowed buildings, quadrangles and manicured lawns. The blue skies and bright sunlight belie the angst that simmers beneath the surface.

The ITC have already released a fragment of information about the date on which the franchise results will be announced.

'It will not be *before* the 14 October,' says David Glencross, the Director General. Beyond this his lips are sealed.

We dine on nursery food, but in the magnificent surroundings of King's College. The Great Hall smells of history and carbolic. The wine is undrinkable, but the buzz of 'insider' conversation is heady stuff indeed.

Michael Grade sits two long tables away from me, looking faintly flushed, as well he might. Only a few days previously he was roundly castigated for accepting an alleged 'golden handcuffs' payment of £500,000 from his employers, Channel Four. This largesse, it seems, is to prevent him being 'poached' by some franchise-hungry adventurer who needs to add lustre to his prospectus.

The *Sun* waxes apoplectic over the issue. 'Rich, isn't it,' the leader screams, 'that the man who presides over a television channel which invades our living rooms with blasphemy, profanity and homosexuality should be deemed so valuable.'

Michael, mistakenly in my view, exposes himself to a packed audience at the Convention and faces some of his critics. They include journalists Peter Fiddick, Maggie Brown of the *Independent*, Ray Snoddy of the *Financial Times* and a clutch of producers angry that their budgets have been slashed by the very man upon whose head these riches have been poured. It is an uncomfortable, bitchy session and achieves little except to expose glimpses of those most unlovely British characteristics, rancour, envy and sanctimoniousness.

Relieved to escape from this bear pit I saunter back to King's College from the Convention hall to keep my appointment with Nick Higham of the BBC who wishes to interview me for the BBC2 *Money Programme*. We conduct the interview from a wooden bench by the river while punts drift lazily past and late afternoon sun filters through the great trees fringing the park. With the slap of water and the ancient Serpentine Bridge in the background the atmosphere is almost Venetian.

Nick, not surprisingly, asks me a string of questions about our bid, which I stonewall, and about my views on takeovers, the post-1974 future and other esoteric matters. I chatter happily, but assume that at least 70 per cent of what is filmed will find itself on the 'cutting room floor'. It is of no great matter. At least my talking head will be seen against an elegant backdrop and not a bland studio set.

On Friday night, back in the great banqueting hall of King's, we eat another school dinner, this time nobly sponsored by Anglia Television. Steve Morrison, Granada's Director of Programmes and Woody Allen look-alike sits at my table and when the subject of an independent central scheduler comes up, we discuss the possible job specification for this new and hugely important role. It is clear, we agree, that if the present deadlock of networking is to be broken and the conflicts of interest negated, the person appointed will have to possess a cornucopia of outstanding qualities: skill, knowledge, creativity, diplomacy, ruthlessness.

For years the ITV network schedule has been the handiwork of five big company controllers (LWT, Thames, Central, Granada, Yorkshire). The conflicts of interest are glaring. The schedule is being constructed by men who are both buyers and sellers of programmes, and this for years has peeved those ten companies outside the magic circle. Even Greg Dyke, LWT's pyrotechnic Chief Executive admits publicly, on the Convention floor itself, that the old system of networking is unfair, secretive and cumbersome.

What sort of superman exists, I ask Steve Morrison, who could fulfil the job of central scheduler? He shrugs, toying with his rapidly congealing school dinner. I decide to prompt him.

'David Elstein of Thames?' I suggest, but this finds no favour with Steve.

'Definitely not the right person,' says he.

Sitting opposite, Charles Denton, an independent producer, pricks up his ears. 'Absolutely,' he chimes. 'Not the man. He would be opposed by the majority of controllers.'

They refuse to be drawn further in spite of my attempt to tease out more substantial reasoning behind their objections. A phrase from the past, describing the late Ian Macleod, springs to mind: 'Too clever by half'. Can this be the reason? The arrival of pudding guillotines further discussion.

I leave Cambridge early on Saturday for a wedding, but later learn that David Glencross of the ITC has challenged the government over their proposed plans for the ownership of ITN. Instead of forcing the 15 ITV companies to divest themselves of 51 per cent of the shares they hold, he urges that the system of 100 per cent ownership should be maintained. Not an easy one to win. The legislation could be modified I suppose, but to perform a complete volte-face is not a manoeuvre the government is famous for.

My memories of Cambridge are many and various. The magnificent buildings, the awful food, the fine weather, Leslie Hill's pale-blue suit (he approaches me at a cocktail party and asks 'Who is this, Georgio Armani?'), Melinda Whittstock of *The Times*, whose legs seem to go on forever, Sir Paul Fox, being described as a 'gold-plated dinosaur' by Barry Cox of LWT, Michael Grade, entering the arena like Androcles to face not just one lion with a thorn in its paw, but a whole pride of journalistic beasts all roaring for his blood. Success in this country is okay it seems, provided it is not richly rewarded. That would be just too un-British.

Finally, the keynote speech by Home Secretary Kenneth Baker on the evening of the first day. For emptiness, vacuity and evasiveness it ranks among the most dazzling of its genre. Here was a Minister, responsible for broadcasting, whose lack of knowledge about his subject bordered on the Himalayan. Perhaps, like his predecessors, he would not occupy that job for very long.

As September dribbles to a close I observe, from the eighth-floor windows of my Knightsbridge office, that the trees of Hyde Park are already touched by the faint patina of autumn. There is talk in London of the ITC's nervousness over the possibility of judicial reviews. Their nervousness is not misplaced. The spectre looms as many bidders for Channel 3 licences have indicated that they will challenge the ITC if they lose. Such challenges in the courts will seriously damage the smooth-flowing transition that the ITC have hoped for. It is also likely to be expensive in terms of legal fees.

Once again the sky grows dark with swooping lawyers, their beaks and claws glinting at the prospect of fresh carrion. Confusion and uncertainty will reign, with winning companies cautious about striking network deals with others whose tenure of licence is in doubt. Consultant Jonathan Davis, who has recently published a study of British television, claims 'in 1993 ITV's integrity could be completely compromised'.

ITC's David Glencross has already written to *The Times* making it clear that the Broadcasting Act has 'instructed the ITC to conduct a much more sophisticated exercise than opening the brown envelopes and identifying the highest cash bid for each licence'.

This is seen by many to be a warning shot. Opt for a judicial review at your peril, it seems to suggest, as all the ITC have to do in court is demonstrate to the judge that they have *followed the procedures* laid down in minute detail. The actual decision remains the gift of the Commission. It is also a timely reminder that the ITC's forefather (the IBA) never once lost a single case of judicial review.

The Economist magazine on 21 September summarises the problem as follows:

> If the commission were to invoke the clause to save Granada (which is thought to be outbid by Phil Redmond) or Thames (also thought to be outbid by Carlton), it would need, according to the Broadcasting Act, to explain that decision in detail. Any such argument would be deeply subjective. If one of the higher bidders sought judicial review – as both would probably do – it might try to persuade the court that the ITC had taken into account an irrelevant fact, failed to consider a relevant one or had acted unreasonably. Any of these would be grounds for a hearing; they might even be enough to win the case.

However, it is clear to most insiders that a losing incumbent from the present 15 contractors would wish to avoid a head-on clash with the ITC. Losing could be expensive and humiliating. There is also the 1994 watershed when the moratorium on take-overs ends. Why not wait until then and go for the jugular of the consortium that has ousted you?

With less than a month to go before 'F' day – or as purists might dub it, 'L' day, depending on whether you believe what is being handed out by the ITC is a franchise or a licence – I attend the opening gala of the spanking new Plymouth Pavilions. The Bournemouth Philharmonic climax their evening's performance with a robust version of the *1812 Overture*. Curiously, the programme is punctuated by two

201

short appearances from the Irish comedian Frank Carson. It is an uncomfortable fit, with Carson's routine more suitable for a night out with the boys.

Earlier, at the reception for VIPs I meet Dr David Owen and his wife Debbie. David Owen is one of our local MPs, for Plymouth and Devonport. We discuss his new book. Then in reply to my question, 'What will you do when you leave the House of Commons?' Dr Owen says,

'I'd like to be the Chairman of a large international company.'

So there. You have been warned.

Two weeks on and ITV executives everywhere are displaying signs of nervous exhaustion. Just when, precisely, are the ITC going to announce the winners of the franchise race?

On 3 October Ken Blyth, Secretary of the Commission writes to all ITV Managing Directors to inform them that on 11 October we will receive a fax message telling us the date on which the actual announcement will be made. It's like being half pregnant. I am baffled as to why we can't have a firm date. Last-minute second thoughts at Brompton Road perhaps?

It is as if every ounce of drama is to be squeezed out of these seemingly interminable October days. Once the results are known however, the press will have a field day. There may even be a few red faces among the more distinguished commentators. Only time will tell.

Lunch with James Gatward, now an ex-Chief Executive of TVS. He is remarkably un-bitter about his recent 'ousting'. James is a very talented producer and I cannot believe he will be idle for long. There is a brief flash of anger in his eyes when I mention his ouster-in-chief, Mr Agnew, the new Chairman of TVS.

'Not a television professional,' says James. 'Doesn't really understand the business. I mean, fancy letting the non-executive Directors decide the size of the franchise bid!'

I find no reason to disagree.

But the lurch towards 'gifted' amateurs as Chairmen is not a new phenomenon, although, thank God, ITV has so far been

202

spared having retired generals or admirals at the helm. Businessmen like Agnew are at least preferable to blimps. But, as in America, businessmen from industry or manufacturing tend to regard television as just another piece of merchandise. Its curious magic and its influence for good or evil seems to elude them. All that matters is the bottom line.

Bruce Gyngell of TVAM and his wife Kathy come to 'Four Acres' for dinner and we have a rollicking evening talking about ITV colleagues. Bruce is a total television professional and has probably more all-round experience than any other ITV Managing Director past or present. We both agree that much of the enjoyment and fun has been throttled out of the business. Those bloody accountants again.

It's Friday 11 October and we are down to the wire. We now know, for certain, that the ITC announcement for the Channel 3 licences will be issued by fax on Wednesday the 16th.

I am sitting in the Colombe d'Or in St Paul de Vence, alone and brooding. Outside it rains with Mediterranean ferocity. In the big dining room the air is heavy with thundery heat and I am gorging myself on roast chicken and ripe cheeses, washed down with house claret. This is the first booze I've taken in weeks as I'm on a sort of slimming kick. The atmosphere in this place is palpable – you could put your mouth on the ancient panelling and suck it out of the woodwork. This is the room in which I have laughed and cried for over 21 years. It is a special place. An original Picasso hangs above my head and to the right is a sketch by Matisse. They are probably worth more than the hotel itself. The room is full of people, mostly Americans, who don't know they are sitting in chairs that have been occupied by Chagall, Pissarro, James Baldwin, Frank Sinatra, Roger Moore and Graham Greene. Fifteen years ago I sat in this corner alone, writing, and Graham Greene himself admonished me for 'scribbling too quickly'. It was a magical moment.

I am here for MIP COM, the bi-annual programme market which takes place down in Cannes at the hideous Palais des Festivals. Two hours ago I received a fax from Gilly Hartley

203

in London with a copy of the ITC's ponderous announcement that on Wednesday the 16th:

A letter from the Chairman giving information in confidence about the outcome of each applicant's own application will be faxed to the applicant concerned on the fax number agreed.
This will be done shortly before 10.00 a.m.
At 10 a.m. precisely the awards will be announced at a press conference to accredited journalists only. Arrangements will be made, however, for the Chairman's statement and the subsequent proceedings to be relayed in sound and vision to the broadcasting gallery on the first floor at 70 Brompton Road.

It is nearly all over bar the shouting (and the weeping). And what a farce it has all been. What a waste of energy, time and treasure.

Earlier, I flew through vile, Wagnerian weather with Paul Stewart-Laing to France and we agree that the tension of waiting has at last got to us both. The Grundy organisation have invited us to a preview of their new mini-series *The Other Side of Paradise* at the Majestic Hotel. When I turn up at the party, only a few hours after landing at Nice airport, the room is full of delegates swilling free liquor and ramming little snacks down their throats. I realise I am late, having failed to change my watch to French time. Within ten minutes all the grub has vanished, not a potato crisp remaining. It is as if a swarm of locusts in designer suits have been let loose and told to take a crack at the world fast-eating record.

I see Hugh Davies of HTV, against whom we are bidding as a shareholder in C3WW. He calls me a bastard, but I know he doesn't mean it. He is Welsh after all and allowances must be made.

The Grundy programme is about men with lots of teeth and women with wobbly breasts, panting and exuding emotion in a Polynesian paradise. It looks a touch like *Neighbours* with volcanoes and Laura Ashley saris. It will probably spawn a

204

long-running series and make a few young Australian actors famous in spite of them having about as much talent as Kylie Minogue and Jason Donovan on tranquillisers.

But what am I saying? It must be the pre-franchise tension that's getting to me, boring a burning hole right through my body, in one side and out the other. It is Reg Grundy after all who has bought the television rights to 54 of my old short stories (most of them written in the days when I believed I could earn my entire living by my pen). What a *fool* I was.

I shall therefore revise my snap judgement of *The Other Side of Paradise*. It is a thoughtful mini-series that explores complex human emotions in a spectacular tropical setting. It is a tale of love and lust and triumph and tragedy. It will thrill audiences from Alice Springs to Buckland Monacorum and immeasurably enrich our store of self-awareness.

I am only here in France for three days as on Monday I have to fly back to London for Sir David Nicholas's leaving party at the Savoy. His ITN colleagues want him to have a rousing send-off in spite of recent difficulties. It promises to be an emotional occasion, and something of a historical land-mark as David's career as a television journalist has been a most distinguished one.

The party will be crammed with illustrious names from the world of politics and broadcasting and it is intriguing to specu-late that by Wednesday at 10.00 a.m. a number of those there may be contemplating early retirement themselves. The press, not unexpectedly, are working themselves up into a feeding frenzy and while I eat a solitary dinner in the Colombe d'Or I receive phone calls from the *Sunday Telegraph* and *The Sunday Times*, both of whom want quotes from me about the ITC announcement. I can think of absolutely nothing to say except the unprintable: 'About fucking time!'

And time is running out. My dreams are of Victorian hour-glasses with sand trickling through their slender waists. For the first time in 18 months I feel bone weary and depressed, as opposed to merely wired with tension.

It rains heavily on Saturday 12 October and Cannes is awash. MIP COM delegates scurry to and from their various

205

meetings in unsuitable clothes, talking in a multitude of tongues about the 'crazy British television auction'.

My old friend Jacques Sallebert who ran Tele-Monte Carlo in the 1970s once told me that in the view of the French, we Brits had a congenital propensity for self-mockery. The television franchise game, 1991 version, is a macabre celebration of that fine Anglo-Saxon quality.

On Saturday afternoon I attend a presentation by the Fox Network. It is surprisingly low-key for such an aggressive organisation: Rupert Murdoch, slated to appear in person, is holed up in New York with a bad back so we have to make do with Jamie Kellner, the President of their broadcasting division. He is a soft-spoken young American who unveils to us his proposals for 'global television programming' where the shows are 'manufactured' with the world audience in mind. The deal on offer is unusual. A network in, say, Spain, or the Netherlands, would receive a Fox mini-series or 'event' programme 'free', in return for surrendering 50 per cent of their commercial airtime in that show to Fox, who in turn would sell it to 'global' advertisers.

It is unworkable in England because airtime broking or bartering are still proscribed practices. But some time in the future? Who knows? I am bound to confess that I shudder when Jamie Kellner talks of 'manufacturing' programmes as if they are cartons of dog food or crates of fizzy drinks. He also confesses, with a winsome smile, that he hasn't read a single book during the past year.

'Too busy with scripts,' he says. '*They* are the television novels of the future.'

I remain mystified as to just where Fox are going to find these 'global' books that appeal to Eskimos, Irishmen, Nigerians and Chinese. Jeffrey Archer? Jackie Collins? The Bible? The *Kama Sutra*?

That evening Fox provide a splendid dinner at the Majestic Hotel and I meet a number of their Australian representatives and my old chum Malcolm Vaughn, who is the Fox Vice-President in London.

When I finally arrive back in the hills of St Paul de Vence

206

the rain has stopped and the purple sky is studded with stars. It begins to feel like the South of France again.

Sunday the 13th, late evening and it is raining again, but with a violence that suggests the gods are very angry. Lightning illuminates the valley below the Colombe d'Or and a fierce wind screams through the trees. It is all very eerie and ominous. Wednesday the 16th looms and ITV's 'F' day approaches. It is now only 60 hours before the ITC makes its announcement. Will it be Armageddon or the sunlit uplands of victory? My Press Officer in Plymouth, Sue Rolling, phones me and reads snippets from the weekend papers. Jane Thynne of the *Daily Telegraph* and Georgina Henry of the *Guardian* now postulate that TSW will lose its licence 'for bidding too high'. How can they know? How can anybody?

The ITC has not leaked or hinted, they have been sealed off tighter than a medieval virgin's chastity belt. It is nothing more than mischievous speculation. But I am depressed nonetheless. I telephone my Company Secretary, Ivor Stolliday, in Plymouth and Paul Stewart-Laing who is staying in Cannes. They both share my sense of apprehension. Paul tells me the palms of his hands are damp and sticky and he is closeted in his hotel room muttering incantations.

I am reminded of something the crazed American journalist Hunter S. Thompson once wrote: 'Never trust a man who doesn't sweat'. Paul and I are sweating now, inside as well as outside, and we'll have to endure it until Wednesday. I refuse to dwell on defeatist thoughts and go down to the bar. It is full of Americans in plastic macs and rubber galoshes. They are admiring the rustic furniture and the photographs of Picasso which decorate the walls. A sudden clap of thunder is followed by all the hotel lights going out. People scream excitedly, but are really enjoying themselves. I drink two Perrier waters mixed with orange juice and when light is restored I decide to leave the Americans chattering among themselves and go to bed.

As I mount the stone stairs that lead to my bedroom there is another burst of rolling thunder and the lights flicker and then go off again. I grope along the corridor to my room and

207

fumble at the lock. Lightning flashes briefly, but long enough for me to find my way inside. I've left the shutters open and they bang against the stone walls outside. The room is cold and there is a small puddle of rain on the old oak dressing table. I blot it up with Kleenex and when the lights are again restored I switch on the television set.

Channel 5 is showing a soft porn movie. In a dimly lit room a man in trousers is crouching over a naked, spread-eagled female form. Her face is obscured by a sheet. Somebody is about to be screwed, but I can't tell who. Is this some sort of portent for Wednesday the 16th? I watch the movie for a while, but it is crass and clumsy, even for the French. Sleep is the answer I decide. Let Wednesday come and let the dice fall where they will – it's too late now to do anything more about it.

CHAPTER 18

A cliffhanger in Brompton Road and Plymouth.
Sir Alan Peacock condemns the auction
process as crazy.

On Wednesday 16 October I rise early as dawn breaks over
Plymouth Hoe. It is bleak and grey outside and the ocean is
dappled with foamy crests. A small ship moves lazily across
the horizon at about the same location that the Spanish
Armada appeared to Sir Francis Drake in 1588. As I feel no
overwhelming urge to play bowls I eat a huge breakfast and
smoke a Monte Cristo cigar instead. Today is 'F' day and one
must be suitably fortified for the triumphs or tribulations that
will surely follow.

I arrive at the TSW studio shortly after 8.15 a.m. and it is
already buzzing with anticipation. Viewers have telephoned
with their good wishes and even my taxi driver, who brings
me to the studio, gives me a hearty thumbs-up sign.

In the first floor executive suite a camera tripod has already
been set up and the furniture rearranged to accommodate
lights. It is my intention to inform all 250 staff in the building of the ITC decision as soon as it comes over the fax
machine – and my message will be relayed live to the 50 staff
in London at the same time.

The mood in the building is upbeat. Executives and staff
arrive and go to their work stations just as they would on any
normal working day, but there is an all-pervading sense of
electricity in the corridors and in the news room where TSW
journalists can already smell a sensational story.

My Press Officer, Susan Rolling, tells me that the *Daily
Mail* and the *Western Morning News* want to photograph me

209

actually 'receiving' the fax. I agree, but make it clear that they cannot know the contents of the ITC's announcement until our staff are informed.

Executive Directors and their PAs gather in the small reception area of the executive suite and we glance anxiously at the clock. The general view is that we shall receive our fax from the ITC at a few minutes before 10 a.m. It is now 9.30 and I detect that the atmosphere is tightening like a coiled spring.

One of our many advisers from stockbrokers Rowe Dartington cautions me that if the announcement comes through early (say at 9.33) it will be hugely price-sensitive until 10.00. Twenty-seven minutes for our aunties to go on a buying or selling spree with this insider information and make a killing! As usual, I believe our advisers are over-cautious, even neurotic, and I say so.

Then, at 9.52, a shade earlier than expected, the small fax machine in the executive suite chatters into life. My Chairman, Sir Brian Bailey, and I watch the sheet of A4 paper emerge slowly from the bowels of the machine. The first thing I see is the ITC logo at the top of the page and I grab it, pulling it out of the tray. This is what it says:

The Independent Television Commission will be announcing today its decisions, in accordance with Section 17 of the Broadcasting Act 1990, on the award of the Channel 3 licences.

The Commission recognises, and is grateful for, the time and effort that went into the preparation of the application from TSW Broadcasting Limited for the Regional Channel 3 licence for South-West England.

I regret to have to inform you that your application was not successful. The announcement that the ITC will shortly be making in respect of the award of the licence is as follows:

South-West England
There were three applicants: Telewest Ltd, TSW Broadcasting Ltd and West Country Television Ltd. It

appeared to the Commission that the proposed services of both TSW Broadcasting and West Country Television would comply with the requirements specified in Section 16(2) of the Broadcasting Act 1990, but it did not appear to the Commission that TSW Broadcasting would be able to maintain its proposed service throughout the period for which the licence would be in force.

West Country Television has been awarded the licence. The amount of West Country Television's cash bid was £7,815,000. The amounts of the other cash bids were Telewest £7,266,000; TSW Broadcasting £16,117,000.

Signed

George Russell
Chairman

I read it through twice, in silence. Brian reads it again and we exchange glances. I feel as if I have just been hit by a three-ton truck.

Outside in the executive suite people are still chattering. They have no idea the fax has already come through. I walk directly to the spot outside my office which has been marked off for my closed-circuit broadcast to staff and I read the whole of the ITC message to camera.

The response is one of dignified and stunned silence. It takes several minutes before the full impact of the news penetrates people's consciousness and then they hug each other, shake hands and a few of them weep openly.

My PA, Gilly Hartley, embraces me, as does Paul Stewart-Laing, my Director of Programmes, but we are all in shock. We start to ask ourselves questions. What does it all mean? Where did we go wrong? Why did we lose?

Years of grinding hard work and hopes for the future cruelly snuffed out by one bleak, uncompromising fax from Brompton Road in London. It seems so unreal, so unfair, so bloody outrageous. And we made by far the highest bid.

'Utterly ridiculous' is the phrase used by my baffled

211

cameraman, Robbie. There are few commentators who, in the next couple of days, will disagree with this verdict.

Within half an hour of learning our own fate we are all glued to television sets to watch the rest of the saga unfold – and I am aware of the painful irony that the first channel to break the news is not ITV, but Rupert Murdoch's Sky News.

Four incumbents have lost their franchises, including TSW. The others are TVS, TVAM and Thames. Both Thames and TVAM have been substantially outbid by rivals, but TVS, like us, have been cast aside even though they passed the pro-gramme quality hurdle and made the highest bid. It is an *Alice in Wonderland* situation made even more fantastic when we digest the full details of the ITC's verdict. Carlton have knocked out Thames with a bid of £43.1 million – Thames' bid was £32.7 million. But Greater London Television, the third bidder, are dumped even though they have bid £45.3 million. They have failed the quality test. The other London station LWT have secured their franchise with a bid of only £7.8 million against rivals, LIB, who have bid £35.4 million. Meridian Broadcasting, a newcomer, will replace TVS with a bid of £36.5 million against the TVS bid of £59.7 million. Granada are secure, in spite of bidding £9 million against Phil Redmond's North-West TV with £35.3 million. At the other end of the scale, little Grampian in the North of Scotland have won with a modest £720,000 compared to the £1.1 million and £2.7 million offered by other hopefuls, the TSB and the British Linen Bank. The smallest ITV company of all, Channel, have survived with a tiddly £1,000 bid, seeing off Normandie Sound, who bid £10,200, but stumbled at the qual-ity hurdle. By contrast, Central, one of the giants, have romped home unopposed with a £2,000 bid as have Scottish with £2,000 and minuscule Border with £52,000.

The press are in no doubt as how to describe the auction process. 'A fiasco' says *The Times* and *Today* echoes this sen-timent. 'A farce' says *Broadcast* magazine; 'A sorry spectacle' says Brenda Maddox in the *Sunday Telegraph*, and the *Observer* dubs it a 'Whitehall Farce'. In the less erudite tabloid the *People* columnist John Smith calls it 'ludicrous' and a 'king-sized cock-up'. Anthony Smith, President of Magdalen College, Oxford, who was a founder director of Channel Four, writes more in sadness than in anger that the auction process was 'A story of subtle political revenge and blind ideological commitment'. And of the system as a whole he writes: 'If it wasn't broke, why the hell did they have to fix it?'

But most poignant of all, to me at least, are the comments of Professor Sir Alan Peacock in *The Sunday Times*:

It is not easy to follow the logic of the ITC's division of the sheep from the goats. It may be a shade too cynical to suggest that it took as its standard some amalgam of current output from incumbent companies, ruling out anything that looked too innovatory.

One staggering anomaly is revealed in the case of TSW which cleared the quality hurdle and made the highest bid, but still lost its franchise. Apart from the quality of TSW's financial plan, for which it took expert financial advice, the only way that the ITC could justify its decision is by ranking the quality of the second bidder as higher than that of TSW. But nothing is said in the Broadcasting Act about a trade-off between quality and the size of the bid.

Sir Alan Peacock is of course the man who chaired the committee on the financing of the BBC, a majority of whose members recommended auctioning commercial TV licences in the first place.

It is Thursday, 17 October. Bruised and in need of a stiff drink I am back in London to join Bruce Gyngell of defeated TVAM at Claridges for his Broadcast Journalist Awards luncheon. The hotel is awash with camera crews, reporters, well-wishers and lots of bewildered hotel guests. It is here that Bruce reads out the famous Thatcher letter revealing her regret that TVAM have lost and expressing how 'painfully aware' she is that she was responsible for the fateful legislation that led up to the present debacle.

213

At least Bruce was outbid, I muse, but I expect no letter of sympathy from Prime Ministers, past or present. Instead I have to be content with a phone call from the ITC's Director General, David Glencross, who says he's sorry, on a purely personal basis. I suppose a kiss from one's executioner is better than no kiss at all.

17 October: it's late evening now and the air is touched with a frosty hint of winter. I am alone in my study at 'Four Acres' surrounded by documents, faxes, telephone messages and the accumulated detritus of the past few months. We have scheduled a board meeting in Plymouth for Tuesday, 22 October, when the question of appeals, judicial reviews and all the rest will be debated. Should we contest the ITC decision? Or accept it with a grimace and a shrug? Right now I am too tired to reach any rational conclusion and I pick up my copy of the *TV Times* to see if there's anything worth watching on the box.

CHAPTER 19

A brush with their Lordships and more drama –
this time off-screen.

The decision to appeal against the ITC's verdict was not taken lightly. We felt we had been 'handbagged' by a piece of grossly flawed legislation and an even more flawed interpretation of it by the regulator.

Shortly after the death-by-fax on 16 October 1991, the Board of TSW unanimously determined to seek leave for a judicial review. By a notice of application dated 7 November 1991, we applied to the courts for such leave. On 13 November, Justice Simon Brown refused our application with the harsh words that it 'was doomed to inevitable failure'.

There followed a brief period of wound licking, but so strong was our feeling that we had been unfairly treated that on 28 November we renewed our application. The Master of the Rolls, Lord Donaldson, presided together with Lord McCowan and Lord Nolan.

Here, for the first time in the history of either the ITC or its predecessor, the IBA, the court suggested it might be helpful if the regulatory body gave some indication of the reasons for its decision. The hearing was adjourned for a week while we scrutinised ITC staff assessment paper 179(91) which had been disgorged by Brompton Road.

Back in the appeal court on 5 December we were at last given leave to appeal, and told that the substantive applications be retained for hearing by the appeal court itself on 20 January 1992.

The days in court were extraordinary. Here was a small ITV company fighting for its life against the bureaucratic might of a government quango. Like most quangos, the ITC prefers to conduct its affairs in a blaze of secrecy. By diligent argument, our QC, Gordon Pollock, was able to peel away several layers of this administrative onion and what lay beneath was curious to behold.

Our main contention was whether the ITC had the right to impose its own assumptions about net advertising revenue on the TSW business plan without having notified applicants of what level of growth it was expecting. We worked on 5.6 per cent, the ITC were wedded to 4 per cent. We had taken expert advice, applied the relevant sensitivity tests and maintained that our forecast was robust. There followed a moment of high farce when the ITC's counsel, Mr Patrick Elias, claimed that the Commissioners of the ITC were fully experienced in the assessment or business plans. One saw these worthy men and women slumped over desks at Brompton Road doing little else during their waking hours.

Our use of the ITC formula in assessing the cost of network programme supply also came under attack. This was a crucial point. By using the ITC's own illustration we had assumed a substantial discount on our programme costs – £2 million a year better than we were currently enjoying. Many other applicants used this formula too (it was in the application document after all), but this cut no ice with either the ITC or their QC.

ITC Chairman George Russell in his affidavit expressed 'astonishment' at our business plan, claiming that our forecasts were 'stretching credulity'.

The detail of the ITC decision-making procedure bolstered our main argument that the Commission members had been misled by relying so heavily on the single staff paper, and our QC described the ITC approach as 'shoddy, incompetent and unprofessional'.

Lord Donaldson observed that the ITC had been faced with a situation in which our bid had produced a comment from George Russell which could be paraphrased as 'Cor, these people are out of their tiny minds'.

In truth the ITC had been dealt a rotten hand by the

government, a piece of legislation that was a far cry from Lord Thomson's 'better way'. Caution was their lodestone. Given the broad discretion granted to them by the Act, they nonetheless felt unable to risk appointing a licence to anyone who might collapse half way through the ten-year licence period. Theirs could not be the entrepreneurial, calculated gamble, they had to play it safe. Thus both TSW and the ITC were working from quite different agendas. On the one hand a company making a straight commercial decision with all the inherent risks and on the other hand a government agency driven by rectitude and prudence. For us, our bid was an aggressive battering ram to ensure success. For the ITC it was a cut too close to the bone.

When both sides had exhausted their ammunition and six days in court had passed like some dreadful dream, Lord Donaldson pronounced that it was a 'complicated case' and he, Lord Nolan and Steyn would need time to reflect and consider. This they did, while staff at Plymouth tried hard to behave as if life was going on as usual and that no Sword of Damocles hung over their heads.

Even then, before the result was known, we were aware that the blind auction had distorted, perhaps for ever, the equilibrium of Channel 3 and its relationship within the network. LWT, a powerful London company, had bid less than TWS and Tyne Tees, but succeeded. Central, already a big player, had secured its licence unopposed with a bid that would scarcely cover the cost of coaching its entire board to London to collect the glittering prize. The ITV system for the next decade would be a lopsided monolith, driven not by a pristine desire to pursue excellence in programming, but by a need to maximise profits. From 1994, in any event, the spectre of takeovers, mergers and conglomerates would cast a shadow over the broadcasting landscape. Things would never be quite the same again.

A week after the appeal court hearing, in a 62-page document, Lord Donaldson said, 'The law and the public interest require' that the ITC should reconsider. His colleagues alas demurred.

217

Then to the Lords, the agony prolonged, the uncertainty compounded. Eventually on Tuesday 25 February 1992, TSW's aspirations to remain a licensed broadcaster in the South-West of England were finally snuffed out.

In an exquisitely panelled committee room at the end of a long corridor in the House of Lords, five elderly gentlemen in suits told four younger gentlemen in wigs and gowns that our appeal against the October ITC decision was to be rejected. Thus ended four months of legal argument, tension, passion, intrigue and soul-searching. As I sat on the plaintiff's leather chair, gold-stamped with the House of Lords' portcullis, a sense of unreality swept over me. A yard ahead of me stood our QC, Gordon Pollock, a splendid lawyer with the build and stance of a rugby scrum-half whose advocacy on our behalf had, in my view, been exemplary. Gordon's wig, which I knew to be a rare antique over 100 years old, looked faintly ragged and thread-bare; not unlike how I felt myself at that precise moment.

The five noble law lords, Keith, Templeman, Goff, Ackner and Lowry had listened to the ebb and flow of argument for three days and taken less than 15 minutes to reach their decision. As Lord Keith, a venerable and softly-spoken man, issued his verdict, a leaden hush fell over the room. It lasted no more than a few seconds during which I glanced at the ITC team seated on our left. They displayed no emotion, no hint of relief, indeed they looked as exhausted as we did. The five Law Lords, having delivered their decision, rose, briefly responded to the bowed heads of the four advocates and filed out – presumably to lunch. I was reminded, perhaps uncharitably, of a line from Alexander Pope: 'And wretches hang, that jury men may dine'.

As we shuffled out of the committee room past two splendidly attired men in Ruritanian fancy dress I was reminded that they were, respectively, the Principal Doorkeeper and his deputy – the Under-Principal Doorkeeper. For a fleeting moment, I wanted to laugh, but suppressed this unworthy impulse. What had all this gilded pomp and solemn ceremony to do with the business of running a small ITV station in the South-West of England?

Why had we travelled this tortuous road and, having arrived, had our journey been really necessary? If I could turn the clock back, would I have done things differently? Hindsight is a tempting luxury, but in the end a barren exercise. It serves no purpose other than self-flagellation.

The most vivid image I have of that last painful week was of the establishment closing ranks and a small proud company being cast down for having the temerity to challenge it.

CHAPTER 20

The end game plus a glance into the future.

After our abortive litigation, a sense of anticlimax descended over the company. The harsh reality of having our bid rejected gradually sank home and practical steps had to be taken to put the company in shape before it ceased trading in December 1992.

There was general agreement that TSW was too small and too remotely located ever to become a player in the independent production game. When our income stream from advertising stopped on 31 December we would be moribund.

The prospect of most of our 300 staff becoming redundant was a chilling one. The successful bidder, West Country, had indicated they would recruit staff from our ranks, but my conversations with their Deputy Chairman, Frank Copplestone, an ex-IBA mandarin and Southern TV executive, suggested that no more than 60 jobs were on offer, if that.

Not unnaturally, staff in Plymouth and London were worried. There were mortgages to be paid, school fees to be met, debts to be serviced. We worked out as generous a redundancy package as we could, painfully aware that shareholders would expect their pound of flesh when we wound up at the end of the year.

Then a flash of good news lifted my spirits. Carlton Television, the triumphant victor in the London franchise battle, announced their intention to recruit a sales force.

I lunched with Nigel Walmsley, Carlton's Managing Director, ex-whizz kid boss of Capital Radio and Marketing Director of the Post Office. Without much prompting, I urged him to hire Martin Bowley, my own young, energetic Sales Director. This he did to my great delight, and then in a remarkable manoeuvre, Martin built *his* new team almost entirely from the ranks of TSW sales personnel. It was unprecedented in the history of commercial television for a sales team from one of the network's smallest stations to be moved *en masse* to spearhead the revenue-gathering of the largest. I took it as a compliment to the excellence of my team, particularly as I had trained the key executives myself in my days as a Sales Director.

As the staff members gradually moved across to Carlton in a phased withdrawal from TSW I appointed a sales house, TVMM, to handle our airtime inventory during the last, dying days of our life as a contractor.

A few of our Plymouth staff decided to leave early and try their hands as independent producers. Tom Keene, one of our brightest executives and a recently-appointed board Director, who was also a bestselling thriller writer, left to form his own company. He had the talent and the contacts to make it work – others would find it more difficult.

Board meetings were now exclusively concerned with the winding-up of the company and ensuring that there was a maximisation of shareholder value. Shares slipped, not surprisingly, and reached a low of 30 pence. In the halcyon days, they had touched 98 pence. By and large the major institutional shareholders were sympathetic. They left us to do what we could in what was little more than a salvage operation.

Relationships around the board table became strained. The natural disappointment felt by us all was soured by brief outbreaks of rancour and bitterness. I found myself at odds with Brian Bailey, who, although he had never worked in a full-time professional capacity in television, was beginning to involve himself in the detailed running of the company. I put this down to post-franchise depression, but it was clear that a once benign and mutually complementary relationship was changing for the worst. His avuncular style and appetite for committee work was always well-known, but I found his methods pedestrian and unhelpful. He was, after all, nearly 70, and television is supposed to be a young person's business!

In the late spring, I took a brief holiday at my villa in Spain

221

and during my absence a board meeting was arranged to discuss an investment proposal concerning the video-taping of cattle auctions. I have scant knowledge of animal husbandry and related subjects, and during a phone call to John Peters, one of our non-executive Directors, I expressed my doubts about the proposal. I also complained, perhaps too sharply, that I objected to board meeting being convened behind my back.

I was due in Plymouth on the following Friday for a pre-arranged farewell lunch with my Director of Engineering, David Jenkin, who was retiring, and this was the same day the special board meeting had been arranged. As I would be occupying the boardroom for my luncheon, there was a somewhat huffy discussion about just where the board could actually meet. In the end, it was decided to cram them all into Brian Bailey's office and perch them on chairs dotted around the perimeter of the room.

After my lunch on Friday which was attended by several outside guests, I joined the board in Brian's office. It was clear they were keen to pursue the cattle video concept. I thought it was hopeless and told them so. We were a television company about to cease trading, our skills and our experience were quite specific.

My refusal to support the projected investment was not popular. I could see why. Many of them, like Lord Iddesleigh, were genuine countrymen and getting involved, even peripherally, with things agricultural had a strong appeal.

The deal on offer was pretty straightforward. Cattle auctions all around the country would be videoed and the pictures relayed to a number of key centres where farmers could sit in comfort, see the range of beasts on offer and buy them via a computer terminal.

Would it work? I had no idea. But the prospect of TSW sinking shareholders' funds into such a venture at this late stage of its life filled me with dismay. I was certain the shareholders would oppose such an investment, as indeed they did, ultimately, at an AGM later that summer.

I returned to the London office, now half empty of staff who had moved across to Carlton Television. There was not a great deal with which to occupy myself as the sales house, TVMM, were taking on the responsibility of airtime sales.

I took my PA, Gilly Hartley, to lunch at San Lorenzo and she told me she detected an 'atmosphere' in the Plymouth camp that was clearly hostile to me. Once I had been the golden boy, cheered on by the board as the company achieved more and more success. Now perhaps I was the fall guy, the front-man who had delivered the fateful bid of £16 million to the ITC. In fairness the whole board had stood behind the level of bid and never wavered. Nonetheless, it was par for the course that the Chief Executive took most of the criticism when the chips were down.

The other 'losing' companies, Thames, TVS and TVAM, were all suffering similar traumas. We all agreed it was a strange feeling going to work every day for companies that were successful and profitable, but knowing their death knell had been sounded by a universally derided piece of legislation.

On 28 April, another board meeting took place in Plymouth and there was further detailed, and occasionally heated, discussion about the way the company should be run down. Paul Stewart-Laing, our Director of Programmes, a talented, irascible man, was particularly critical of the Chairman, Brian Bailey, and with tempers fraying it was clear that the non-executive Directors, who were in the majority, were uneasy about these little explosions of hostility.

I shared Paul Stewart-Laing's concern over the role of the Chairman. The relationship between a Chief Executive and a Chairman is always a delicate one and although Brian and I had worked smoothly for nearly eight years, he was trespassing more and more into my territory. Of course he denied it and made a passionate statement to the board that he had no wish to usurp the Managing Director's function.

With the passage of time between those events and the setting of them down in writing, I have concluded that Sir Brian's motives were well-intentioned, but at the time his nit-picking approach rankled deeply.

The non-executives on the board began to grow restive. They were after all the custodians of the shareholders' interests and were also there to monitor the performance of the full-time executives. As usually happens on most boards of public companies, there were two or three very articulate directors with clear, uncompromising views. The remainder tended to say very little at board meetings and generally went with the flow.

Keith Sykes, a lawyer and businessman, was perhaps the toughest nut. Clever, articulate and numerate, he often lectured colleagues at length, occasionally being described as 'pompous and long winded' behind his back. Gareth Keene, another lawyer and West-Country businessman with a passionate interest in the arts, also spoke on all subjects with vigour and conviction. Finally, there was David Johnstone, a merchant banker from Bristol with a first-class mind and a polished, almost ecclesiastical style of delivery.

Along with Commander Douglas Hale, R.N., a retired navy pilot and owner of the Flambards Leisure Complex, and John Peters, the 73-year-old ex-Gillette Director and Lloyd's underwriter, they were the major decision makers whose views, when they all agreed, tended to prevail.

I was invited to a private luncheon with all the non-executive Directors at a hotel in Kingsbridge where the Chairman was not present. I was asked to give chapter and verse to my concerns about the role of the Chairman and my own as Chief Executive. I received what I felt was a sympathetic and supportive hearing. Sir Brian would be 'spoken with' and all our difficulties would be ironed out.

What followed was somewhat bizarre. A board meeting was scheduled for Tuesday 28 April and after normal business was concluded I was asked to leave the room while the non-executives had a 'closed' discussion. I was then sent for and we discussed, among other things, my redundancy package, pension arrangements and just what I would be doing for the last few months of the company's life. It was a friendly, low-key meeting and after we had finished I went back to my office.

Ten minutes later, Sir Brian loped in looking downcast and lachrymose.

'The board have decided that there isn't much else for you to do now that sales have moved to TVMM and the next few months will be straight administration and winding-down. How about going early – in June?'

I was surprised but not devastated. It was quite true that my *métier* was not that of a liquidator or compiler of inventories. My style and my talents were probably redundant in a company that was in a terminal slide to oblivion. So I accepted the offer with what I thought was good grace and caught the Brymon flight back to London. A few details needed attention in my last few weeks and I set about tidying them up.

Just over three weeks later, I received a handwritten letter from Brian Bailey which in effect fired me. I was clearly unable to be of any further service to the company and so, after 30 years in the business, I was being put out to grass by a septuagenarian ex-trade union leader, not face to face, but by means of a hand-scrawled note. I was to leave in mid-May, two weeks earlier than anticipated.

Boards of directors in PLCs of course have a perfect right, even a duty, to remove executives from time to time. That they had the right to remove me at the eleventh hour is not in dispute. Their judgement may well have been correct. There was little more I could do for the company and in truth my ability to contribute was probably finished. But their collective handling of the affair was clumsy in the extreme. All my business life, whenever I had bad news to impart, or was required to dismiss staff, I did it face to face, in person. It is the only proper way.

After Brian Bailey's letter, I received a number of incredulous calls from senior managers in Plymouth, but not a whisper from any of my non-executive Directors with whom I had worked for over ten years. At the time of writing, not one of them has picked up the telephone to talk with me even though all past disagreements have now faded and I have mostly fond memories of my time with the company.

225

Not long after I had left, I was holidaying in Venice and heard that Paul Stewart-Laing, the Director of Programmes, had departed from the company. Never an easy man for the board to cope with, Paul was something of a maverick and given to expressing his opinions with all the subtlety of a howitzer. He had transformed the TSW programme output by a combination of skill and ferocious cost-cutting and in my view was an outstanding creative executive. But diplomacy and team-playing were alien to him. If he encountered a brick wall, he refused to scale it but preferred to try and head-butt it over. Needless to say, this management technique caused a multiplicity of bruises and broken heads.

It was clear that without a Sales Director, Programme Director or Chief Executive, the company was virtually in free fall until its wind-up on 31 December.

Ray Snoddy, the doyen of TV correspondents, paid me a handsome tribute in the *Financial Times* during July: 'Harry Turner is not being replaced as Chief Executive at TSW. He is irreplaceable'. I was still feeling bruised, but Ray's piece lifted my spirits.

Time heals, and there is still a lot of living to be done. New challenges beckon and there are new peaks to be scaled. I look forward to the next decade of television with interest and more than a little apprehension. The politicians meanwhile, whatever their political stripe, will continue to eye television with a mixture of envy and despair. The Broadcasting Bill was conceived in a hostile frenzy by an administration that hardly ever watched television and as the fruits of their folly ripen over the next few years, coupled with whatever vindictive damage they inflict on the BBC, their attitude, far from being one of regret, will be one of studied indifference.

Perhaps I am being Canute-like if I suggest that television's slide into a subculture of cheap, moronic, lowest common denominator populism can be halted.

So I won't.

It can, however, be slowed down. Brakes can be applied. Here are the ten first steps necessary in this process of damage limitation:

1 No accountant should ever be a Chief Executive of any TV organisation. Fire or retire them *all*.
2 The BBC should scrap all its regional TV and radio stations and concentrate on its core business, BBC1, BBC2 and Radios 1, 2, 3 and 4 only.
3 Move ITN news back to ten o'clock.
4 All channels should only employ presenters and announcers who speak *English* properly. No more chirpy yobbos or impenetrable Glaswegian accents you can cut with a knife. (Incidentally, there are *no English* accents on Scottish TV.)
5 Scrap *EastEnders*.
6 Scrap *Brookside*.
7 Wind-up the ITC for failing to monitor ITV quality.
8 Scrap the BBC's 24-hour news service. An expensive disaster.
9 Invest less in management and bureaucracy and more in creative talent.
10 Send Chris Evans and Ben Elton to the moon in a sealed rocket, but only after giving both of them a good smack.

Seriously, however, the future lies in the hands of a new generation. The challenges are enormous and the opportunities to return to a pursuit of excellence unparalleled.

Whether the young practitioners of our trade will have as much fun as I have enjoyed during my time as a television journeyman, is open to question. The signs are not good. Ominous even. We live in stern times from which all hints of élitism must be expunged.

This is the age of the common man and the day of the maverick is done. Pity really, because, speaking personally, 'How dull it is to pause, to make an end, to rust unburnished, not to shine in use'.